Putting the Pictures in Picture Books : Helpful Hints for Children's Illustrators and Authors

Terrie Sizemore

Putting Pictures in Picture Books : Helpful Hints for Children's
Illustrators and Authors
This is a work of non-fiction.
Copyrighted by Terrie Sizemore ©2025
Library of Congress Control Number: 2025909280

Printed in the United States of America
A 2 Z Press LLC
PO Box 582
Deleon Springs, FL 32130
bestlittleonlinebookstore.com
sizemore3630@aol.com
440-241-3126
ISBN: 978-1-962101-20-2

DEDICATION:

*To all those who do
and love GREAT art!
And to all want to create
a great picture book!*

Contents

Foreword

    This little book is meant to inspire everyone interested in the creation of children's books – particularly picture books. Yes, everyone. At first, I meant to create a book for just artists to glean ideas for creating beautiful and fun art for children's literature, but also feel the authors may glean ideas here as well. It doesn't matter if authors are illustrators themselves, the art that contributes to their projects is important. In fact, I know the 'words' we put into our children's books are crafted for each book, but it is my opinion the art brings those words to life! And, as this book took shape, I wanted *everyone* to be inspired.

    I am an author and writer of award – winning children's books myself as well as have published not only my personal books, but over 100 picture books for authors spanning the globe. I am also an artist, however, due to the number of books A 2 Z Press has published, I have relied on artists from around the globe to contribute their talent to make each book I publish special and spectacular.

    Many of my authors are educators and the artists that bring their words to life are talented and some are parents themselves. They have all helped me be a better author, illustrator, and publisher.

    I created this book as a springboard for great ideas to flow for artists to find ways to create the art every child can enjoy. The talented artists I have worked with over the years have thanked me for helping them develop their skill as well. They are artists! I tell them the creativity is inside them.

    I attended the Institute of Children's Literature many years ago and learned a great deal about the creation of children's picture books. Every artist and author I work with teach me daily.

    Not only have I had great fun creating stories for children, I have enjoyed a lifetime of new adventures and newly creative projects. I see every day as a day to do something fun and every season as a reason to celebrate!

    I believe the world is before us and all we have to do is open the curtain to find a new adventure, a new way to create beautiful things! Thank you for reading, the Author, Terrie Sizemore.

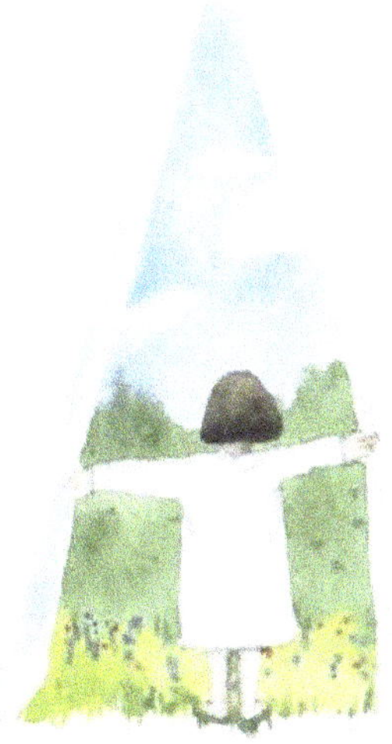

    I hope every reader enjoys this book as much as I enjoyed creating it! Every day is a great day for creativity! I'm also looking forward to my next project!

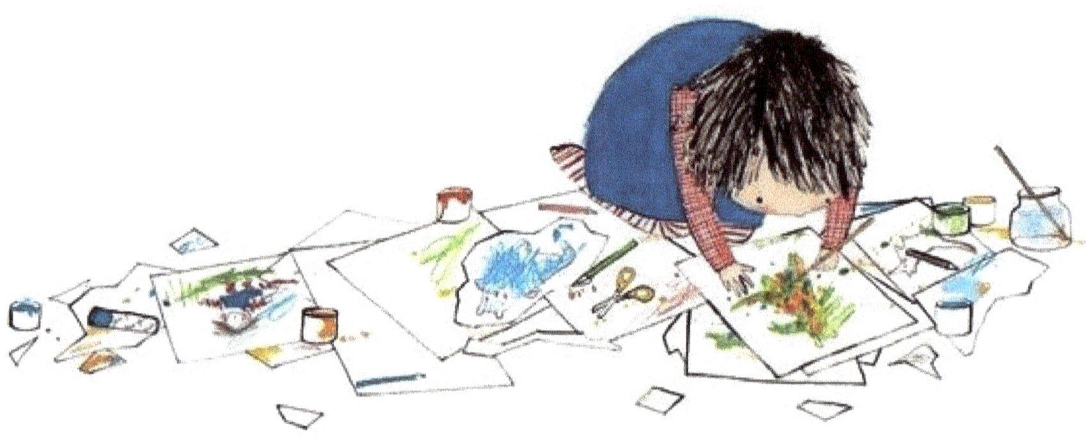

Picture Books are FUN!

Picture books should make the reading experience fun for every child! If a child's first experience with reading is a negative one and looked at as a chore, it may make reading appear to be work rather than fun. This may hinder a child's love for reading and their progress from picture books to chapter books. It also may make them not want to explore the joys of what reading provides to every reader.

What makes picture books fun? The pictures of course! The stories make reading fun as well, however, let's look at *A BOY, A DOG, and A FROG* by Mercer Mayer. This little book is the first in his series of books that have NO words, but the stories are simple and easy for the young reader to understand and follow by illustration.

Let's take a look at some of the illustrations that make *A BOY, A DOG, and A FROG* so special -

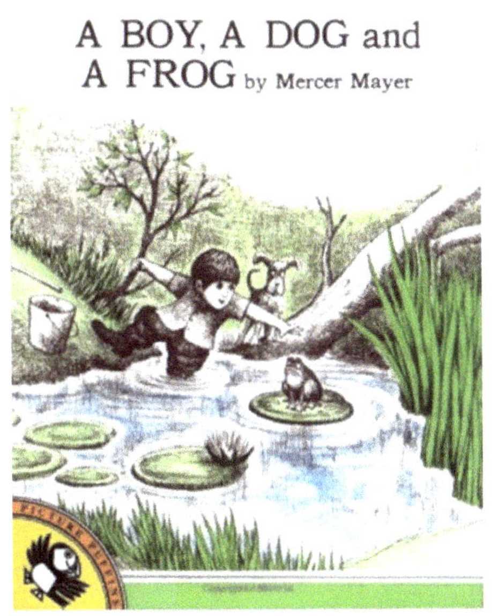

A BOY, A DOG, and A FROG is a fun series with a little boy trying to catch a frog. This little book shows how important the illustrations are to a story. I am including a few of the pictures from this little book to show how cute it is and how FUN picture books are. Picture books have the basic elements of storytelling – including characters, a setting, a plot, and resolution. This allows children to understand the beginning, middle and ending of a story. It also helps children learn how to create their own stories.

A BOY, A DOG, and A FROG, as well as all picture books, is an ideal introduction to storytelling and eventually reading. This small book shows how the illustrations tell the story.

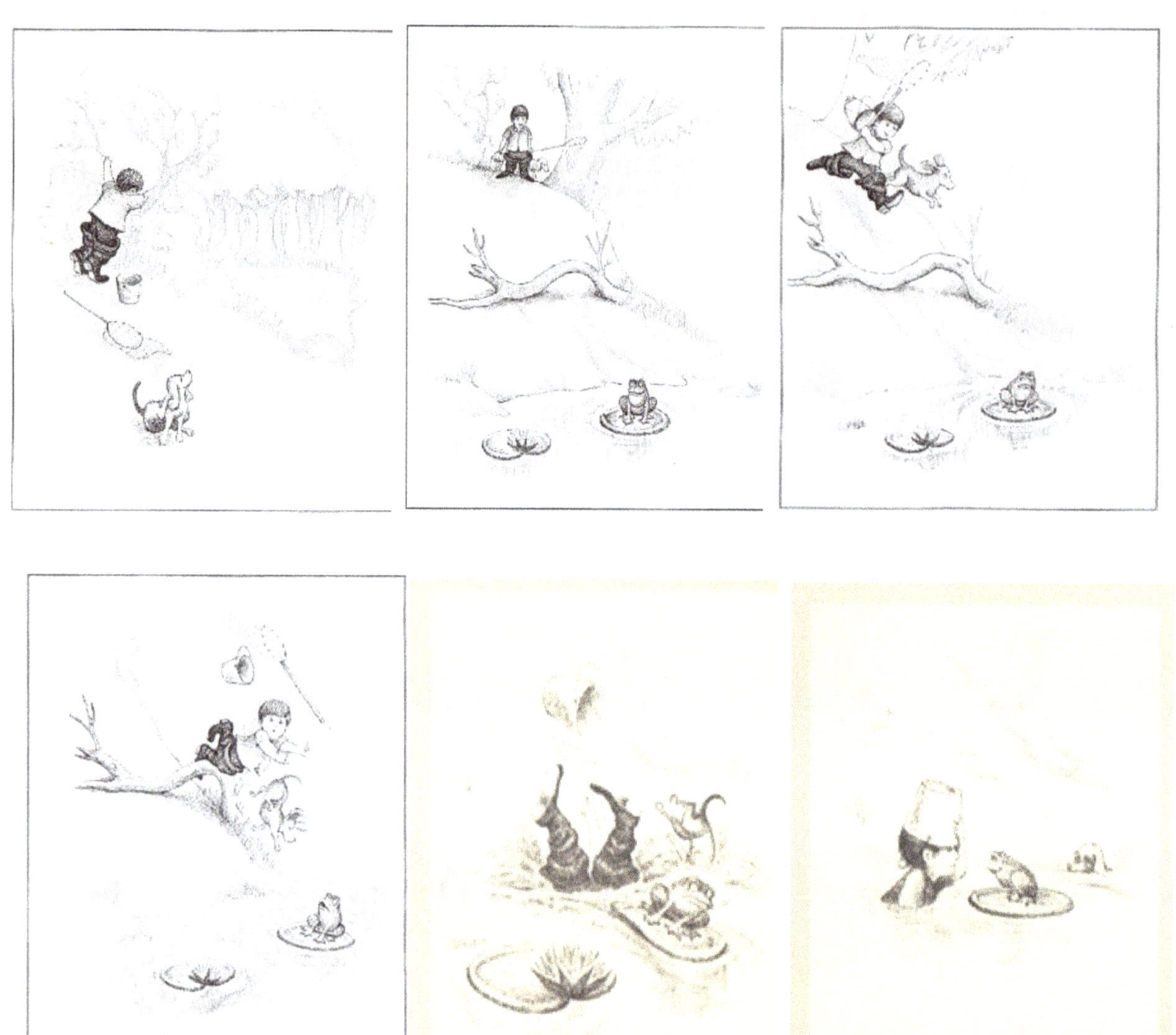

Sorry for the difference in shading, The older pictures are tainted, however, show how cute the illustrations are. As a young reader can see, the story starts with a boy and his dog off down a hill. They spot a frog and, after several attempts to catch that little frog on the lily pad, the boy and his dog topple into the pond. There's a face-off between the boy and the frog, but the boy tries several more times to attempt to catch that little frog.

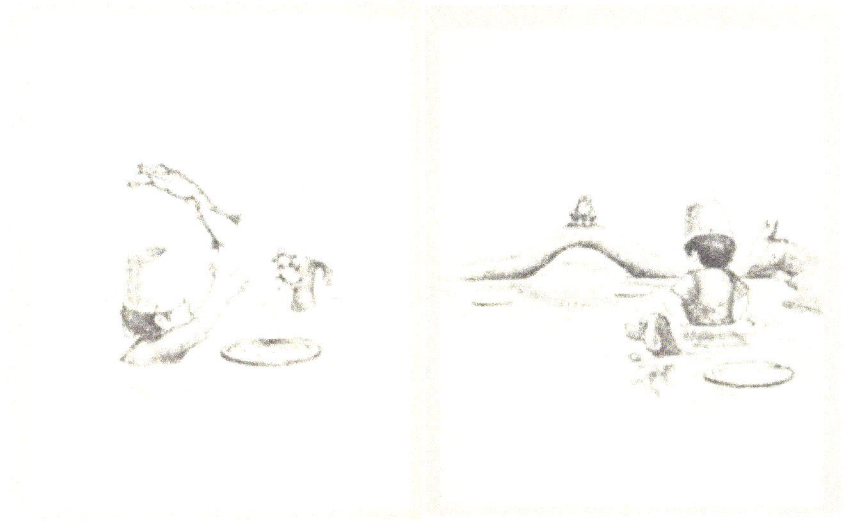

The frog happily gets away and the young boy is very frustrated.

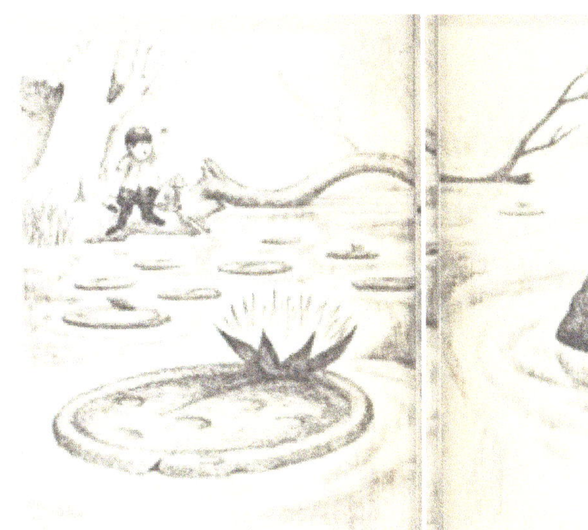

And the boy does

not want to play…

A lonely frog walks…

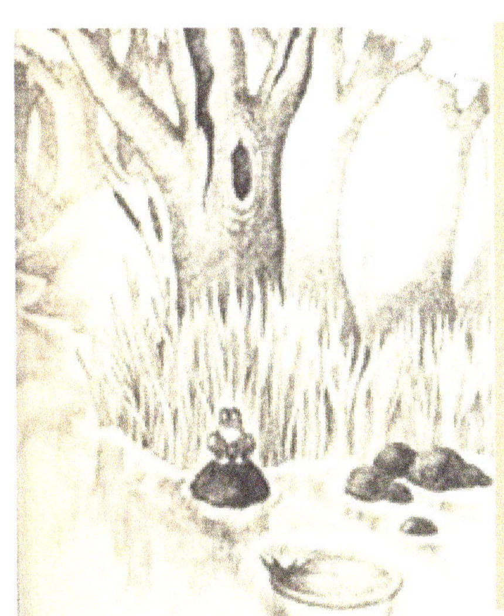

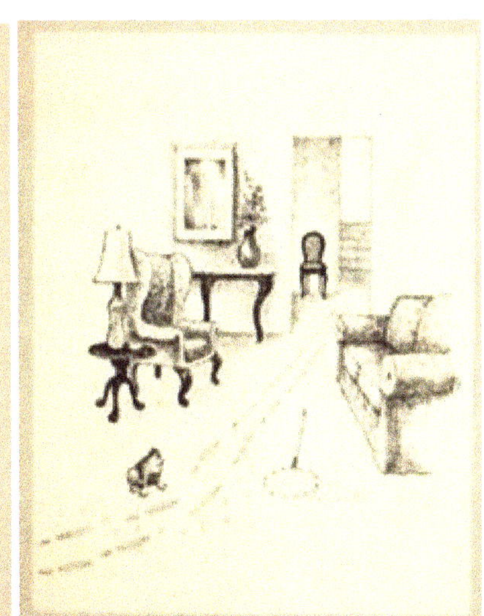

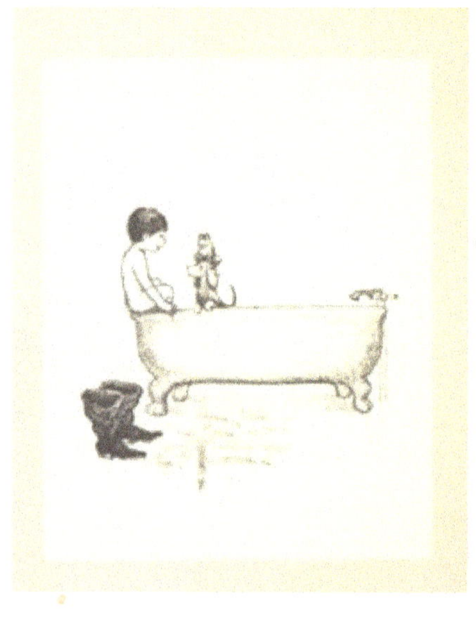

….and finds the boy that wanted to play with him.

Funny, engaging, and beautiful images in picture books make reading FUN! Picture books are an ideal introduction to reading and language skills.

Despite not having any words, *A BOY, A DOG, and A FROG* do begin to introduce the concept of reading in a child and the love for reading. Children look forward to fun things – as we all know. My authors have created many different types of picture books. One category I especially like is my 'Just for Fun' category.

Let's check out a few titles with illustrations that make the books as fun as the stories within – First – David R Morgan's book, *TV Mouse,* is just for fun.

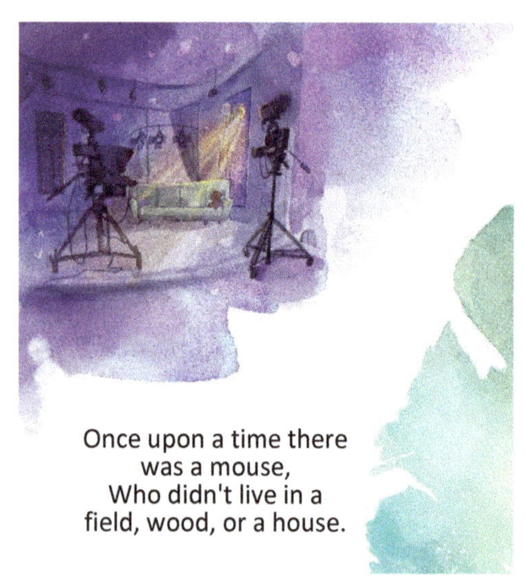

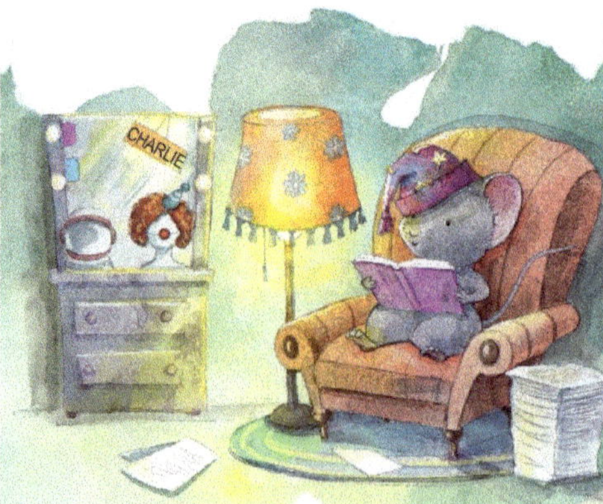

Charlie not only lives in the TV studio, he is part of all the activities there - clever.

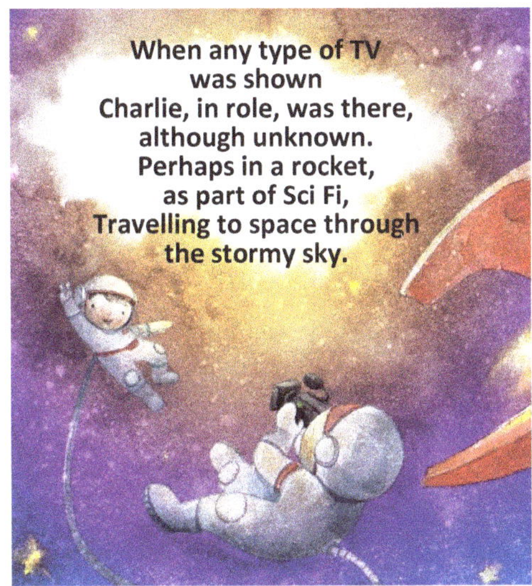

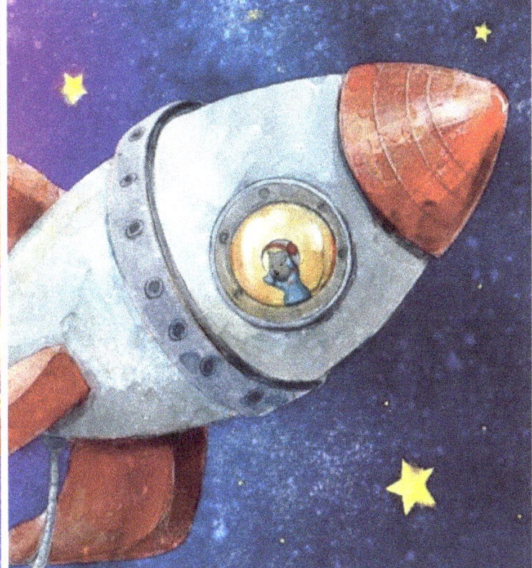

Charlie flies

though space…

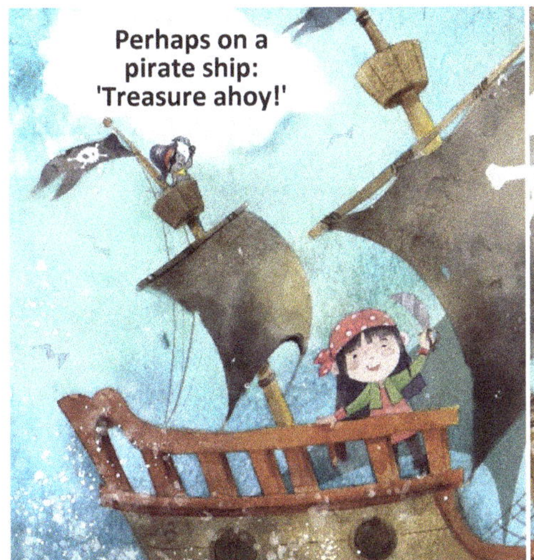

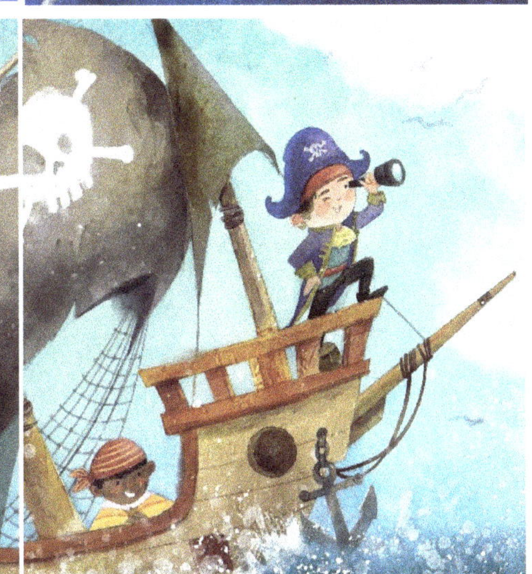

…and serves

as a look out

on a pirate ship…

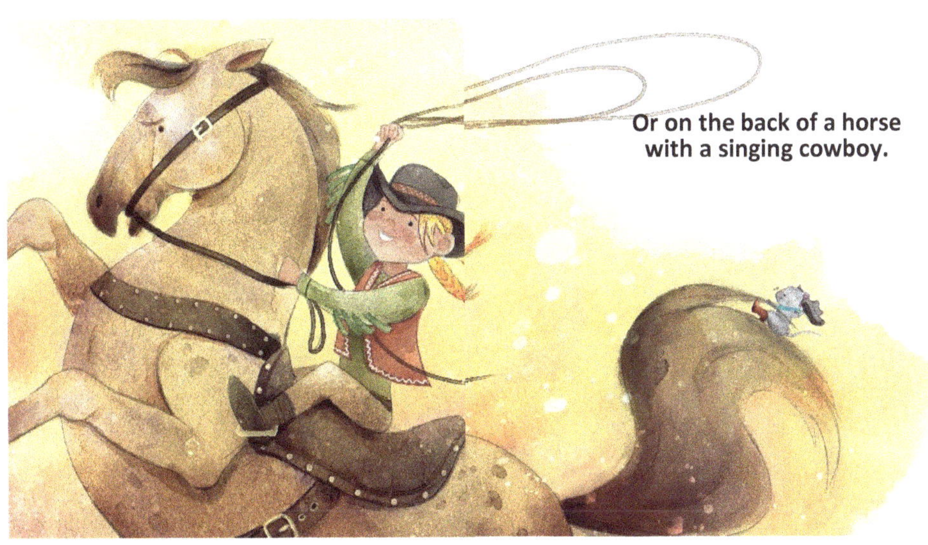

…. And is a

rootin'
tootin'
cowmouse!

Charlie also competes in a game show and magic show, watches filming from the rafters, rides roller coasters, and more! Making reading fun invites children to develop a love for reading. See *Joe's Astral Holiday* -

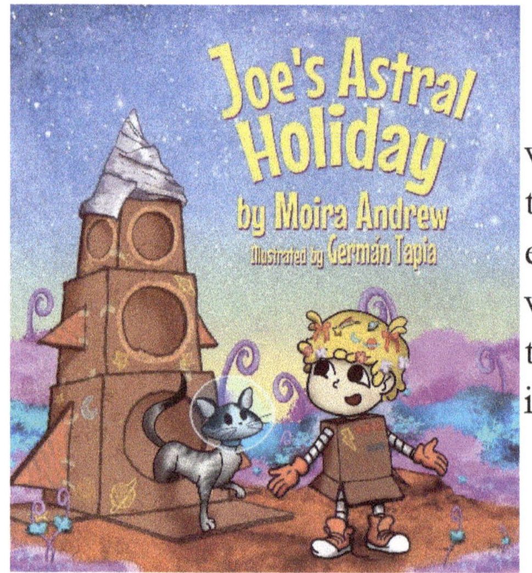

In Moira's cute little book about Joe – who wants to go to the moon and wants to go with his cat, the text is simple and the illustrations are darling to engage the young reader in a fun way to make them want to pick up this book and ask for it to be read to them over and over! Come look at a few of the illustrations –

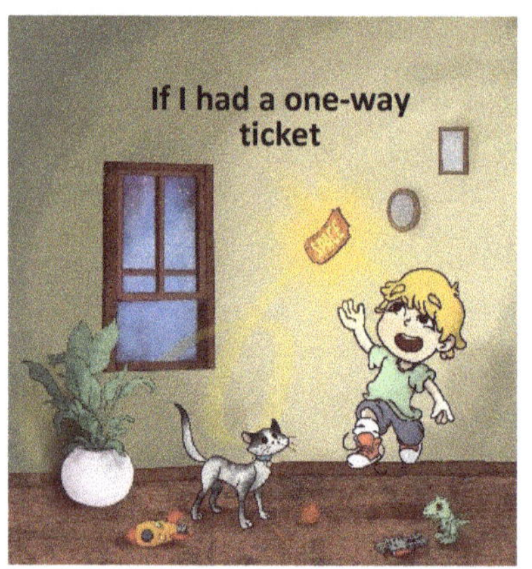

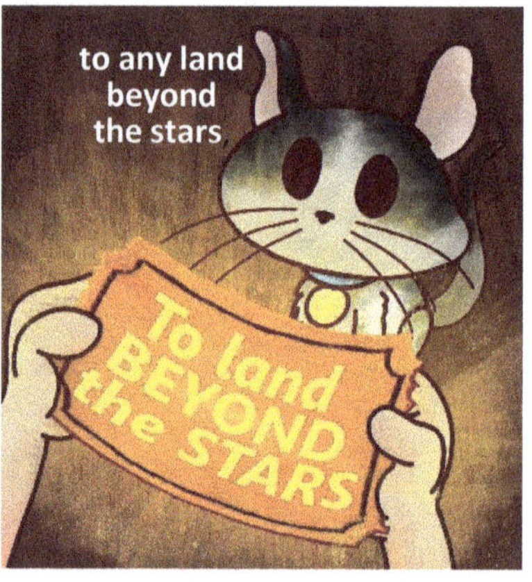

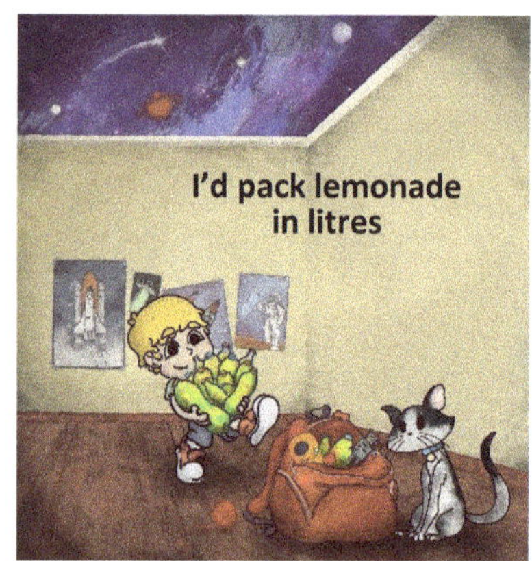

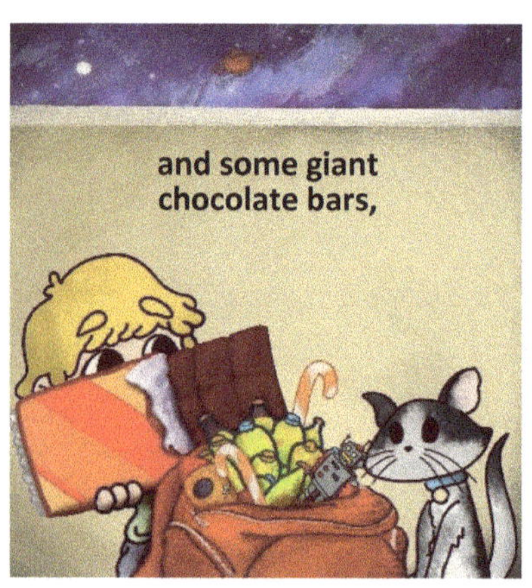

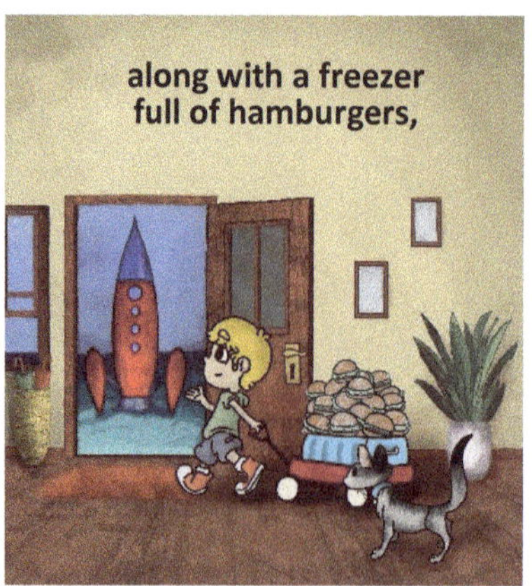

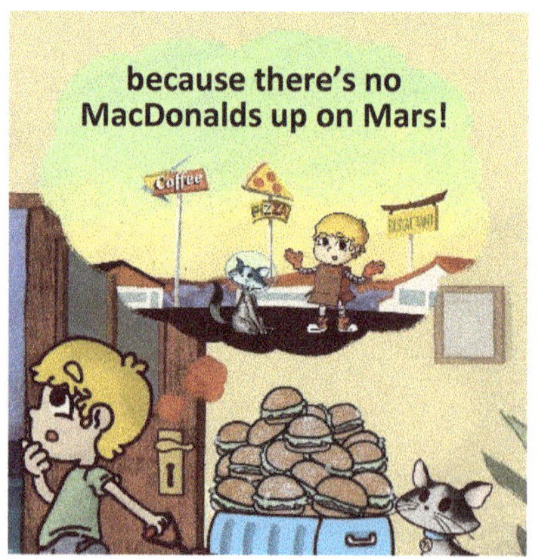

Moira writes stories that are simple and cute with fun things to make her books something young readers want to pick up again and again.

Just like Moira, Réne Curtis brings her 'just for fun' story to the young readers in *Wendy's Pajama Adventures* – where Wendy and her beloved cat, Mr. Snuggles, have great adventures in her bedroom in her pajamas! Let's take a look -

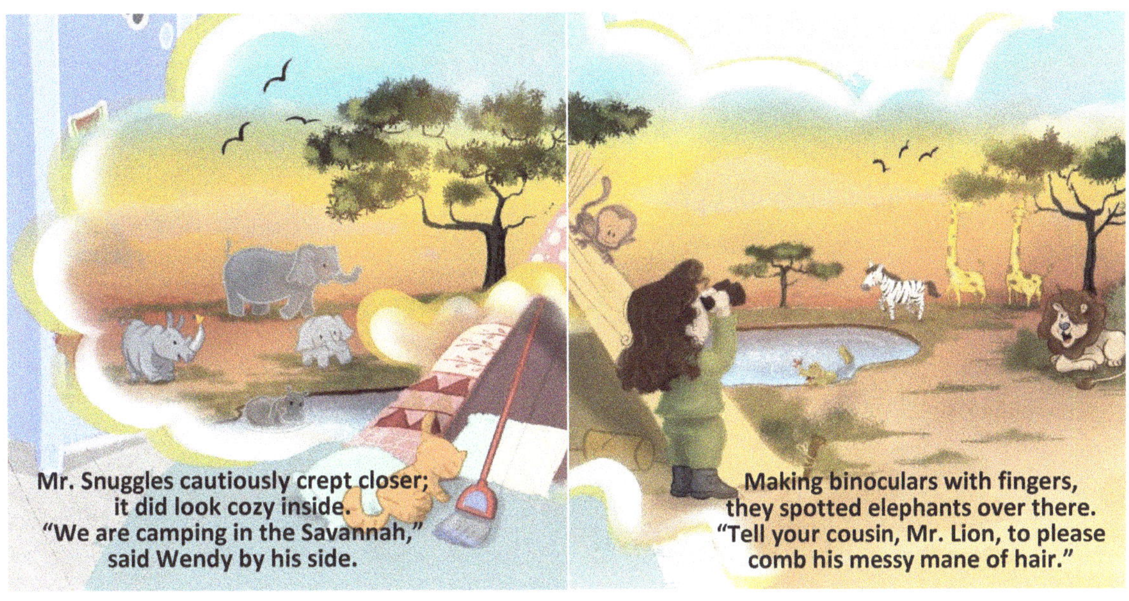

Réne has Wendy having soooo many adventures and imagination is great for children.

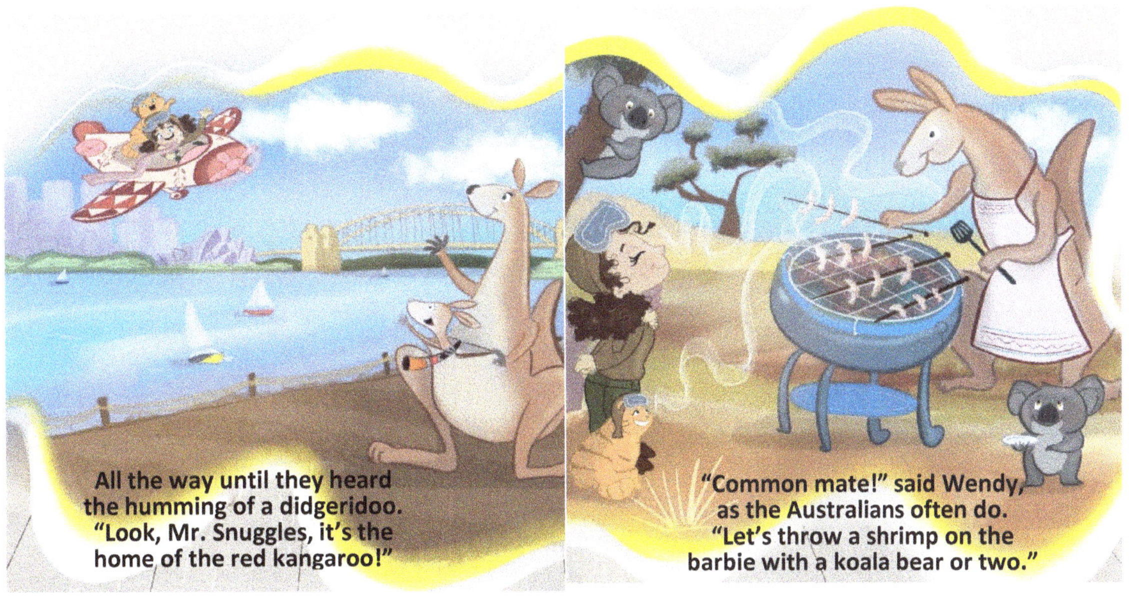

Children's book authors and illustrators have done wonderfully to make picture books a tool for parents and educators everywhere. Illustrations help tell the stories the author creates and the children enjoy. In this book, both are emphasized, but we are showcasing 'picture' books that make reading and learning fun.

Some picture books make us laugh – like *The Silver Balloon* by Moira Andrew that needed help back to the sky after she – the moon - fell *out* of the sky -

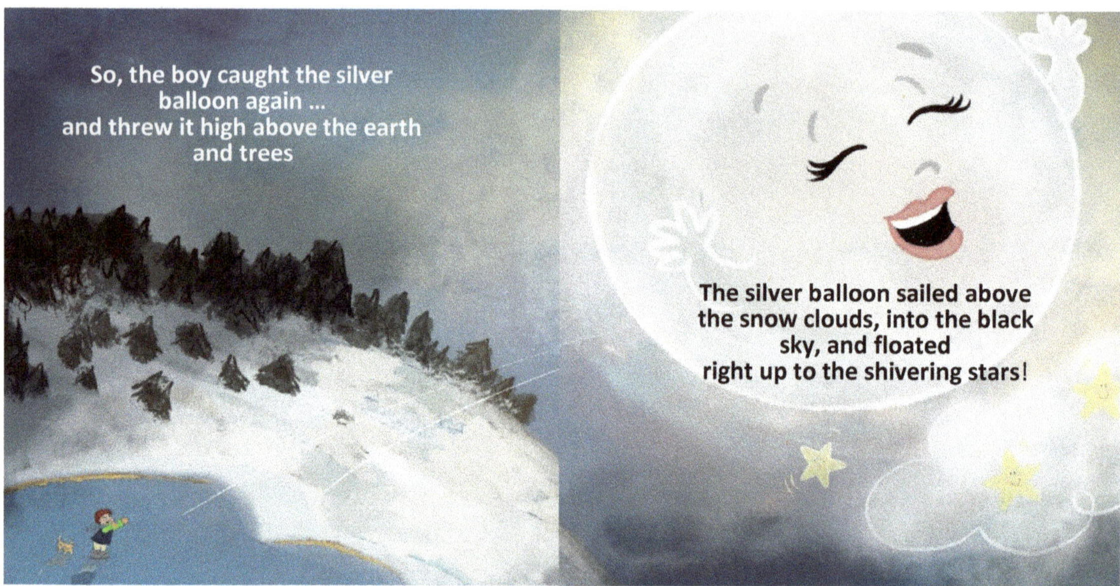

And some tenderly help us cry about losing important people in life like David R Morgan's *Grandma Snowflakes* he wrote for his daughter after she lost her grandma –

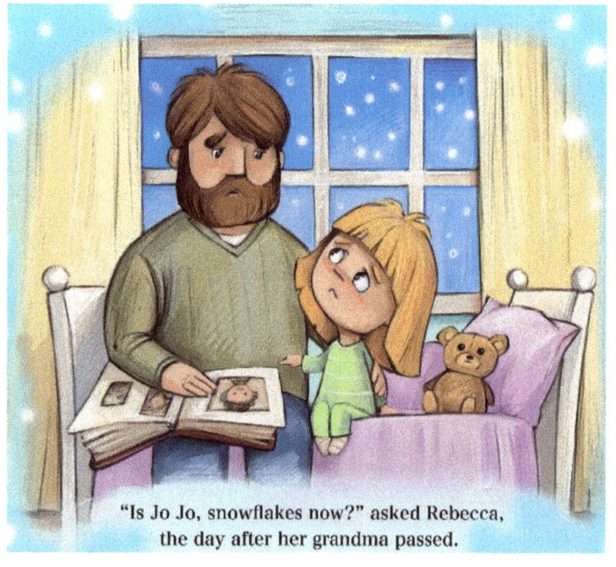

Perhaps not a 'fun' topic, but done in a manner to help children through difficult moments.

David does well with difficult topics.

2

Picture Books Need Pictures!

I'm a kid at heart. I think being young at heart is the secret to staying young – thinking and acting young! It thrills me to create a new story for a picture book.

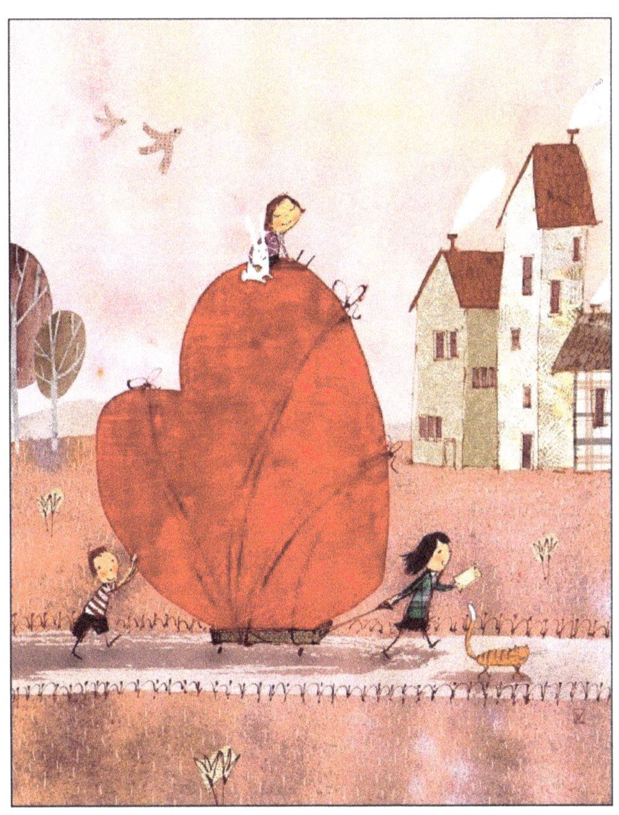

A picture can have many meanings to different children, but this is the beauty of art, it's just fun and beautiful. I would like to talk about the art in general.

Everyone in the 'industry' knows the beautiful artwork and stories of Beatrix Potter. Her work is still enjoyed by children today. In fact, I understand Beatrix Potter's stories are the best – selling picture books of all time. What brings her stories to life is the art she created – those little bunnies with blue jackets and little gold buttons and kitties with bonnets!

And almost all of us know, "I will not eat them in a box, will not eat them with a fox, I will not eat green eggs and ham!' by the infamous Dr. Seuss.

In addition to Miss Potter and Dr. Seuss, many talented authors have created picture books on every imaginable topic and they are treasures for the lifetimes of children everywhere. Come, join the long list of children's authors and illustrators to create more treasured picture books.

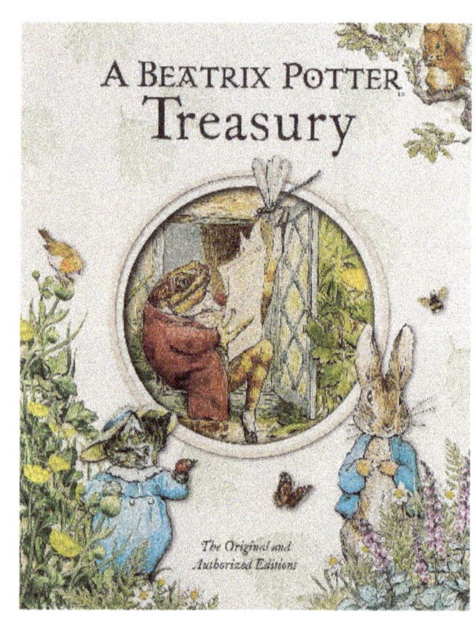

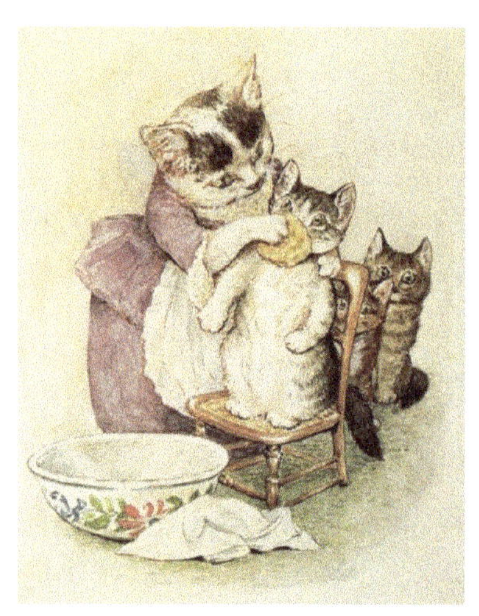

Beatrix Potter was creative with her illustrations as she tenderly has mama cat caring for her little ones and Mr. Frog cross-legged on a lily pad fishing with his fishing gear.

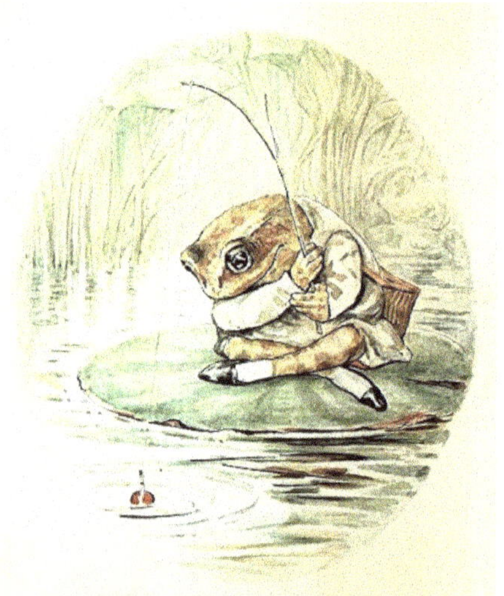

Beatrix Potter added this colorful suit and red vest to the fox and Jemima's bonnet are darling additions to her characters to make the books even more delightful.

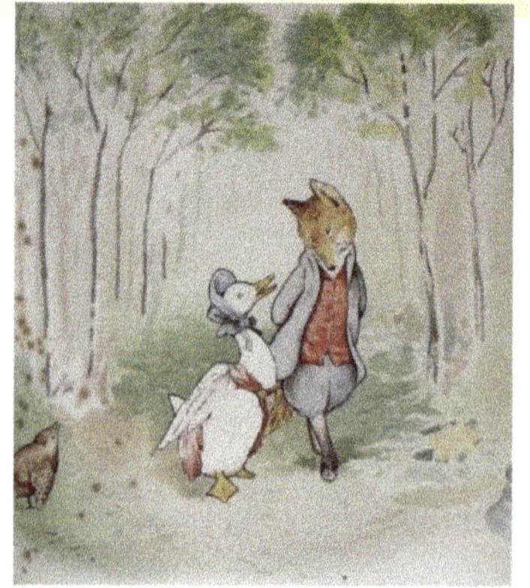

My authors have created many priceless picture books. For instance, Moira Andrew has over 100 titles to her credit and her award-winning book for illustration, Jelly Baby, is a treasure.

In addition, she published several other picture books with stunning illustration. Like….

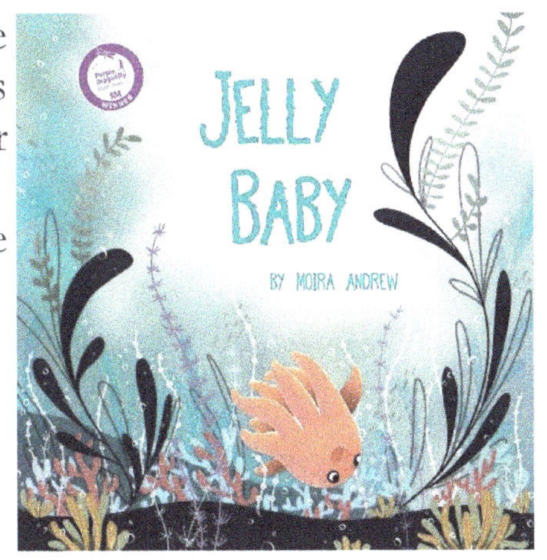

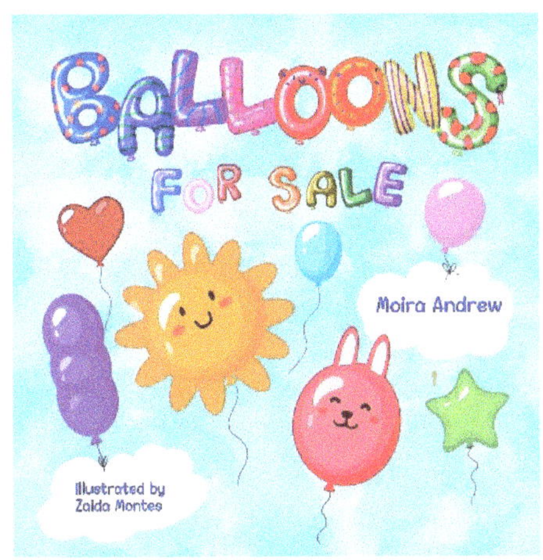

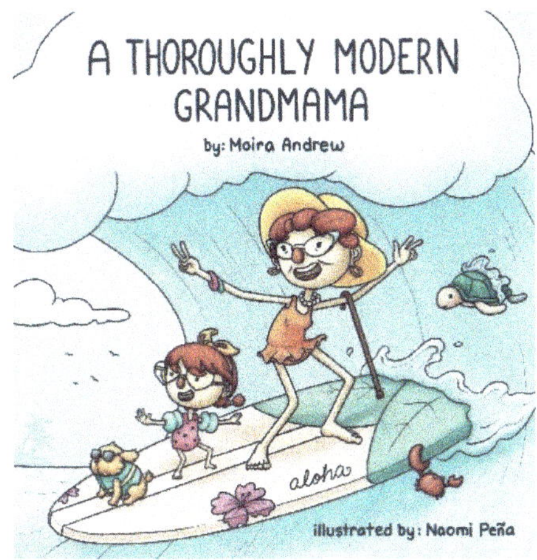

Moira agrees that art brings her cute poem stories to life and each artist brings their special talents to do so.

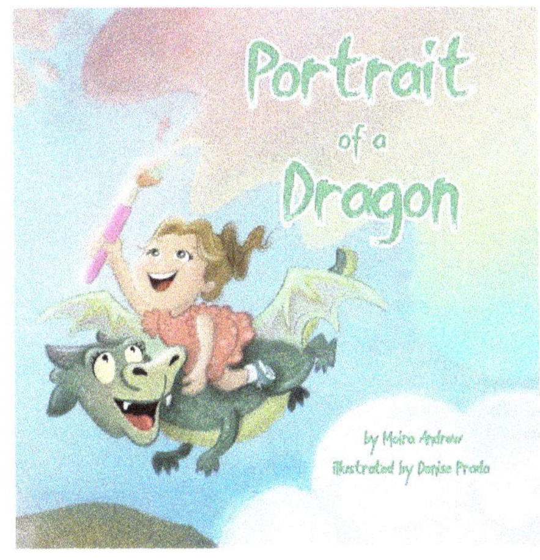

These two small but precious books were created by Moira Andrew and are written in rhyme and also with pictures that bring her stories to life.

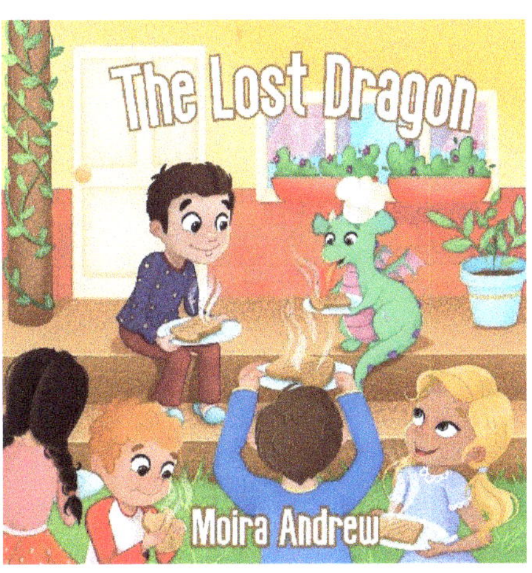

DJ Stutz is a podcast host of Imperfect Heroes, Insights Into Parenting where she promotes family values and has written three books for families to share and invite conversation about subjects such as different emotions that children experience and may not know how to verbalize like Roman does in Roman is BIGGER :

In Roman is BIIGER, Roman has Harley, his pal.

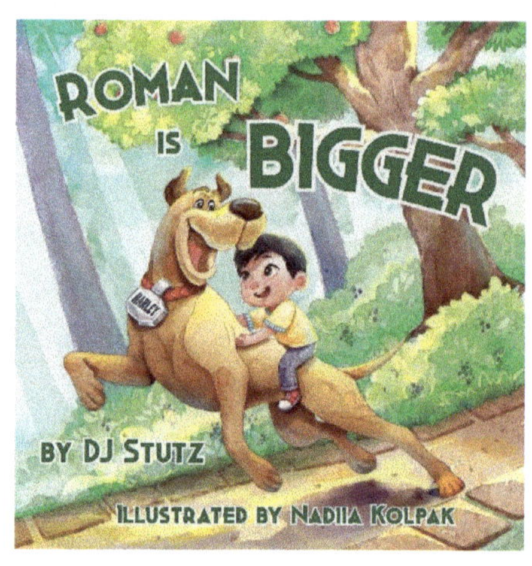

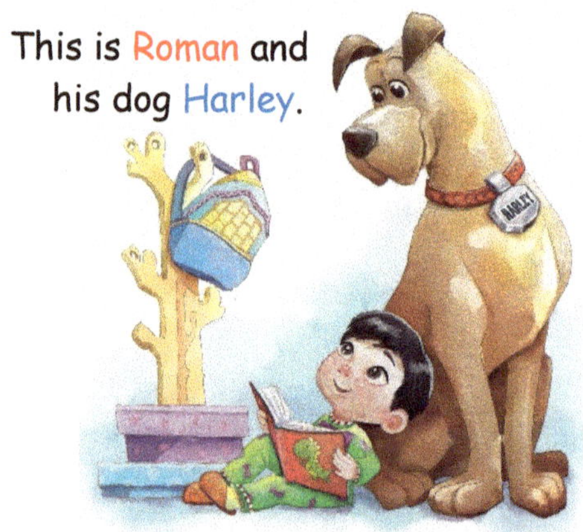

And, with Harley, he experiences the COLOSSAL size of Harley, ANGER when Harley destroys his toys, and HEARTBREAK when Harley is lost …

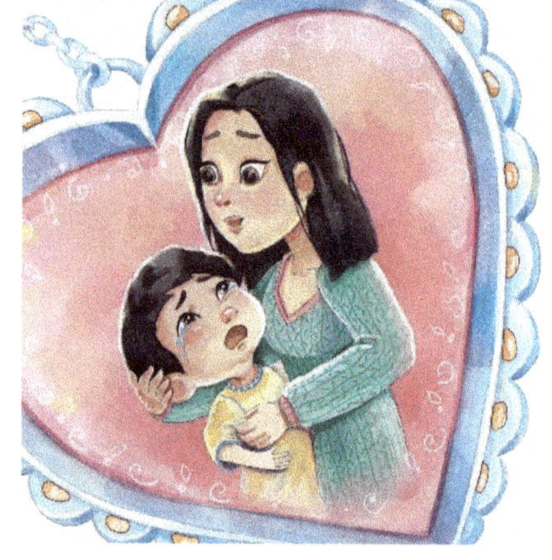

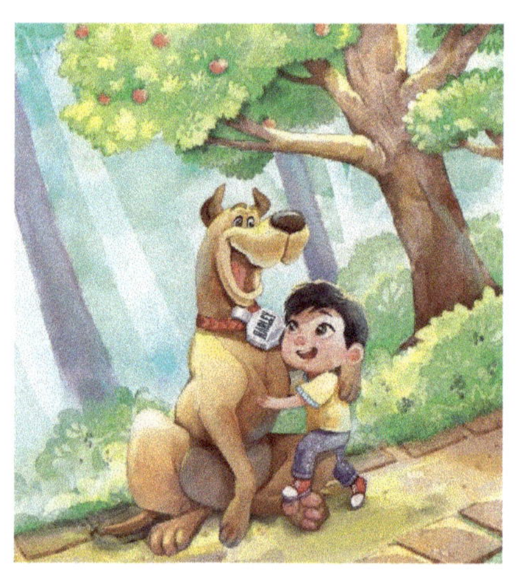

And ECSTATIC happiness
when Harley's found!

All the different emotions DJ Stutz adds
to her book, are illustrated beautifully by
Nadii Kolpak..

Award-winning author and poet, Sheila Marcotte, has created many books with sensational illustrations. Her 'There is a Poem Inside of Me' is a Moonbeam award-winning book with clever pictures:

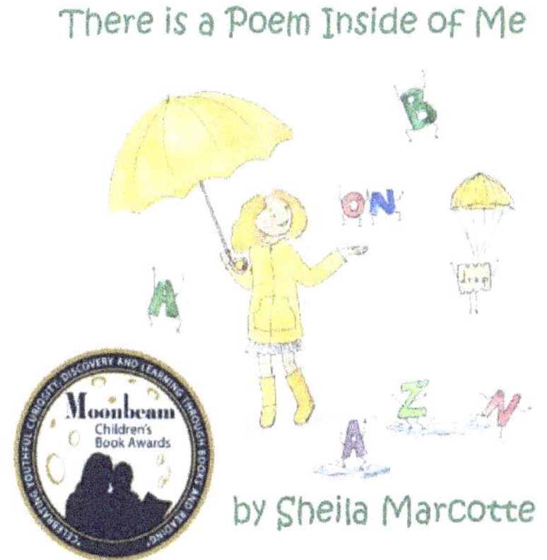

Sheila also created 'I Want to Look for Bugs' with many illustrations that resemble the art style of Beatrix Potter…

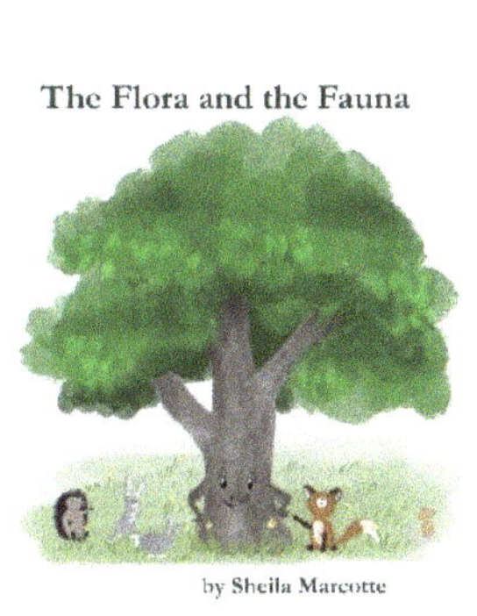

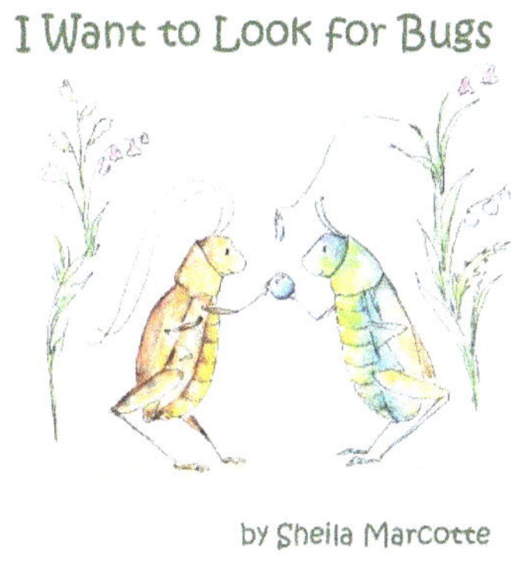

The *Flora and the Fauna* is straight out of the forest onto the pages of her delightful book… and includes different trees and animal friends.

And her book about Grandma's Garden and Grandpa's Tool Bench are filled with clever pictures that are educational as well as entertaining….

and with interesting facts.

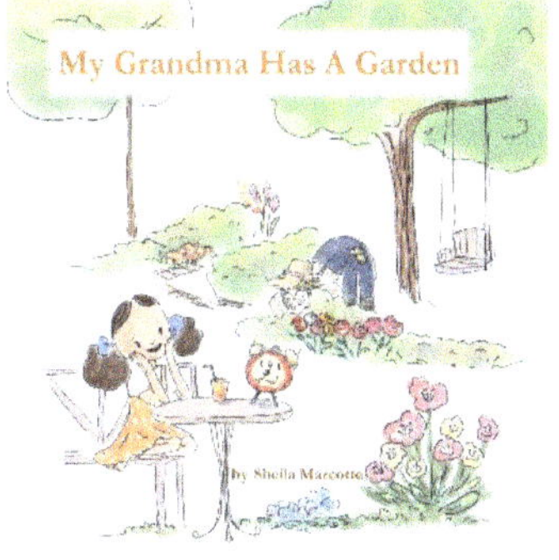

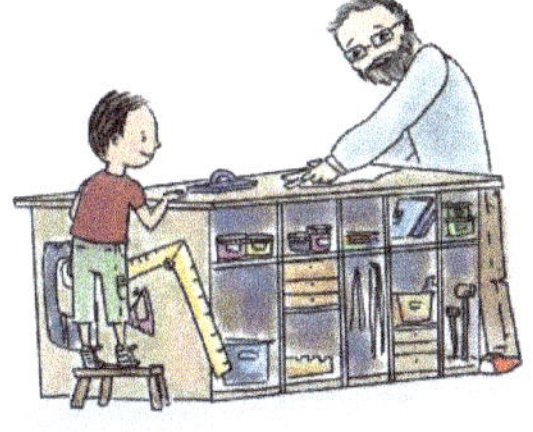

And, Shiela also entertains and teaches the young reader in her 'The Day That I Went To The Zoo.' The art brings each story to life and inside the pages are picture after picture of different zoo animals doing zany things.

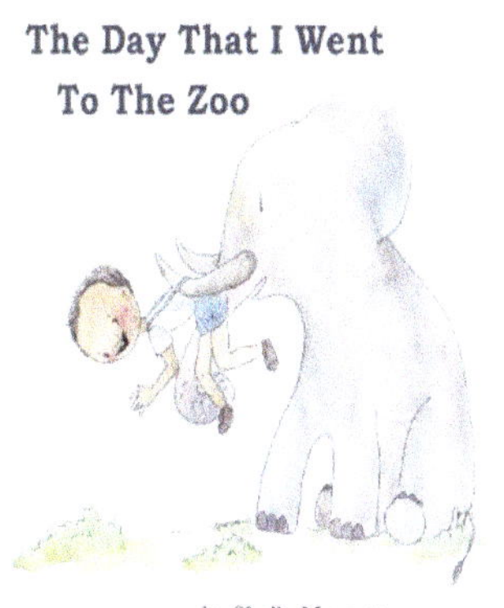

Alexsandra is the artist that created the clever work.

David R Morgan is an award-winning author who created a series of wonderful picture books featuring the adventures of Winnie and her beloved dog, Waffles. The two don't let anything deter them from adventure and doing great things. In his first book, Winnie's Wonderful Wheelchair, the illustrations bring Winnie's adventures to life….

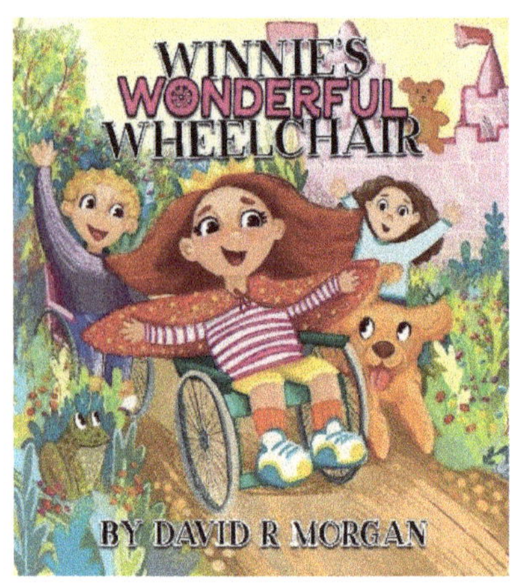
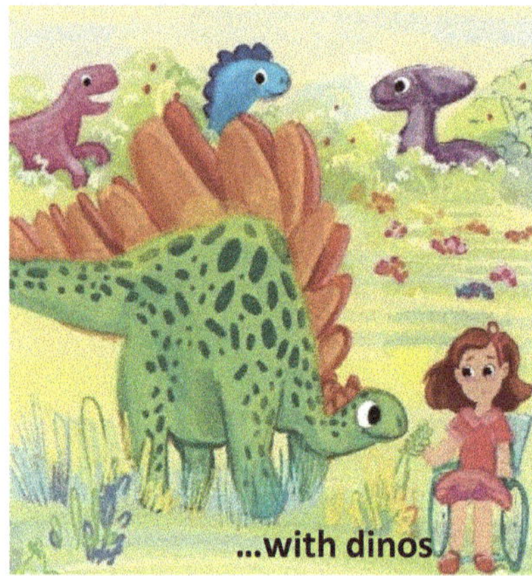

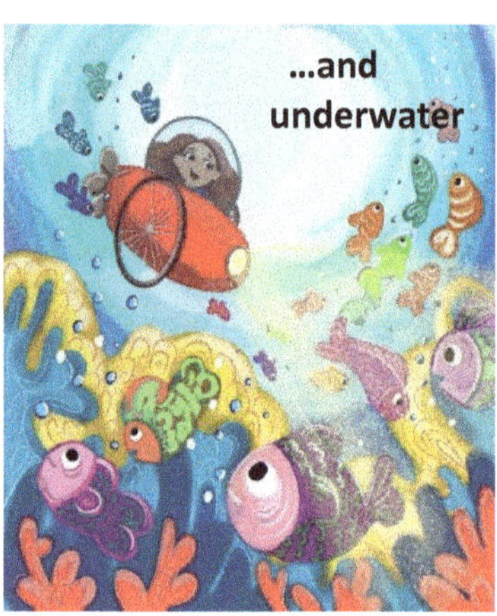

In another of the seven-book series, Anna brings David's words and Winnie's adventures to life as he writes about Winnie's Winning Week ….

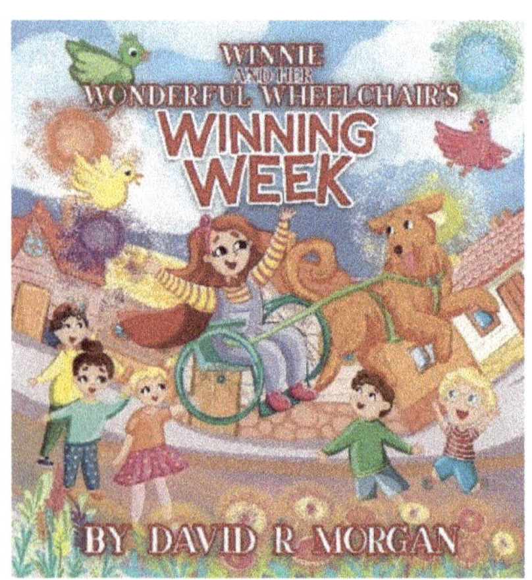
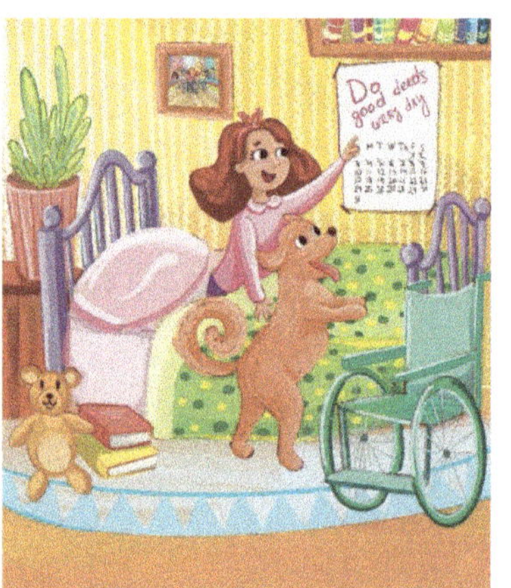
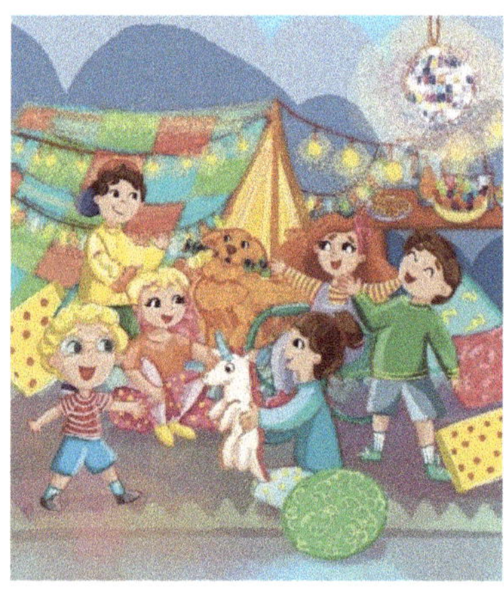

…where Winnie plans her week and, during that week, spends time with lonely children. She has a very exciting week.

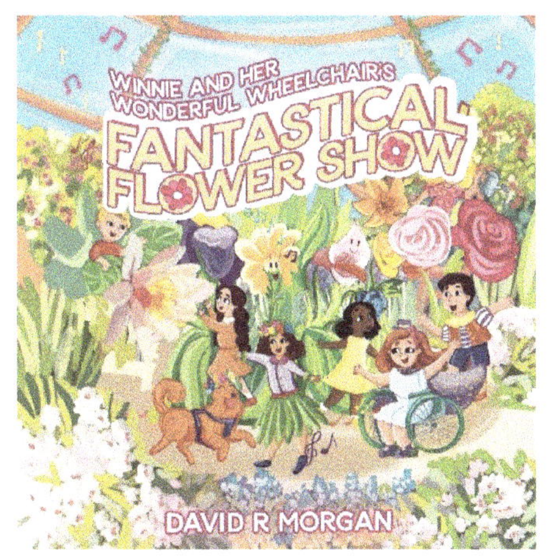

David also wrote about Winnie and her fantastical flower show. The illustrations bring the story to life about Winnie and Waffles and their friends experiencing a magical flower show with music in the garden with many different flowers and musical intruments

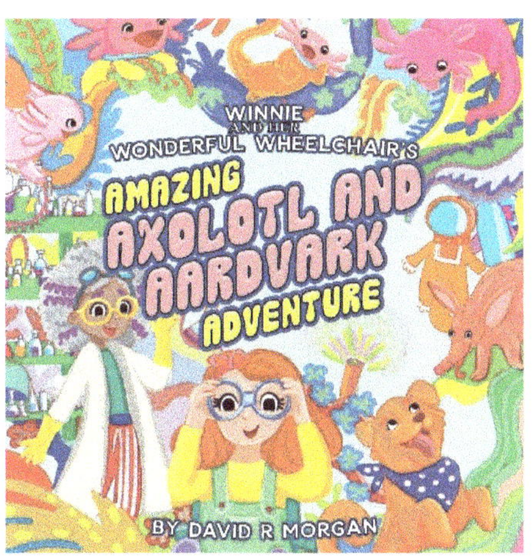

In the series, David also wrote cute books about Winnie finding some missing axolotl and aardvarks, Winnie and having fun in all the four seasons of the year…….

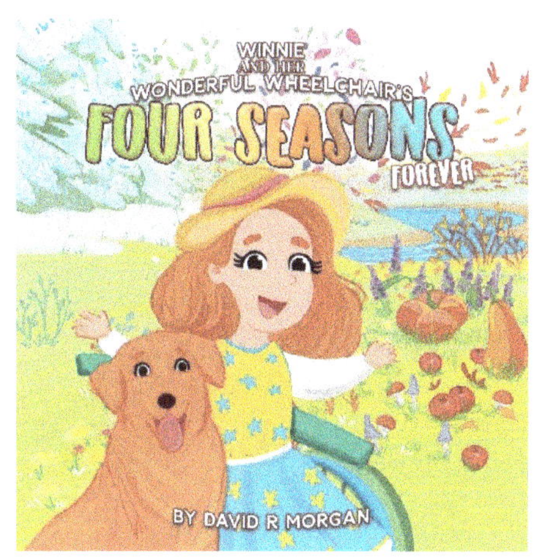

…Winnie taking a time trip, meeting famous people of the past, and a Christmas book where Winnie saves Christmas. We decided to have the same artist for all of the books in the series.

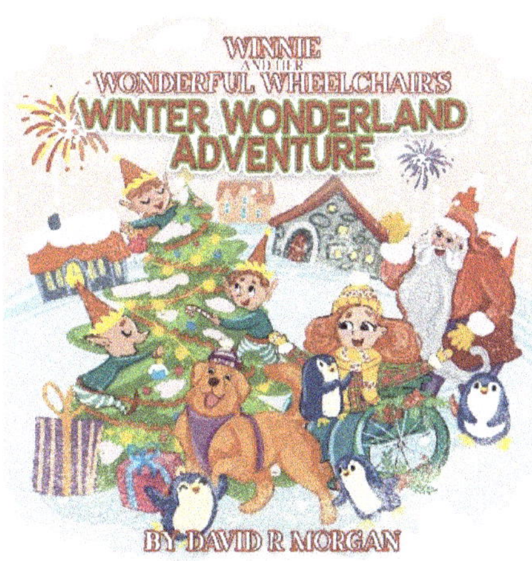

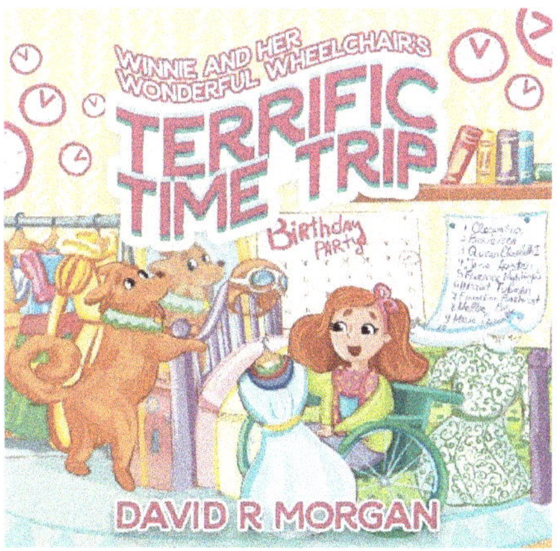

There's an artist for every book. I search until I find the perfect style for each book I partner with an author to create. For variety and fun art, there were several artists

who drew for the 24-book alphabet series created by Paula Curtis-Taylorson, who created Finding A-XYZ : The Great Alphabet Hunt and the styles include…

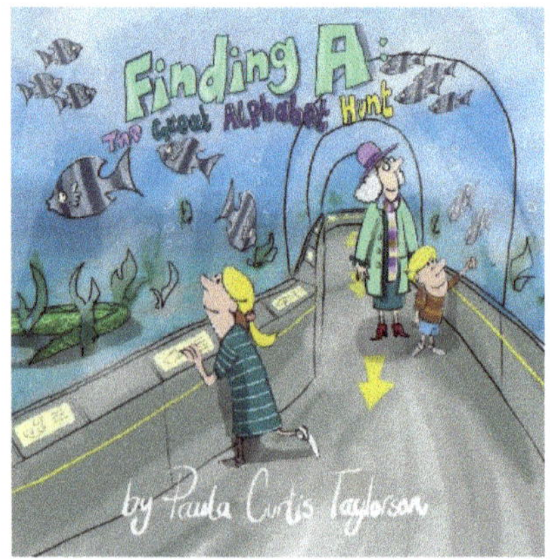

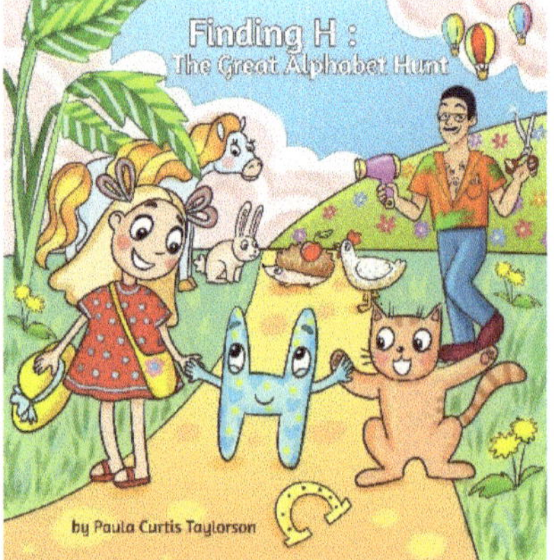

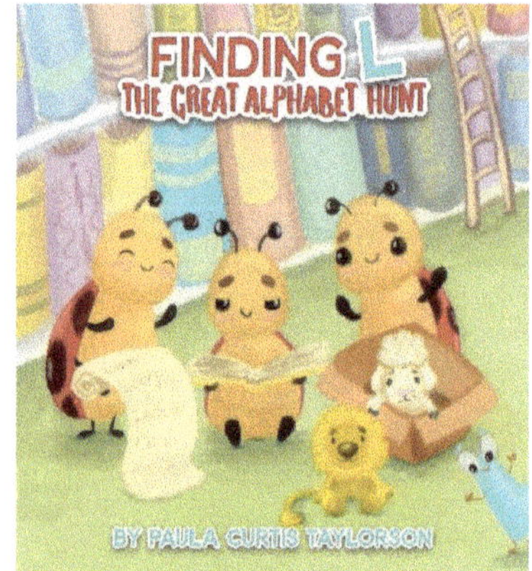

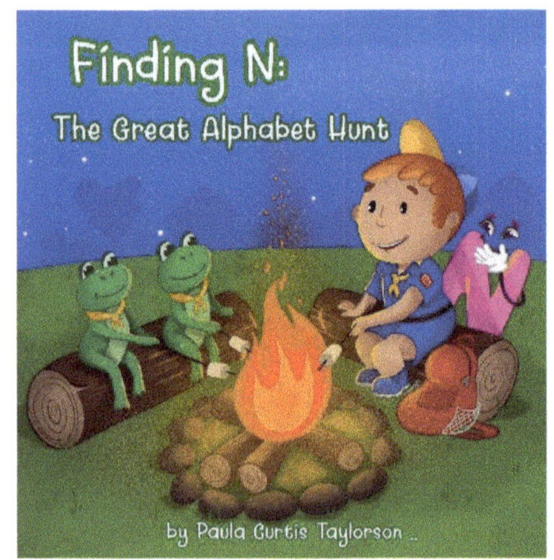

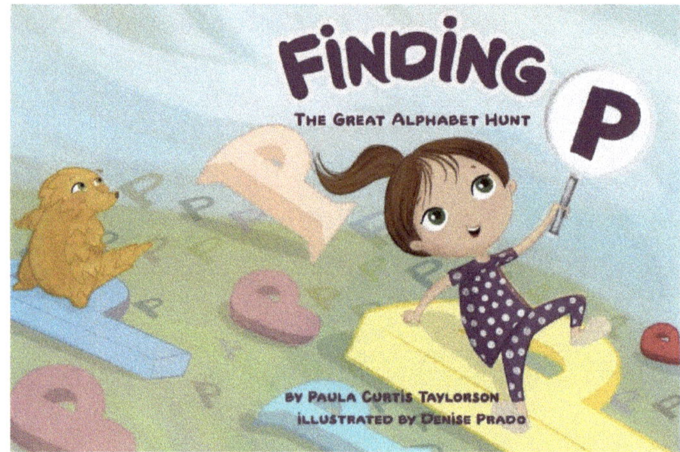

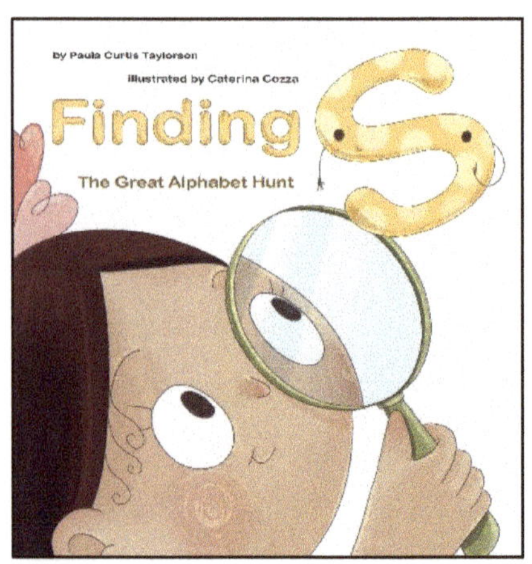

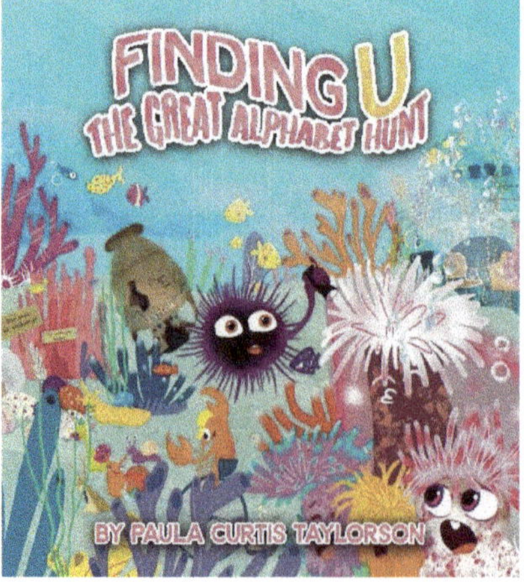

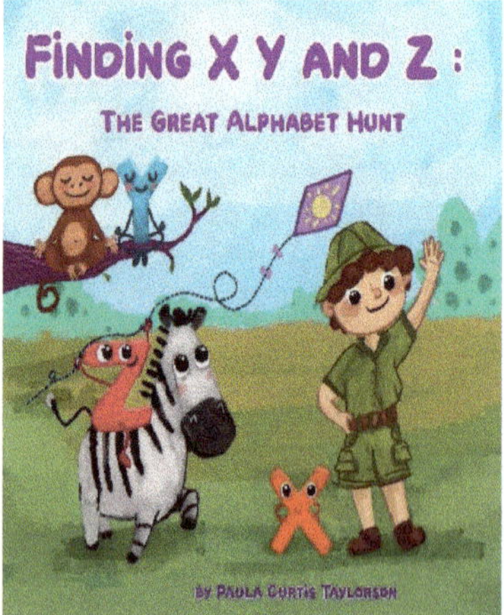

Copying art can be difficult for some, but Anastasia seems quite skilled. She finished several books for me. A couple examples are from *Fascinating Fungi*…..

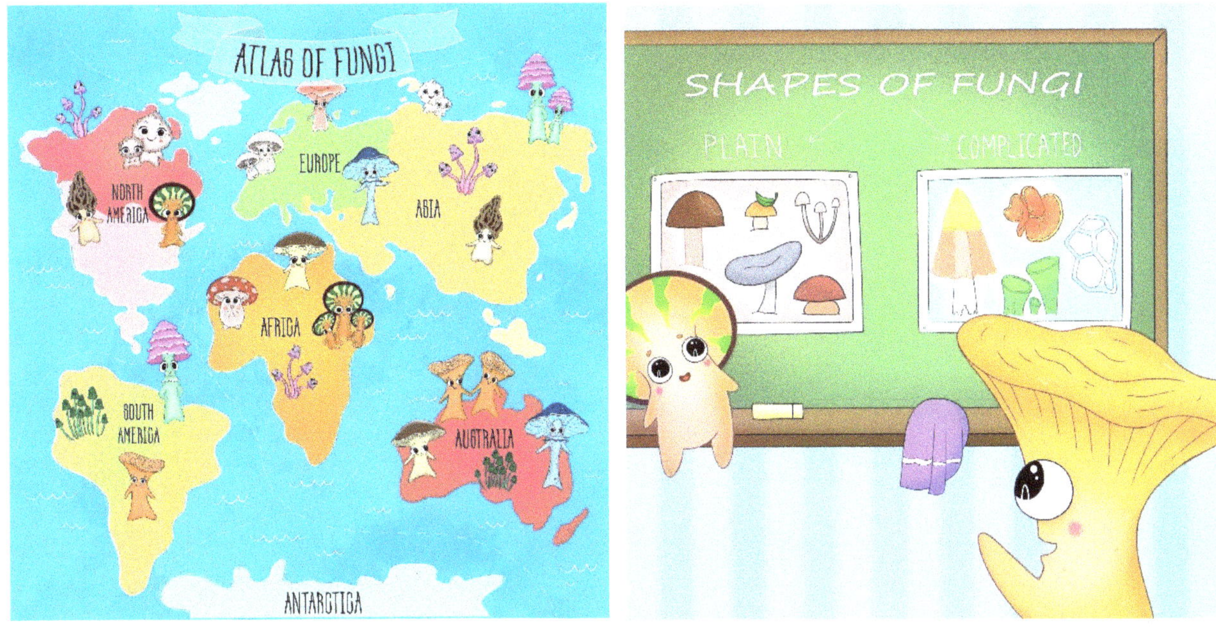

…and *A Week of August Weather*… The original artist's art is on the left above and below and Anastasia copied the 'style' to match and finish the book. Sometimes artists can't finish a project for one reason or another. It can be very difficult to find someone who can match the style closely enough to finish the project.

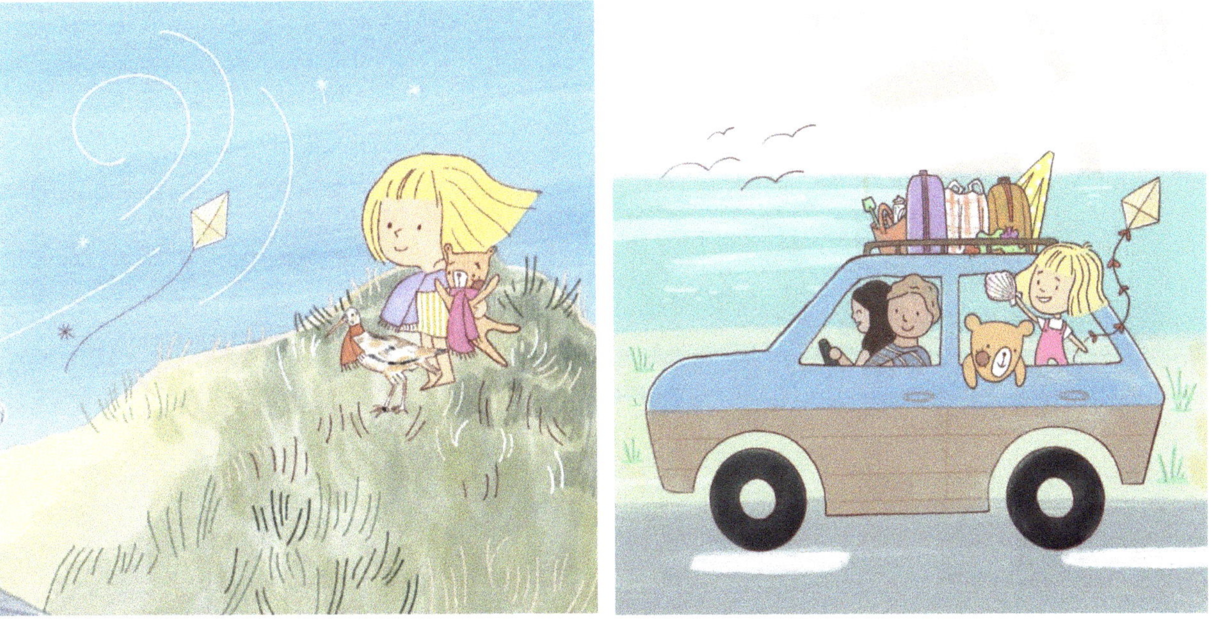

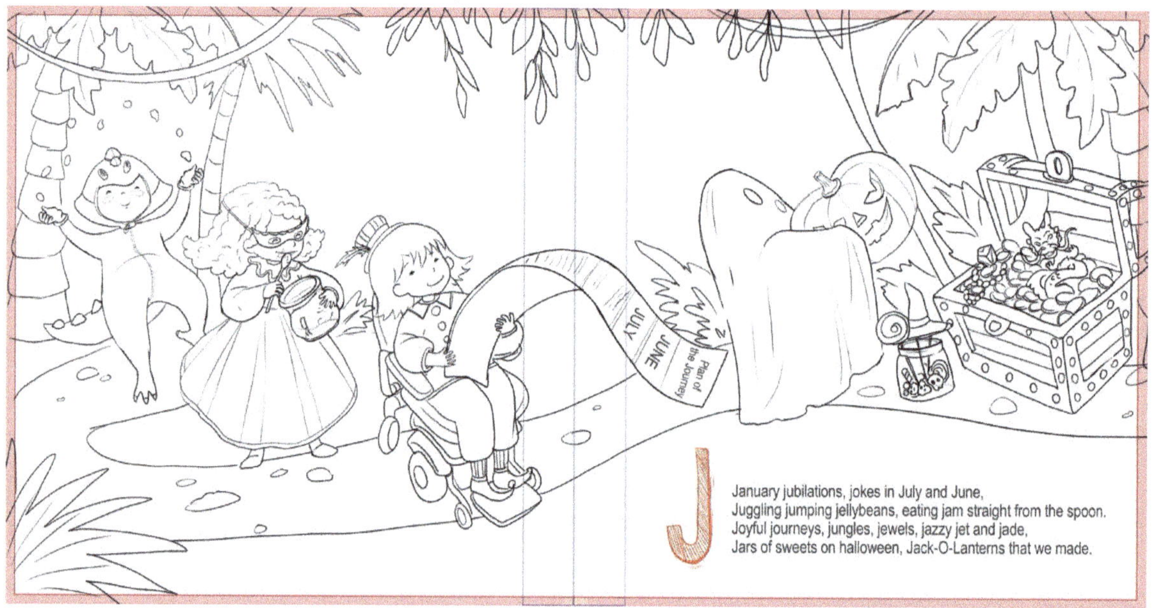

January jubilations, jokes in July and June,
Juggling jumping jellybeans, eating jam straight from the spoon.
Joyful journeys, jungles, jewels, jazzy jet and jade,
Jars of sweets on halloween, Jack-O-Lanterns that we made.

When my artists create my 8 inch x 8 inch picture books, some create 16 inch x 8 inch spreads. When they do, they leave room in the center for where the binding will be and if important art is here, it will be lost in the binding or difficult to see, so they give themselves margins to work within. Also, this particular artist allows enough room for placement of the words. This allows them to be read easily and they are positioned in a place that will not be in area of the 'binding' either.

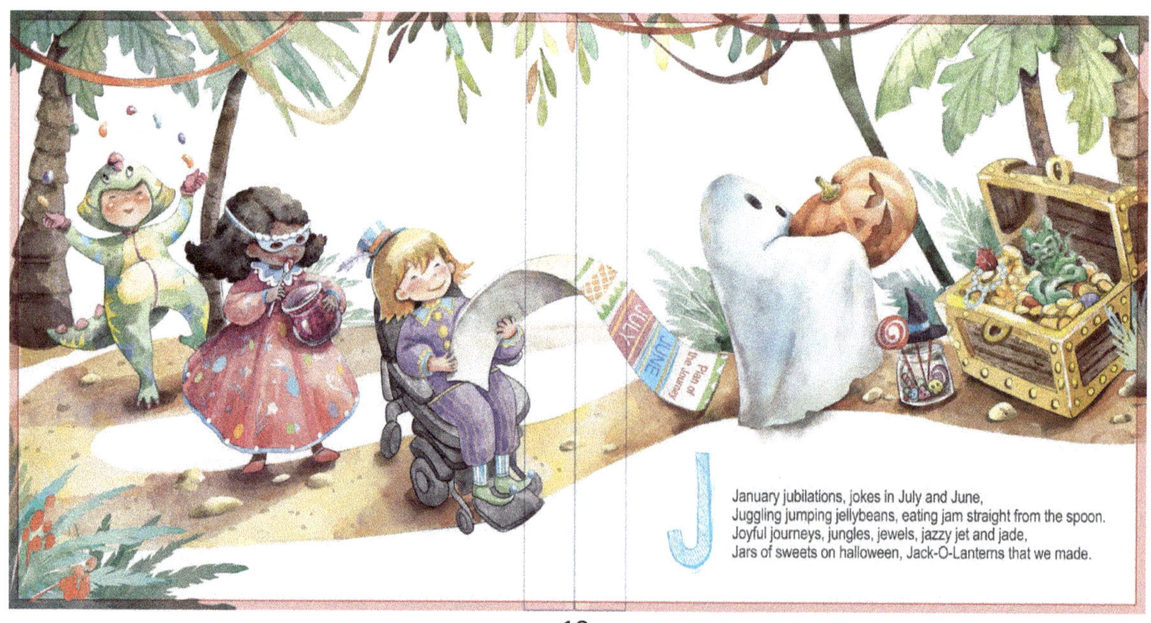

January jubilations, jokes in July and June,
Juggling jumping jellybeans, eating jam straight from the spoon.
Joyful journeys, jungles, jewels, jazzy jet and jade,
Jars of sweets on halloween, Jack-O-Lanterns that we made.

After these rough sketches and colored samples, she splits the pictures into 8 inch x 8 inch files for me to create the book as I do in my book creation software program. I add the text after I receive the pics.

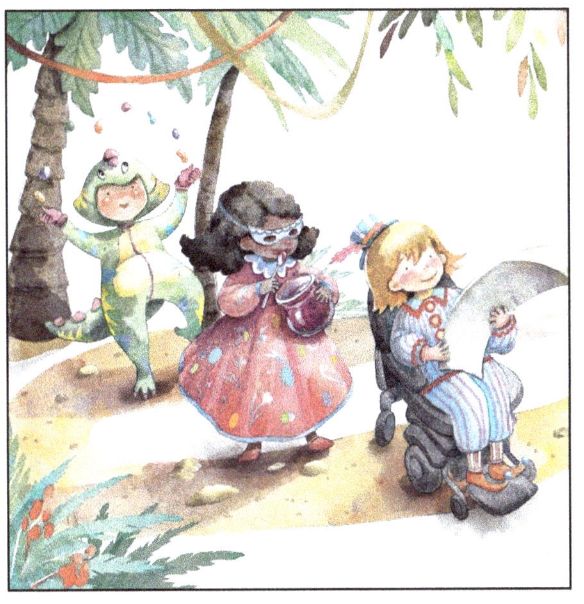
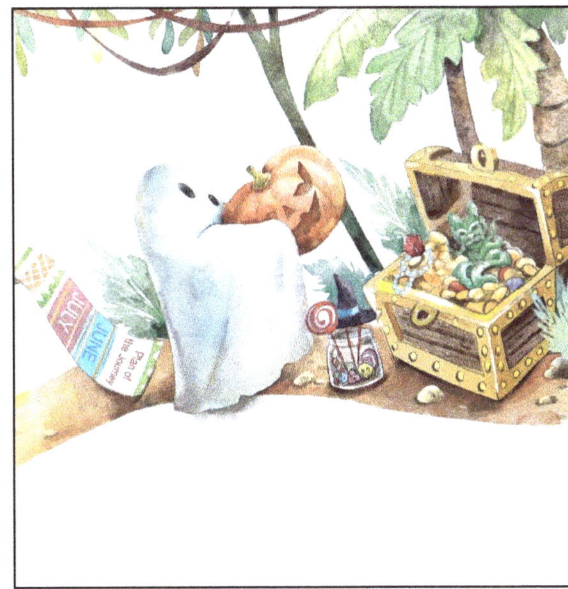

So, we can see how the pictures bring the story to life! And, no matter who's doing the art, it is the special part of children's picture books.

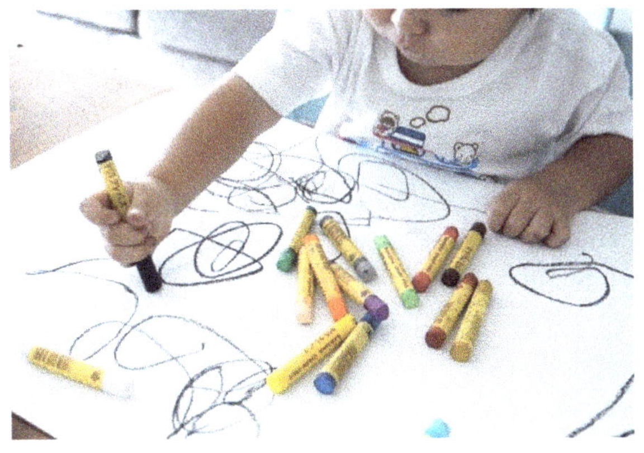

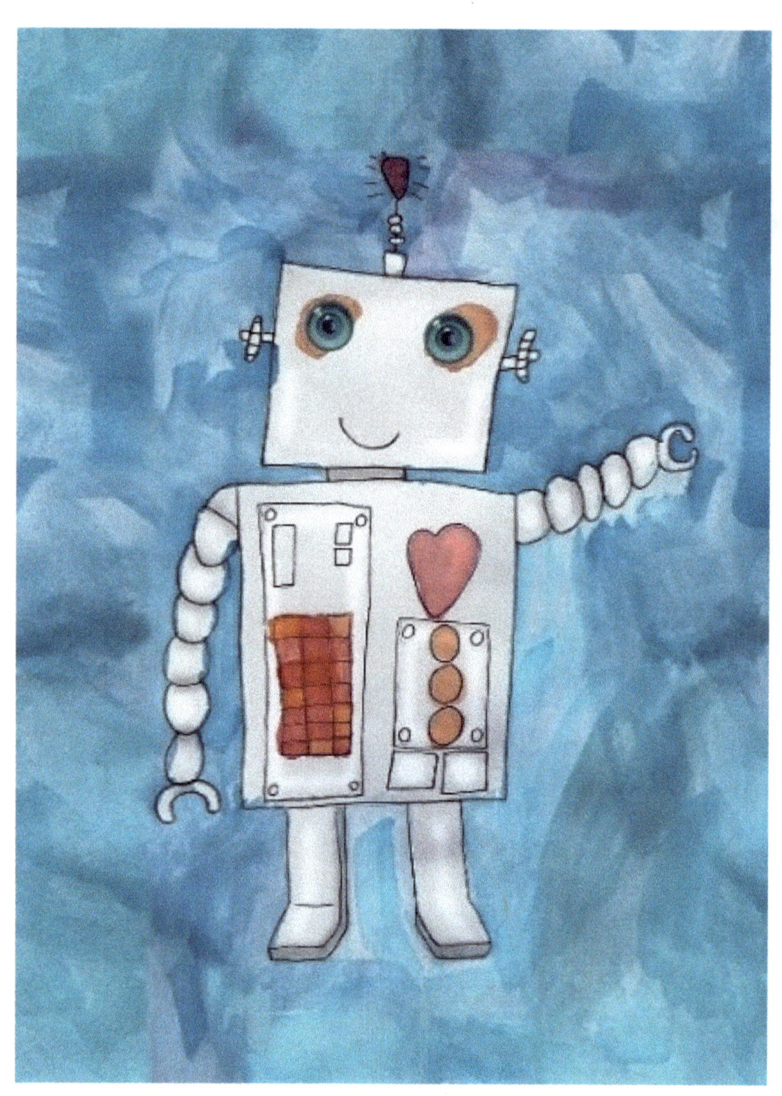

3

You've Got Style

**Each artist has a style and
manner in which they do their work.**

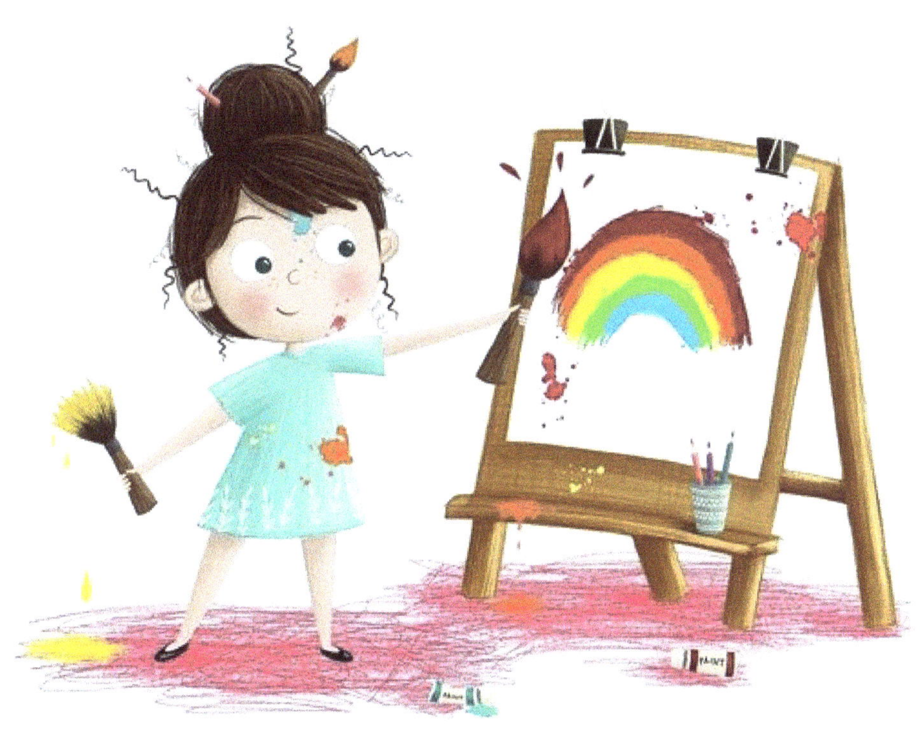

Let's take a look at different art styles.

Every artist has a unique style. Some can do more than one style.. One artist seems to be able to copy any art style I ask her to. There were a few times when an artist was unable to complete a project and I had part or most of a project completed.

During my search for artists for different projects, I received many different styles. Some were cartoony, digital, realistic, or some artists created their art by hand and completed individual work. Most artists work in a program that allows them to make changes easily. I will elaborate as I continue in this chapter.

Sometimes when I viewed sample art, I was overwhelmed. For example –

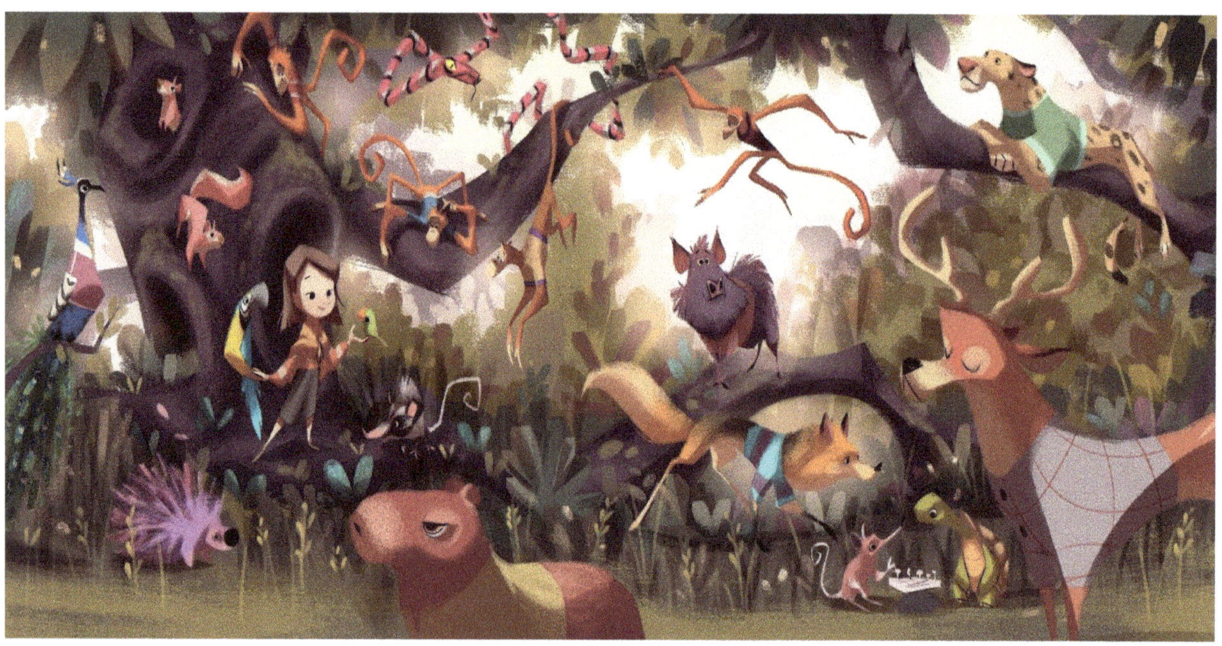

There is so much detail in this. It's a little darker than I prefer for children's literature, but I just LOVE all the detail and the action and interaction in this art sample.

I think this art is stunning and the talented artist that sent this to me was willing to partner on a picture book project, but the art he submitted was not this style. It is confusing to me when I appreciate a style and want to contract for that particular style and the art samples sent for a project don't match. This happens frequently and it makes me think perhaps the artist for a sample is not the same artist for a project. I'm still not certain, but when submitting samples, I think artists should represent the 'style' they are able to provide for an entire picture book.

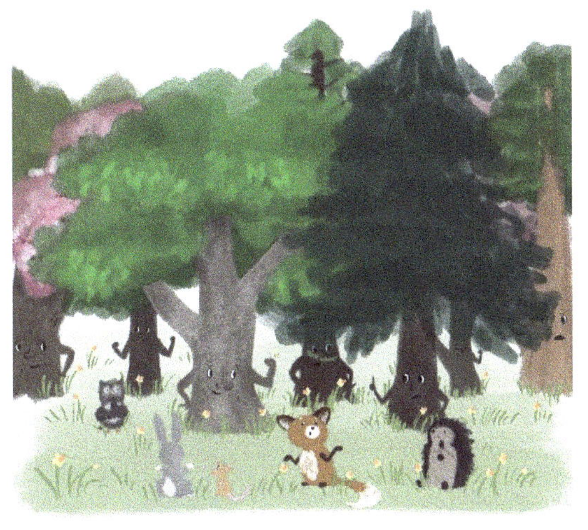

This artist partnered on several projects and her style is simple, but cute with details.

Alexsandra's art is simple. She hand draws and watercolors as seen here.

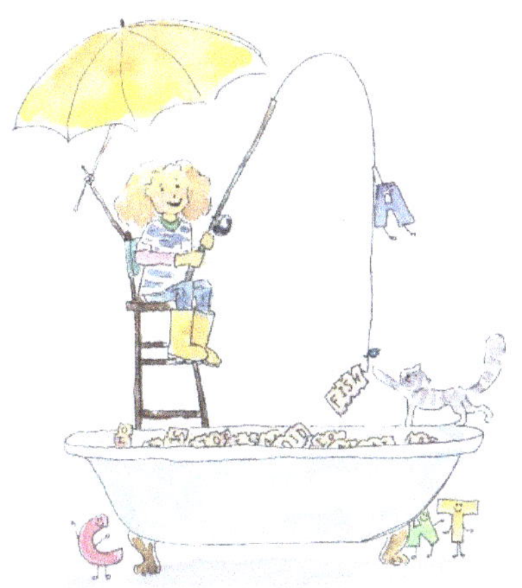

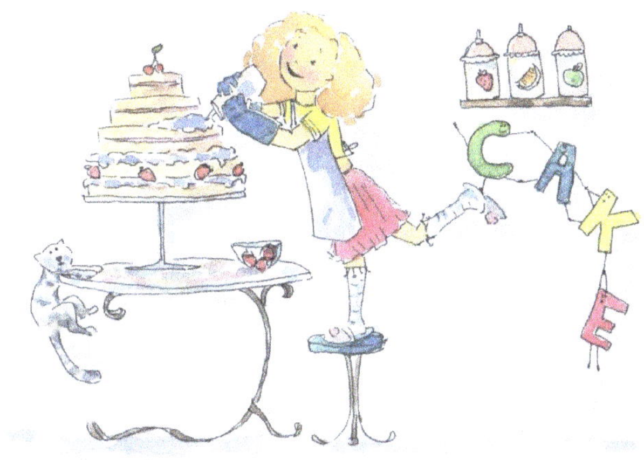

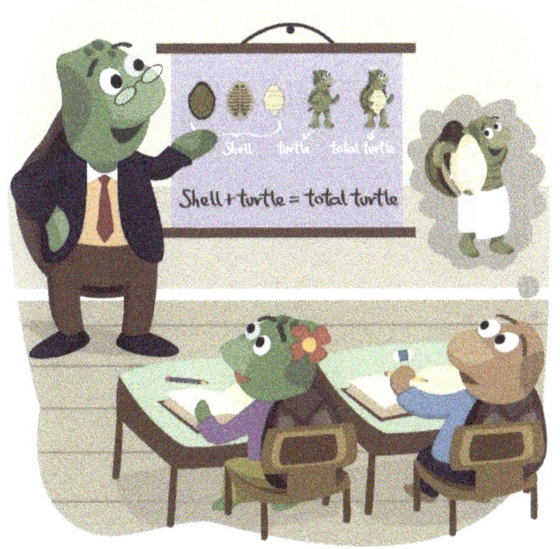

The artist for the book *Turtles and Tortoises are Tremendous* created cute pictures of the turtles and dressed them in cute clothing and added the glasses for the teacher.

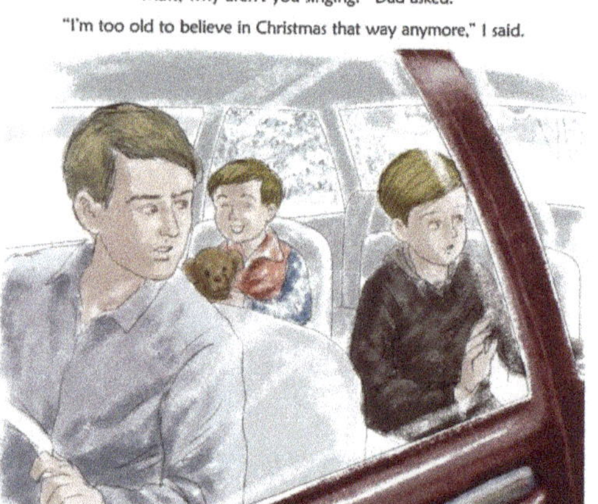

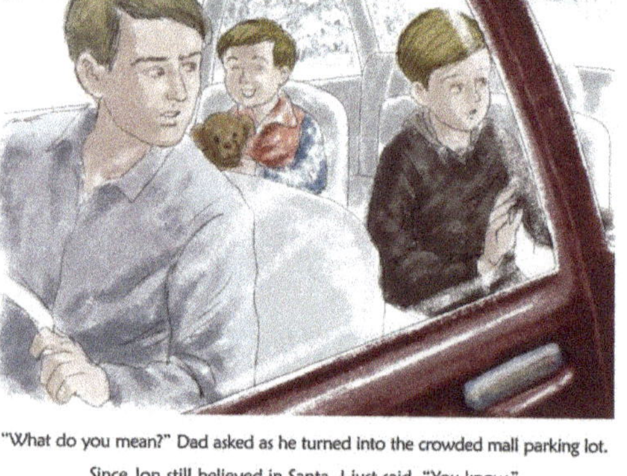

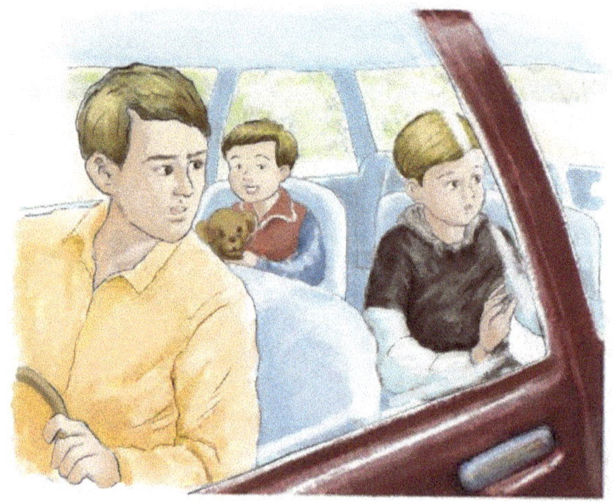

I first met talented Olesya when I needed pictures from one of my personal books recolored. I'm sure you can see what a difference she made. Since we met and she helped with these, she has partnered with me on many other books. Her style varies, but the one style I really appreciate is her 'soft' edges style like in *Finding L......*

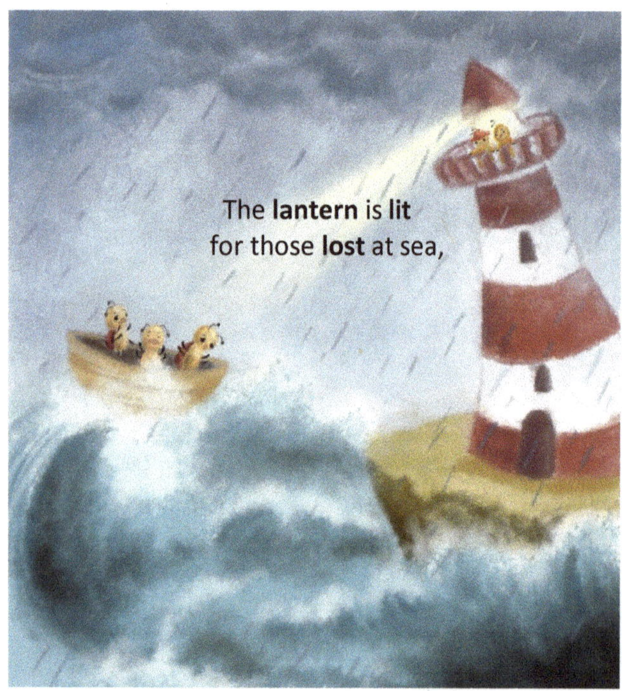

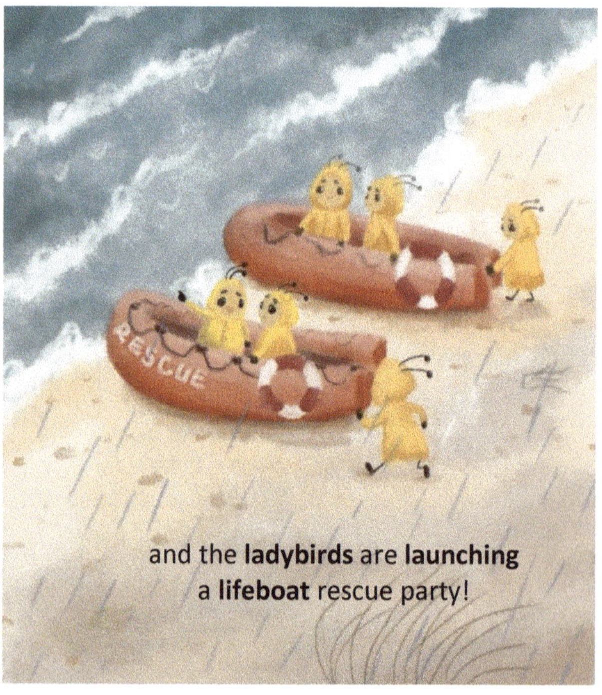

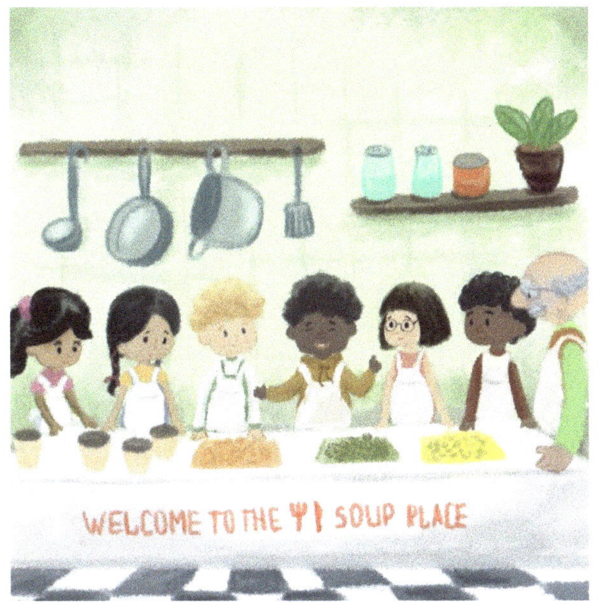

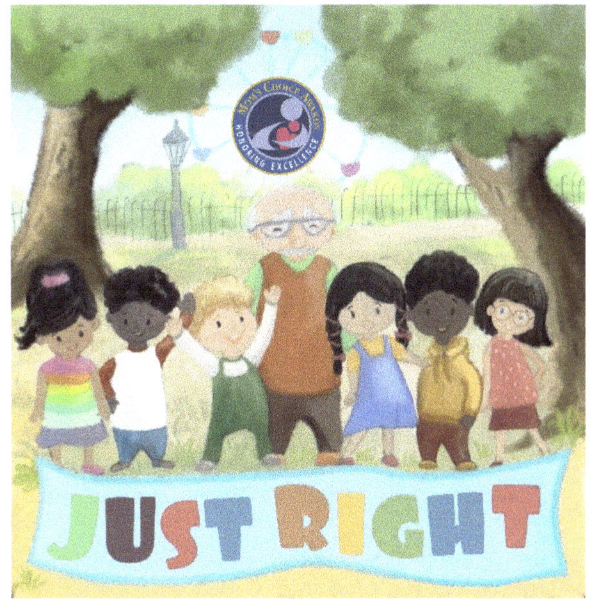

Just Right is a 'Mon's Choice Award' silver medal winner. It was not awarded a gold medal due to the illustrations appearing 'blurry,' however, this is the intended 'look' in this book and the softer style I really love. Her style is different than Timm's artwork below in *'Animal Academy'* where the animals come to school. He does lovely art and outlines all his characters and structures he adds to his work. It is crisper.

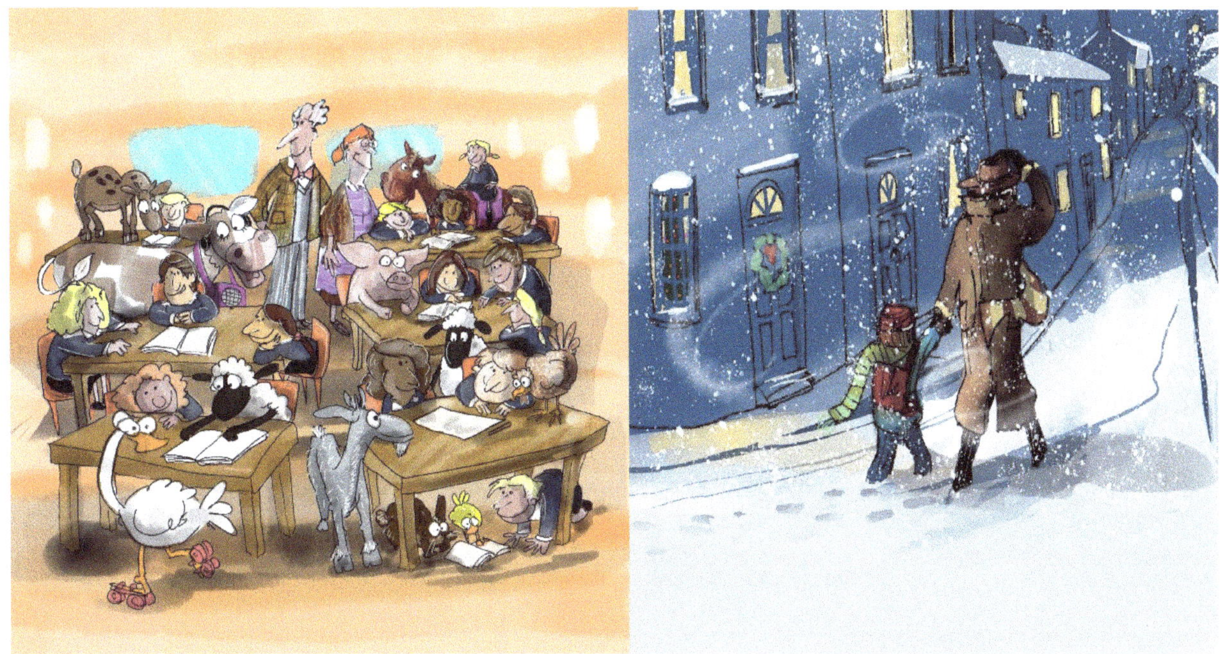

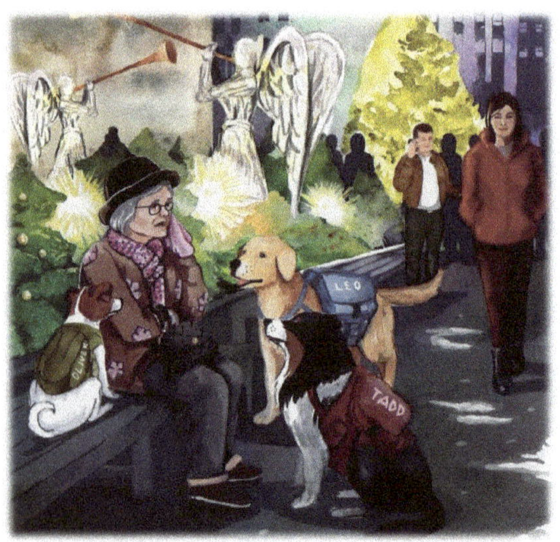

We huddled close together in New York. We found Emily.
She was crying. "I lost my little dog, Tiny," she said.

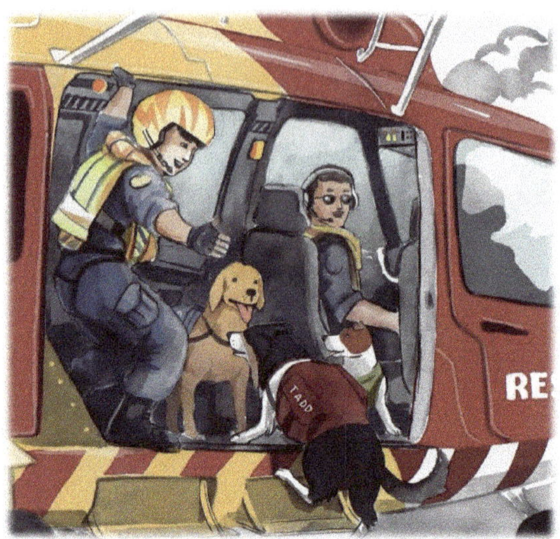

We flew in Jack's helicopter to the tallest mountains in the
world! "We have to find him fast, boys! A big storm is
coming in!" We understood and were ready to rescue.

I found Indra for my book titled *In Search of Christmas* where three search and rescue dogs from Minnesota, USA overhear their owners claim we've lost Christmas. They jump into action and travel the globe meeting people like Emily who love them. They jump in helicopters and more to journey to find Christmas. Indra was recruited for the second book *In Search of Easter* where the family has grown, the dogs have pups, and their owners have adopted little Scottie who searches for Easter with one pup.

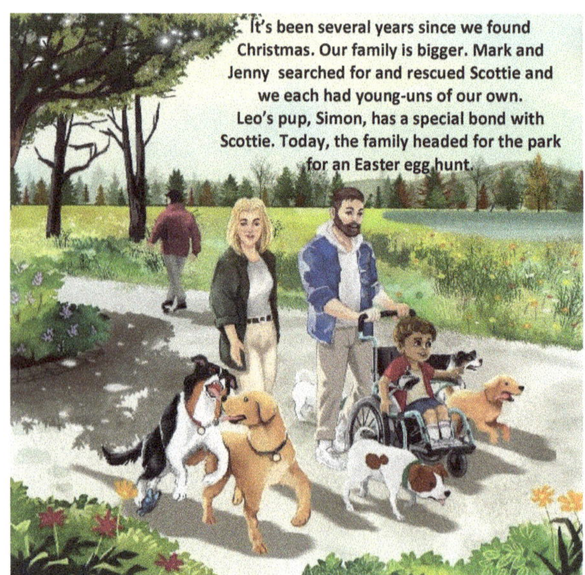

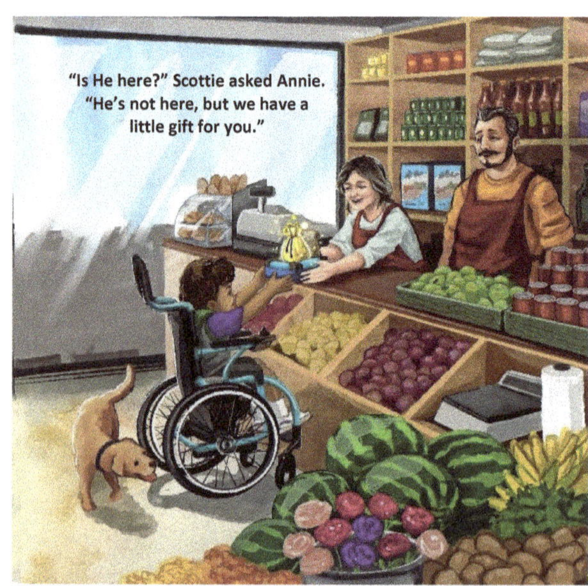

Indra's style is realistic more than most children's books, but it matched these books.

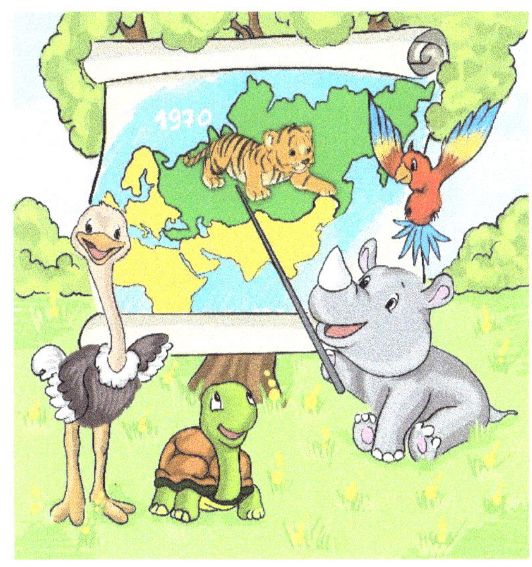

Some like a little more cartoon-like look for their book. This little book is about animals that have become extinct and the artist made all the animals look like they are straight out of the nursery and cute.

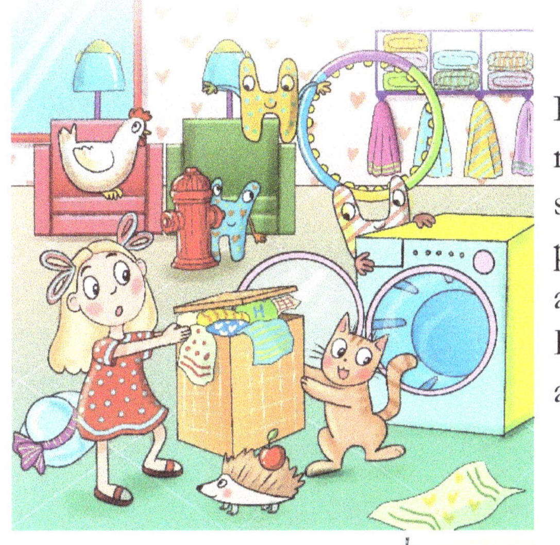

In Finding H – it happens at the hairdresser and many things go wrong. Anna Naboka brings the story to life and you can see how much detail she puts in each page. Fun stuff with the kitty helping and the wash becoming a chore. She also placed H items in the picture- like the hen and hydrant and hat and more.

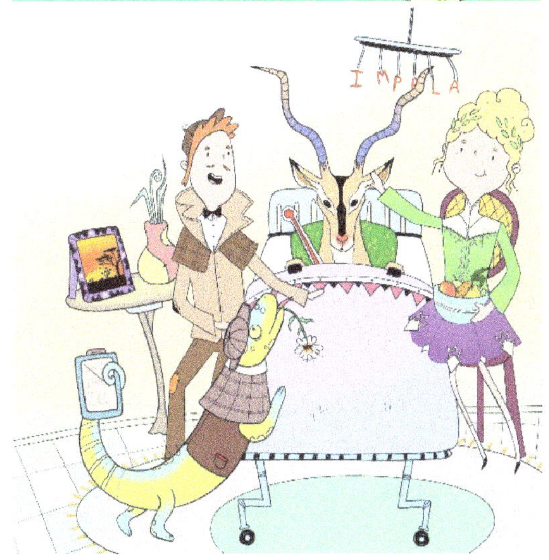

This is *Finding I* – it's about an inspector and his iguana side-kick visiting an impala in the hospital. We wanted the books to be different in settings but also different in their style of art so they were more interesting. This is always the author's choice, especially when a series is created.

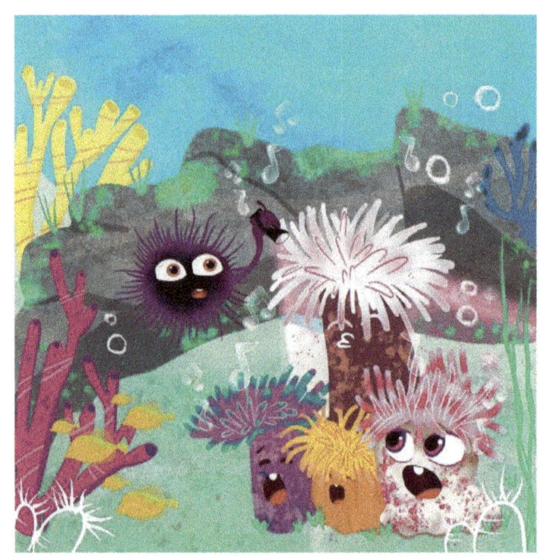

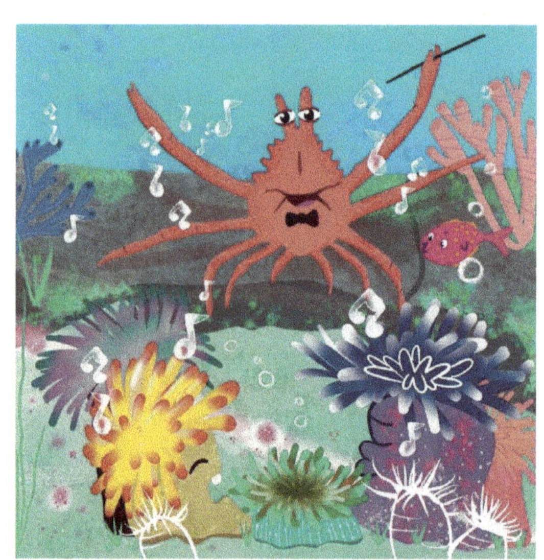

Finding U is interesting because it is set in the world under the water.

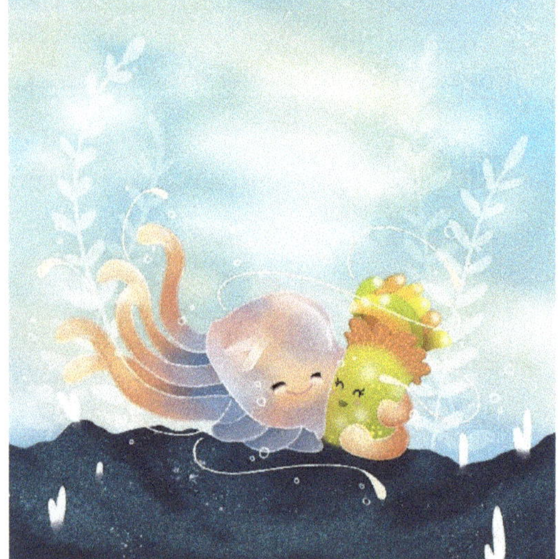

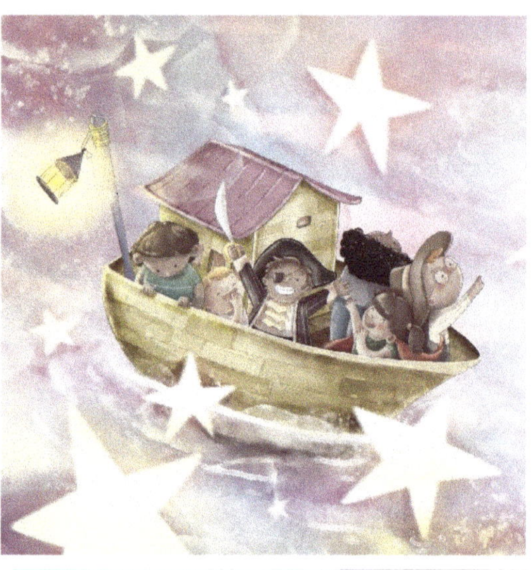

Caterina created the art for two books and they are marvelous

and her art style is perfect.

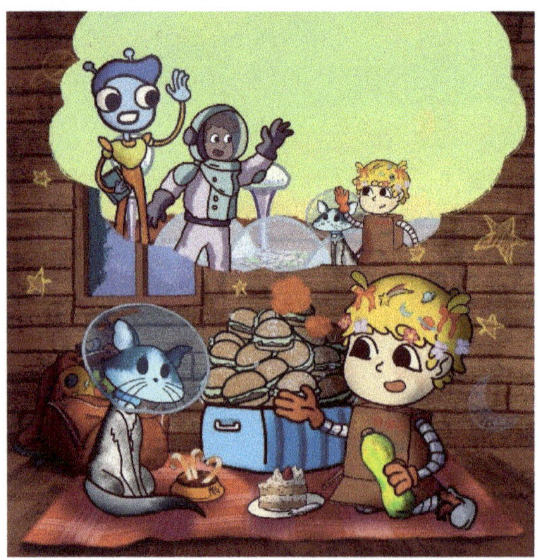

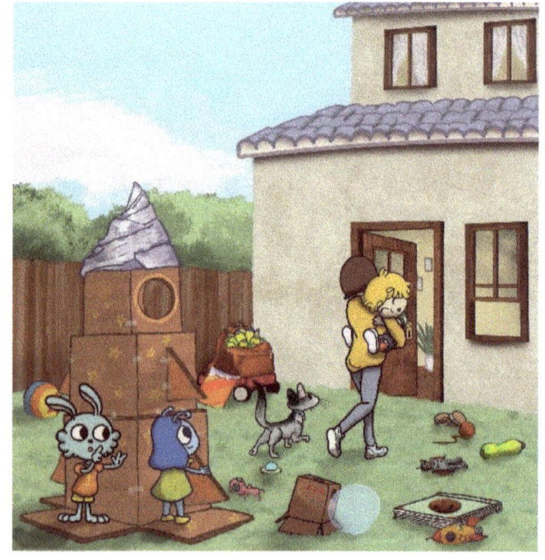

Germaine created a really cute book about Joe's trip to space with his cat too.

4

Storyboards

What is a storyboard? It's any way an artist and author have of making illustration suggestions for each page of a children's picture book. This is one example -

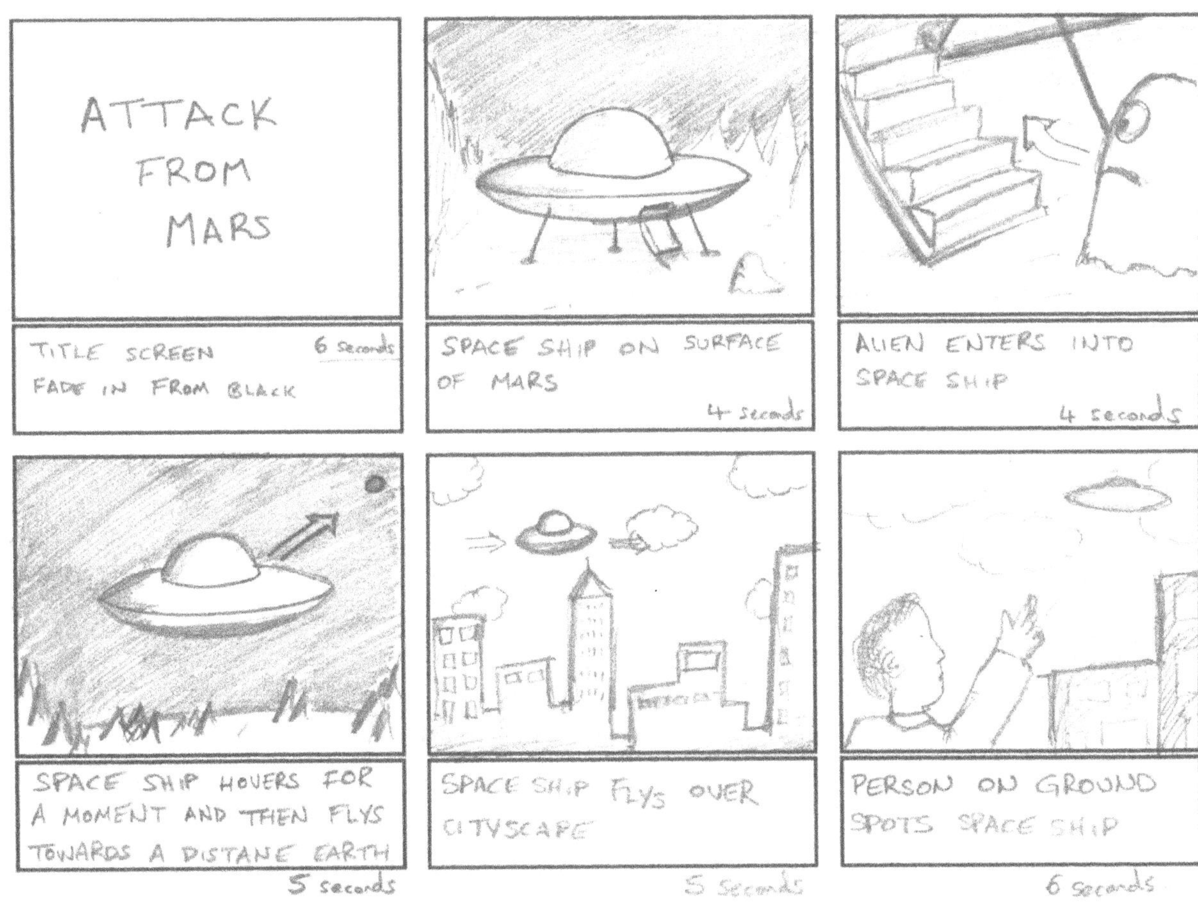

Storyboards can be actual boards with pictures drawn on them like this or they can be on a computer program if the artist works on such a device or sample sketches.

Storyboards are helpful to convey thoughts and ideas about the direction of a story's illustrations. It's a tool to understand everyone's vision is for the book. There have been many times when I appreciated an artist's 'style,' but when I asked for a simple sketch of characters or a sketch showing the artist's vision for the book, their ideas didn't match mine or the author's.

Obviously, a storyboard starts with the story. Authors send their stories for consideration to partner to publish their work. When they send the story, I review it and decide if I feel it's a project I can partner on. If I accept the story, I count the words and then I divide the sentences into 32-33 pages. I realize the industry standard is 32, but I like to end my illustrations on the right side of the page, so I add one extra illustration. Artists have been agreeable with this extra page. I then have the books, lines, and illustration ideas approved by the authors I work with.

After I create the page numbers the sentences / lines will be placed, I send this to the artist and author for their approval. If either make changes, I review those.

Then, I begin the process of written storyboard ideas. I write what I feel should be included in each illustration for each page and send these thoughts to the author. They make suggestions and we finalize the storyboard. I have included a partial example of one storyboard created for *Oscar's True Friends*. The story lines are BLACK, my thoughts are RED, and the author's thoughts are BLUE.

- In the vibrant waters of the coral reef lived Oscar, the most beautiful fish you'd ever see. Some of his scales gleamed in the sunlight. Other scales were bright beautiful colors that matched the coral reef. His long, elegant tail swished gracefully as he navigated the ocean currents. Just show Oscar swimming peacefully in the sunlight layer of the ocean. I think he should be special – and others should look at him with envy- the other ocean creatures? Jellyfish? Dolphin ? swordfish? And the coral reef beautiful around him

And this is what was illustrated –

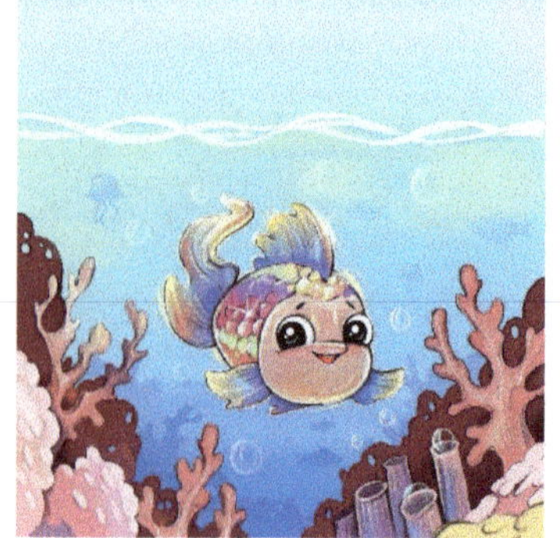

We didn't add any other characters in this picture I suggested in my note.

Another example of a written storyboard is for *Never 'TOO' Wonderful* written by me and illustrated by Nina – the text is black ink and my thoughts are RED -

Page 1 Kevin was a busy, busy boy
No matter how he tried and tried
He was forever in the same old rut
and "TOO" was all he ever cried   I WOULD APPRECIATE YOUR CUTE THOUGHTS HERE ABOUT HIM BEING BUSY AND CUTE – THESE ARE 8X8 PICS I THINK FOR EACH PAGE -AND HE CRIES 'TOO' -HE NEEDS A PET – A CAT OR DOG MAY BE OK, BUT MAYBE A CUTE AND UNIQUE PET ? PARROT THAT SAYS TOO TOO! MAY BE CUTE – THE BIRD SAYS WHAT KEVIN SAYS SOMETIMES

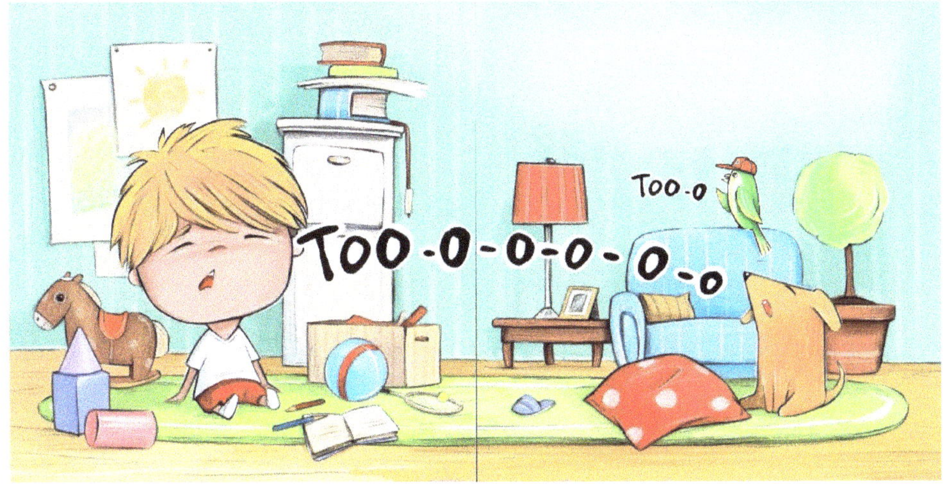

And this is what Nina created. She added the hat on the bird and has the bird and dog saying 'TOO!' very cute and more than I asked for in my written ideas.
Great detail too.

Page 2 The oatmeal was too hot
while the milk was way too cold   HOT CEREAL – SMOKE OVER THE BOWL, CHILLY CHATTERING TEETH WHEN HE SIPS THE MILK – THE BIRD IS CLOSE

Again, Nina took what I suggested, but she added the cutest details – the hat on the bird, the dog and bird saying TOO COLD/ TOO HOT

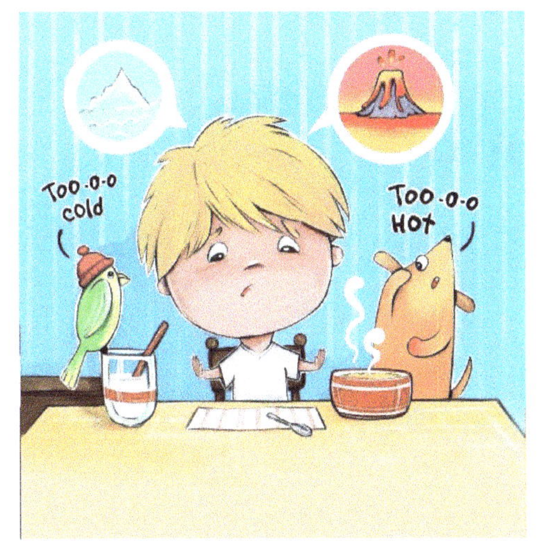

Page 3 the bathroom floor too wet
and the bath soap too slippery to hold HE'S IN THE SHOWER AND THE FLOOR IS WET AND OVER HIS FEET? HE'S DRESSED IN A BATHING SUIT WITH A FLOAT AROUND HIS WAIST ?? AND THE BATH SOAP KEEPS JUMPING OUT OF HIS HANDS AND HE'S NOT MAD, BUT FRUSTRATED -THE BIRD HAS AN UMBRELLA AND SAYS SLIPPERY SLOPE

Nina added a shower cap on the bird – cute add.

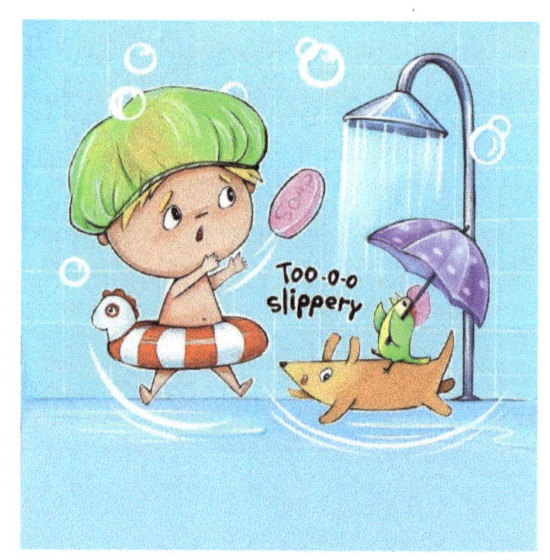

Page 4 Waiting for the bus takes TOO Long
and the other children are much TOO loud
Kevin mumbled everyone thinks I'm TOO impatient
But this is much TOO large a crowd! THE OTHER CHILDREN ARE THERE AND HE PUSHES TO THE FRONT OF THE LINE AS THE BUS IS ARRIVING AND THE NOISE ? HE HAS THINGS ON HIS EARS FOR THE NOISE- Nina added ear covers for the bird as well as the bird says 'TOO loud' – she leaves room on the pages for the words as well

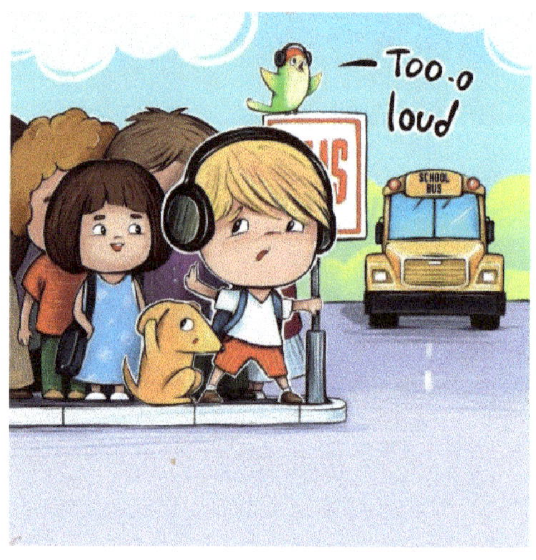

Page 5 Kevin often sits to think of all things TOO
There were pencils that are too thick or too thin
And it was either TOO cloudy or the sun too bright
And that's just where Kevin would begin HE'S IN THE BACKYARD – IN THE SUN WITH SUN GLASSES AND LEMONADE AND THERE ARE PENCILS THICK AND THIN AROUND HIM AND THE CLOUDS IN THE SKY AND SUN ARE THERE TOO - FUN THINGS AROUND HIM? PETS AND HIS BIRD -WITH THE THICK AND THIN PENCIL SHOWING HIM EACH OF THEM

Nina adds cute hats and the pals reinforcing the words in the lines.

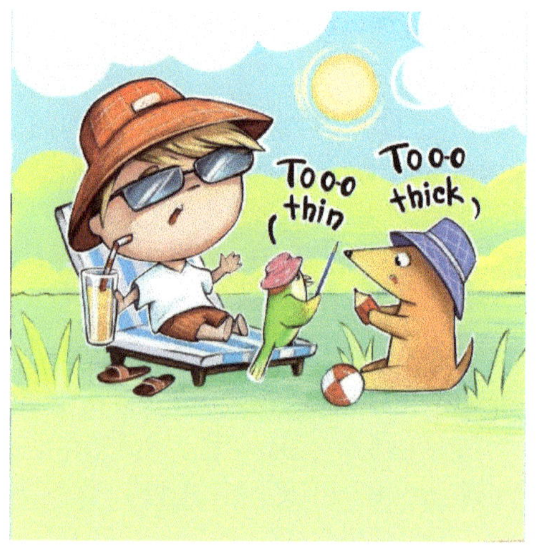

Page 6 When Kevin wanted to play with others he was TOO tired and TOO bored he'd say Kevin was TOO silly and sent his friends away Kevin said we'll play some other day HE'S IN HIS ROOM – UNDER THE COVERS WITH HIS BIRD UNDER WITH HIM AND HIS FRIENDS ARE AT THE BEDROOM DOOR WITH MUM Nina didn't do exactly what is suggested but she does a really nice job because his mum at the door is just fine and the pillow over the bird's head is cute. Some artists need every detail written and some – like Nina – are excellent at creativity.

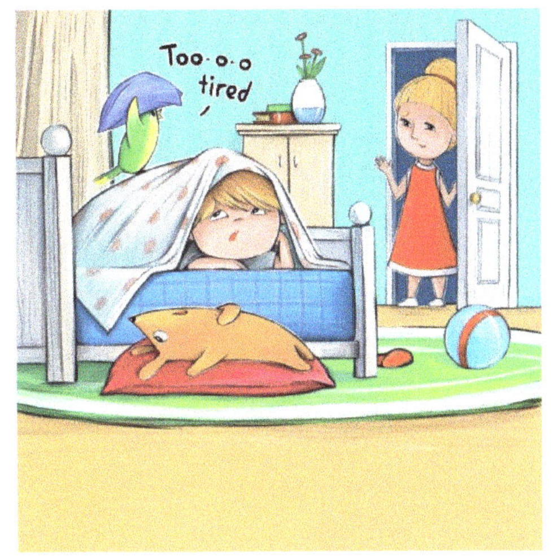

Page 7 Kevin always said hiking hills were TOO difficult to climb HIM AND THE BIRD HIKING – DRESSED IN HIKING CLOTHING AND A SMALL HILL – HE'S COMPLAINING ABOUT
Page 8 His bike was too big and too red MUM AND DAD GIVE HIM A BIKE FOR BIRTHDAY AND IT'S RED AND NOT THAT BIG BUT BIG FOR HIM?? AND HE PUTS HIS HAND UP AND THE BIRD PUTS HIS WING UP TO SHOW TOO BIG
9 His kite would fly way too low
And I'm too frustrated is what he said KEVIN'S KITE FLIES LOW AND GETS INTO SOMETNING? THE CLOTHESE LINE OR THE NEIGHBOR'S PICNIC- AND THE BIRD IS FLYING ON THE KITE TOO WITH BINOCULARS TO SEE AHEAD   Below is Nina's vision for this book and she cutely adds a bike helmet in the left pic and a flyer hat in the right illustration. These small details are great.

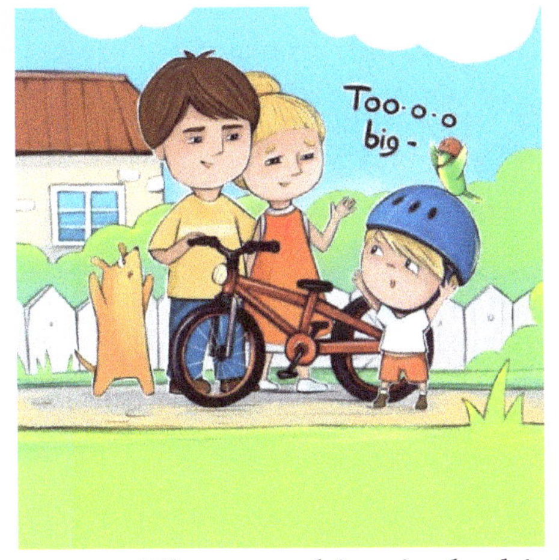

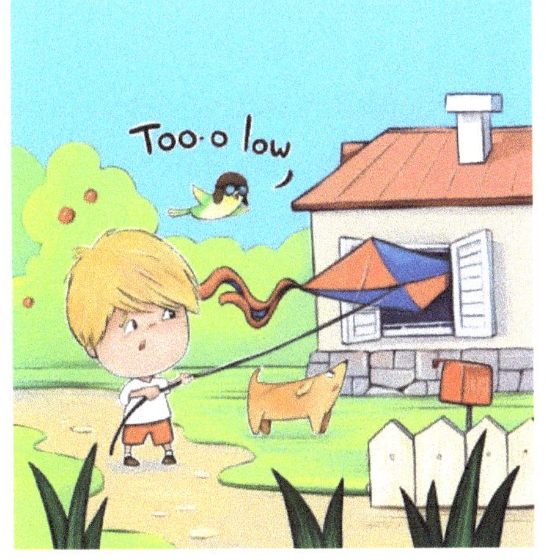

The cute thing is the bird showing BIG as well as Kevin.

Small details may not be specifically outlined in each line of written storyboard, but I always encourage artists to add their creativity. Artists are creative by definition – that's what an artist is – a creative person. Nina not only had these cute hats on the bird and added details of the dog and bird helping Kevin with his 'TOO' dilemma, she added these hats as well – fire hat, Santa hat, Mexican and cowboy hats and more.

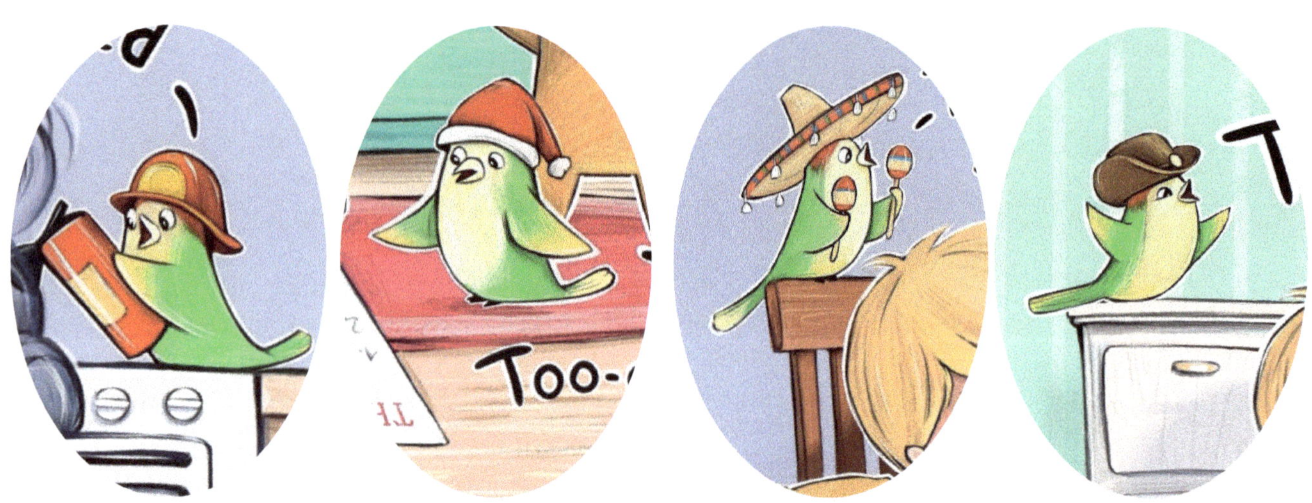

Aren't they cute? She gave the little bird a hat for every picture – one he has a graduation cap for the topic of intelligence. And with the Mexican hat, she added the Morroccos for spicy food.

Some artists prefer every small detail be included in the storyboard for every picture, but that's exhausting to do. I feel an artist should be able to create beautiful children's art with what I consider are 'guidelines.' After working together or doing a couple pictures with sketches, most of the time an artist acquires a 'feel' for what a publisher or author would like so the working relationship develops nicely with time.

Some artists create the entire storyboard themselves. I really appreciate when this happens because it is difficult at times to create new ideas. Some stories are interesting themselves and lend to cute and creative art, however, some are plain and it's nice when an artist can give a story a creative twist. Everyone has different ideas on how to make a story come alive on the pages and no one does this better than the creative force of the artist themselves. I have grown as an author from relationships with my artists.

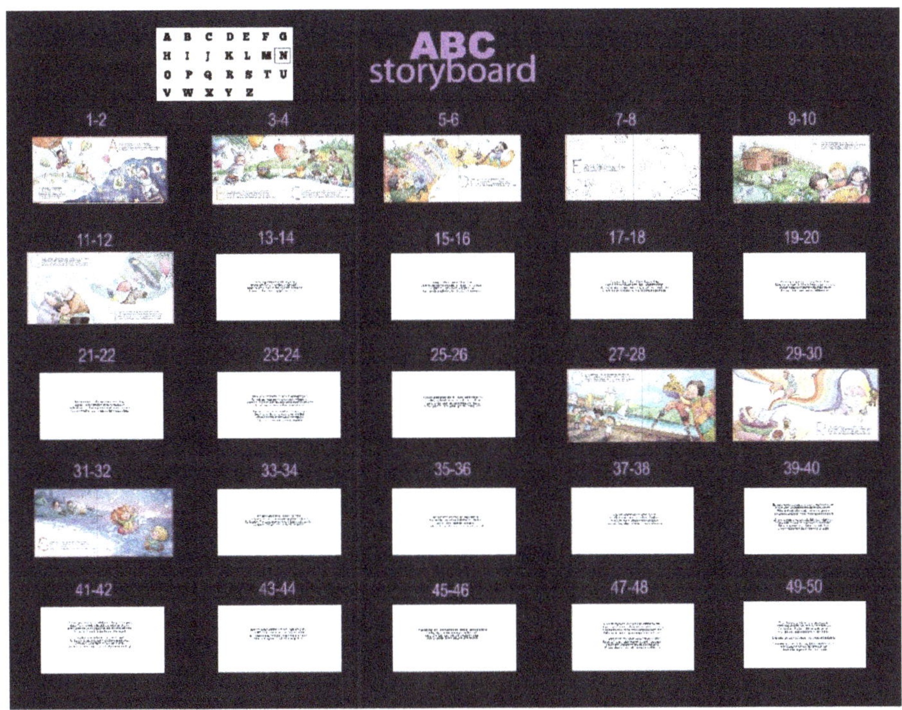

One of my favorite artists provides a storyboard for the illustrations. She sends a division of the words into pages and her ideas for how the art will be created – mostly as two-page spreads. Then, she sends me updates until it's all finished …

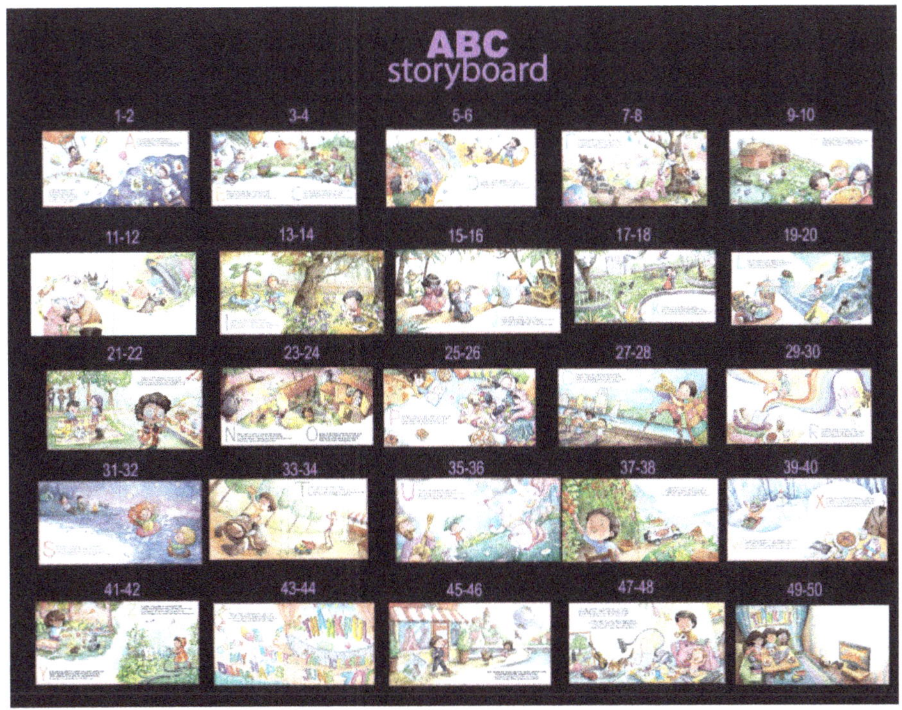

However, some stories don't lend themselves to two-page spreads and the art is created as single pictures such as this partial storyboard for *Come and Go Steve-O* where some of her illustrations are two-page spreads and some are single 8x8 inch illustrations.

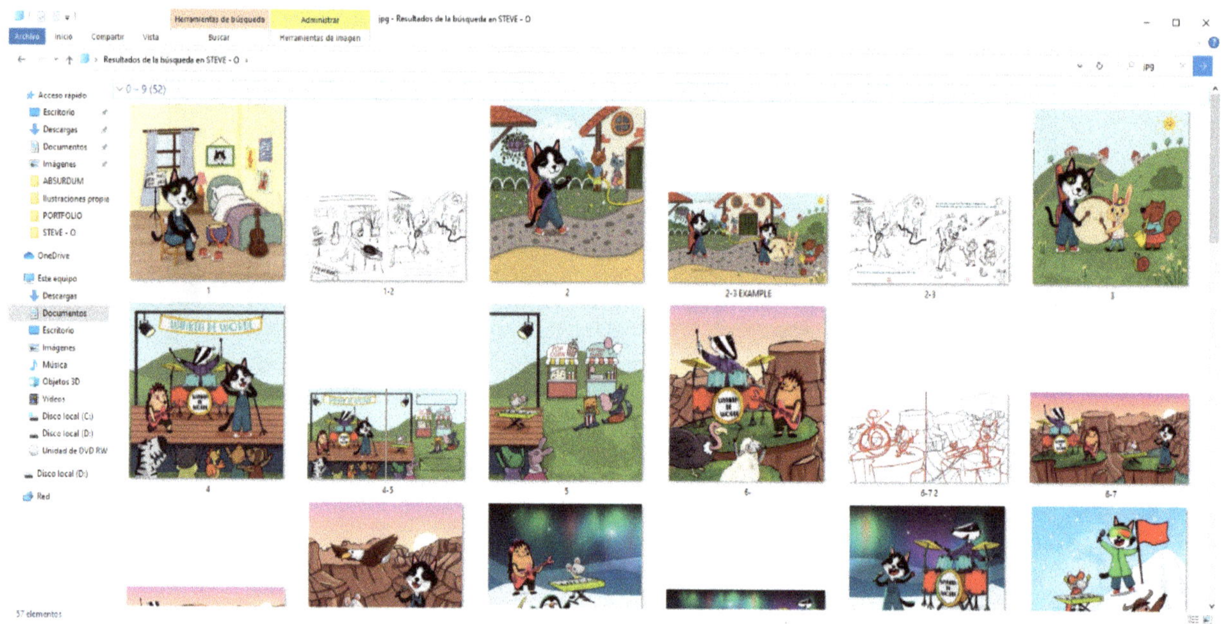

Some artists do their work one frame or picture at a time. They send a sketch and after that is approved, they beautifully color it as in *Not All Fairies Are the Same*.

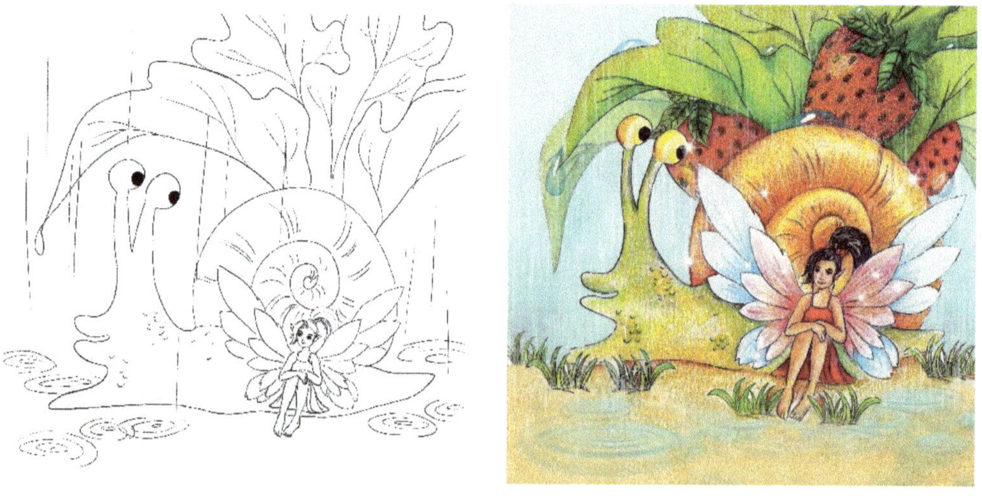

And some artists send multiple sketches at one time if they are not sending all of them.

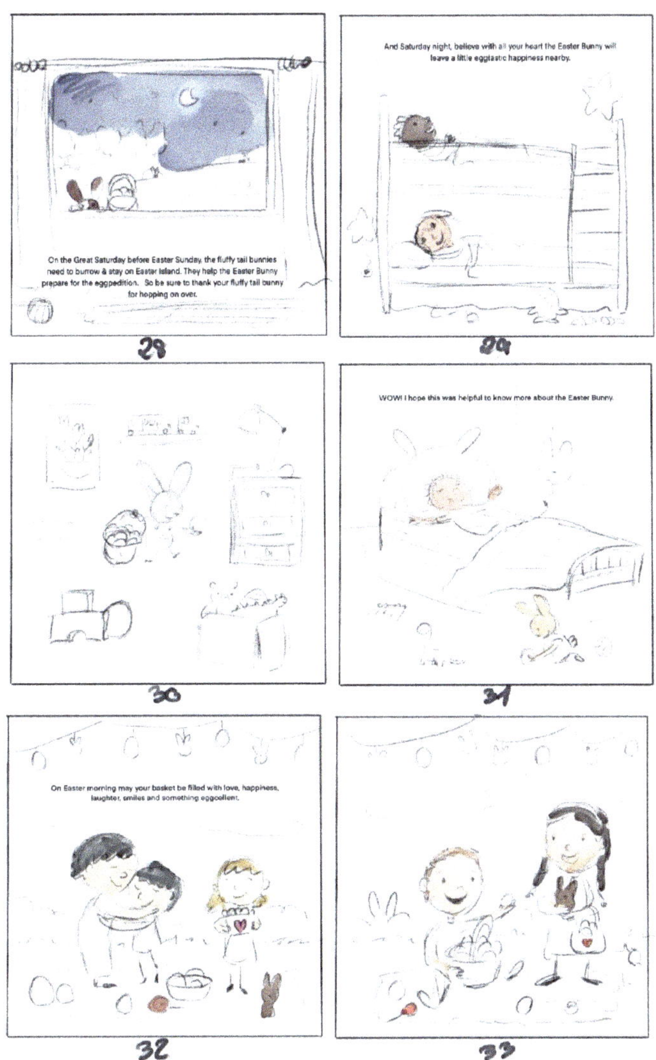

This is a way for an artist to break up the pages into a manageable number of illustrations for them to work with. Some do several pages at a time instead of one at a time or working all 28-32 illustrations – which is the industry standard. The number of pictures an artist works on at one time is individually decided by them. This works well if all the pictures are approved, however, it can be confusing if changes are requested and the details are lost in the number of illustrations elected to work on at one time.

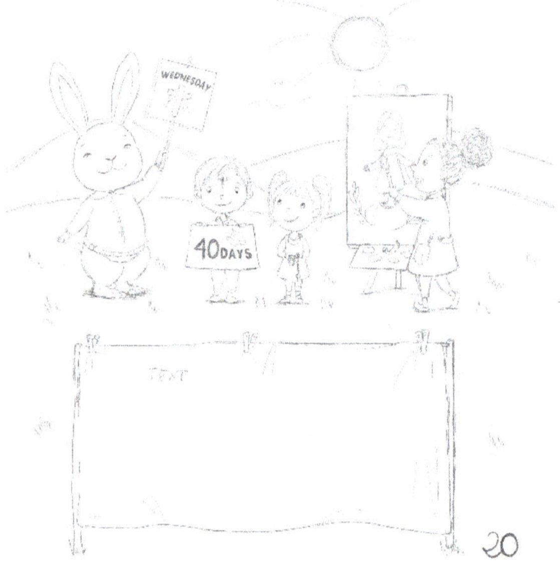

This sketch is difficult to visualize because it's light. However, it is also difficult to visualize what it will look like colored. This can be frustrating to an artist because when they submit this for approval and it is approved, it is frustrating when changes are requested but as is demonstrated below, the coloring makes a difference if an illustration is given a final 'thumbs-up' for acceptance as can be seen in the two colored pictures below.

As can be seen, the large 'white' area that is now easier to visualize in the colored version was not something the author felt she wanted in this picture. Since this artist works on a digital device, she was able to make the change very easily. This change can be frustrating because when a sketch is approved and then colored, it can be extra work to make requested changes.

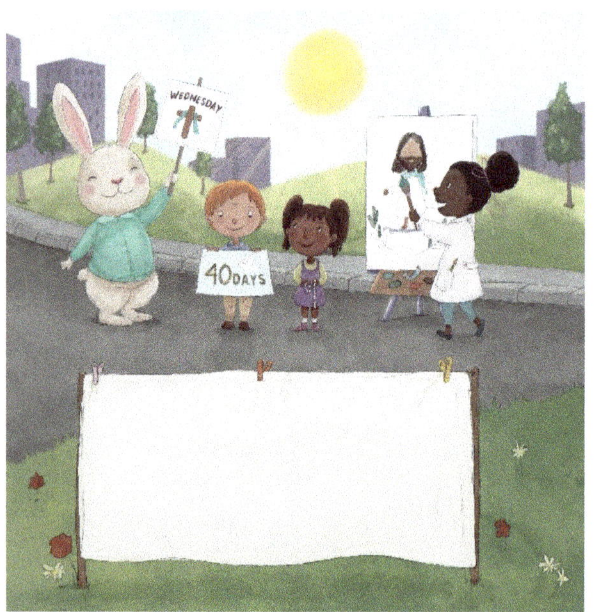

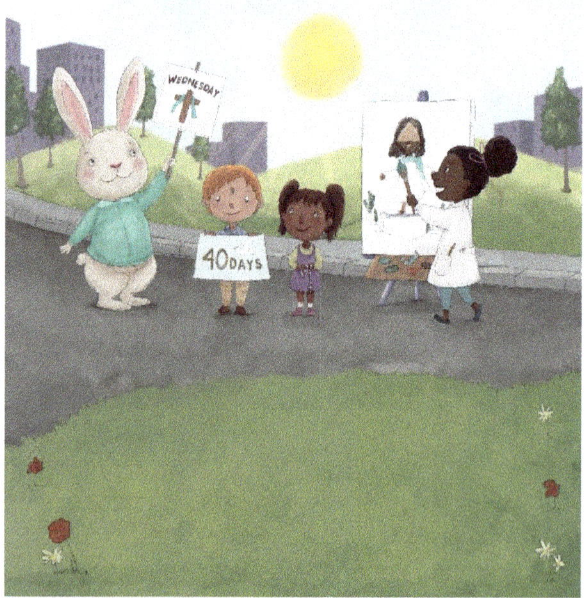

We've seen several different styles of storyboards and ways artists make use of them, so, work with your author or publisher and utilize a storyboard if you like them!

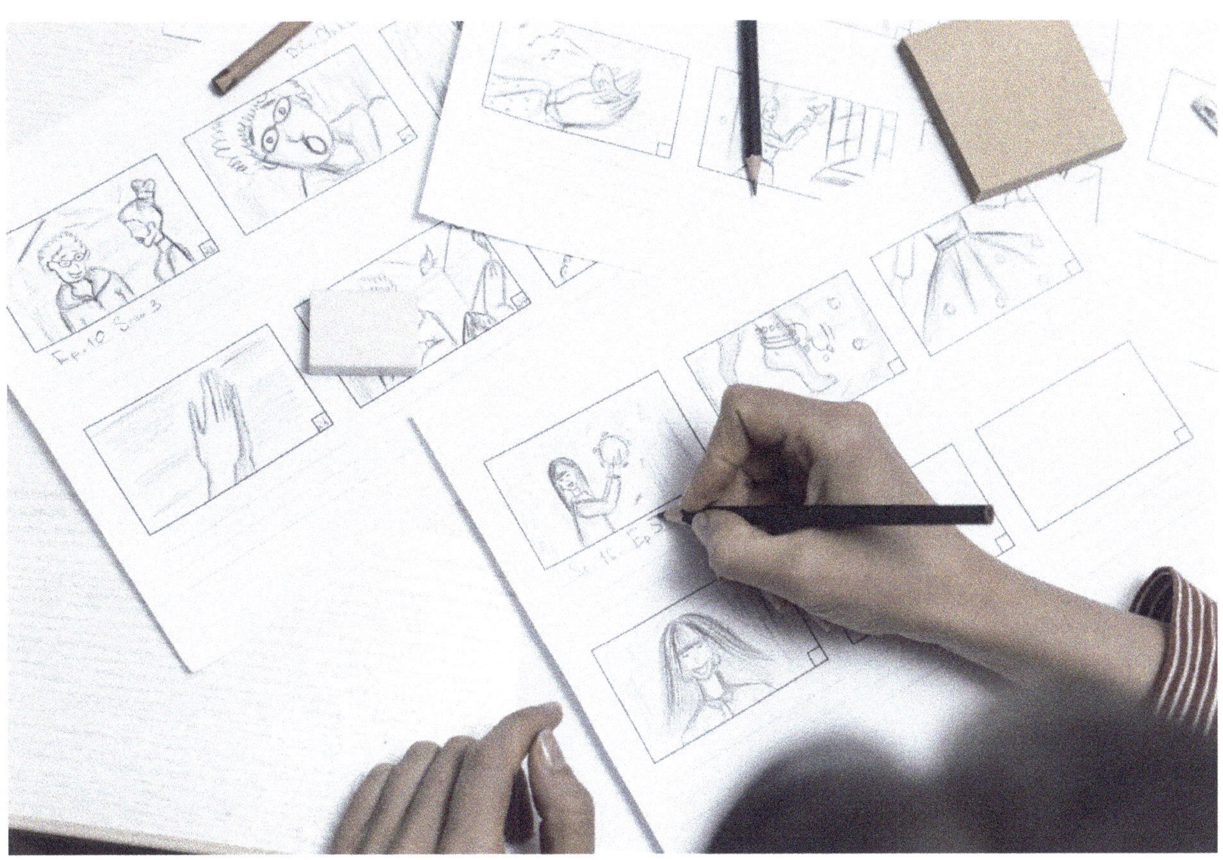

And create beautiful art!

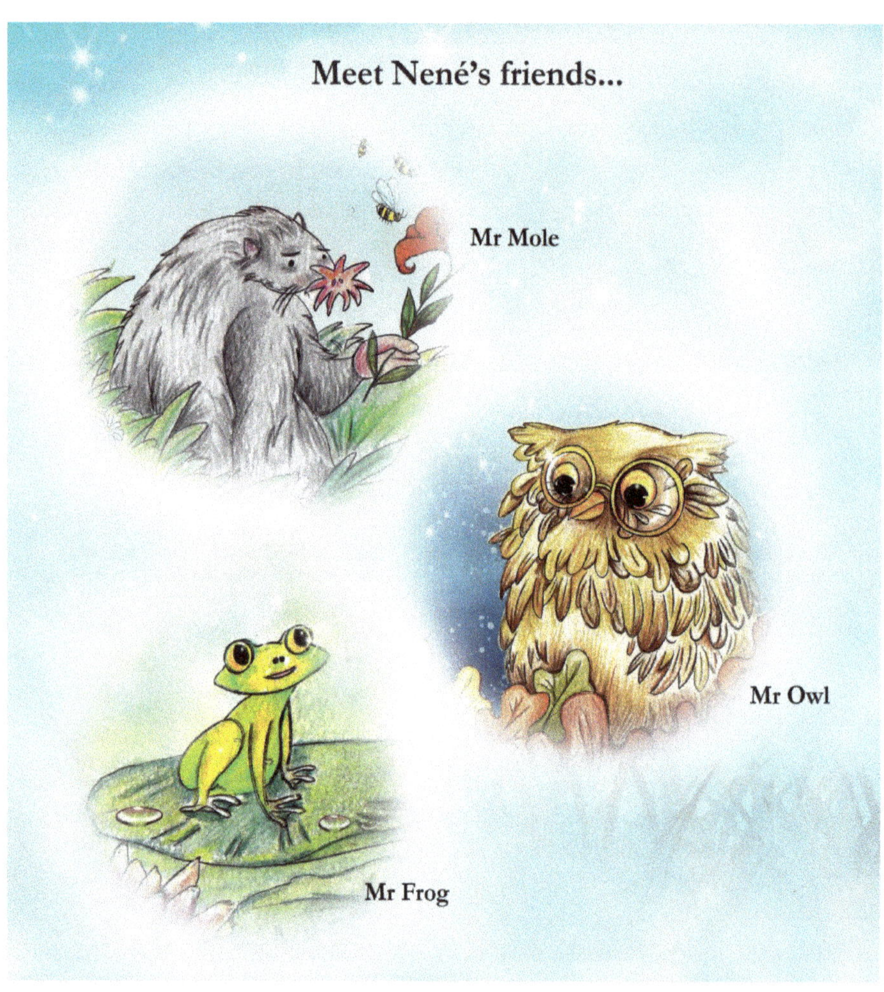

5

Unleashing Your Creativity
The Cute Factor

If you are an artist or author, you are CREATIVE!! You have lovely and wonderful talents within you. I say this to all my artists and authors. I want to share some of the truly beautiful art that artists from around the world have graciously given me to make the books I have published special.

This is Alexsandra. She was the first artist that taught me the art of art. She made everything clever and cute –

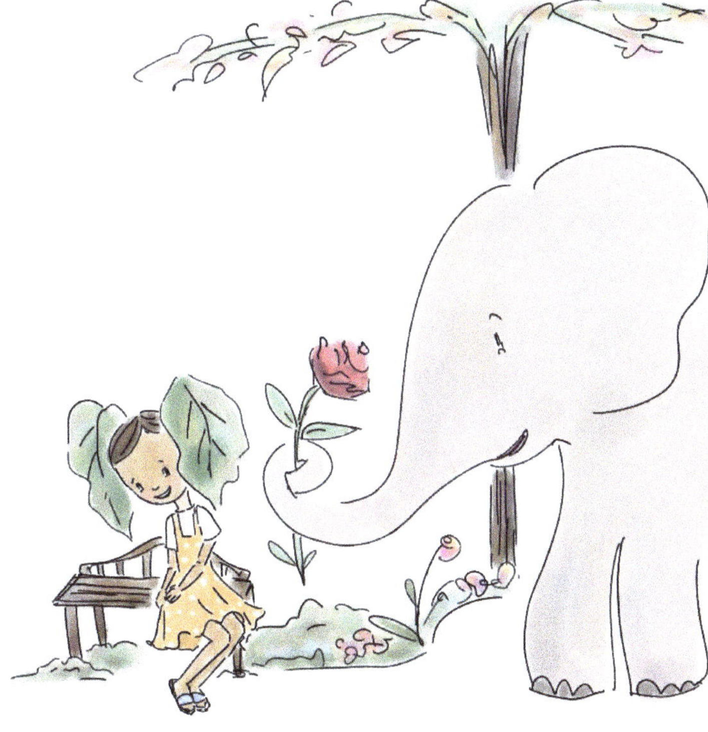

The lines that relate to this picture are, "Elephant Ears provide some shade, But look a little silly," from *My Grandma Has a Garden.* When she drew art for elephant ears, she put the small version of the leaves on the main character's ears and added the elephant to give her a rose. This is clever and creative. Alexsandra taught me how to make ordinary things extraordinary.

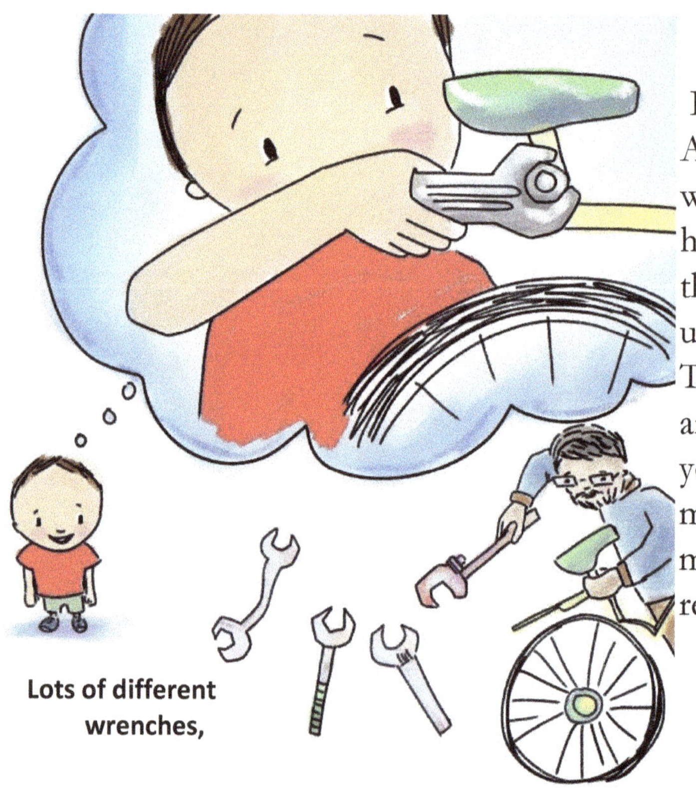

In *My Grandpa Has a Tool Bench*, Alexsandra was clever as she went through the different tools his grandpa was using and how the young boy imaged himself using the different tools as well. This picture is of wrenches. The art is simple, but really allows the young reader to identify with the main character – which I try to make the same age as the target reader. This is 4-7 year olds.

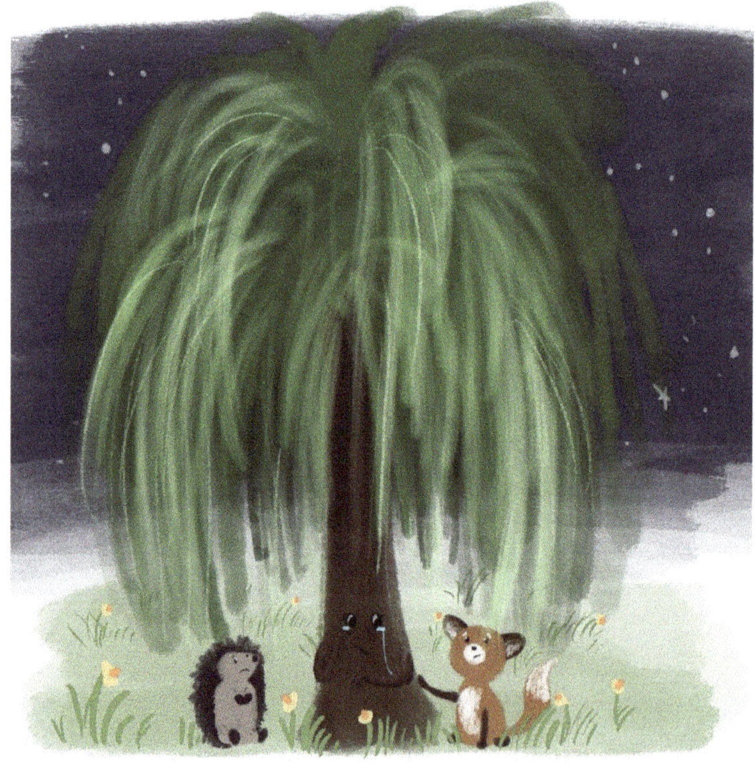

'The Willow Tree was weeping.' is the picture from *The Flora and the Fauna*. Fi drew the cutest weeping willow and put little tears on the face on the tree as well as added two cute forest animals to add to the story. Simple but very cute.

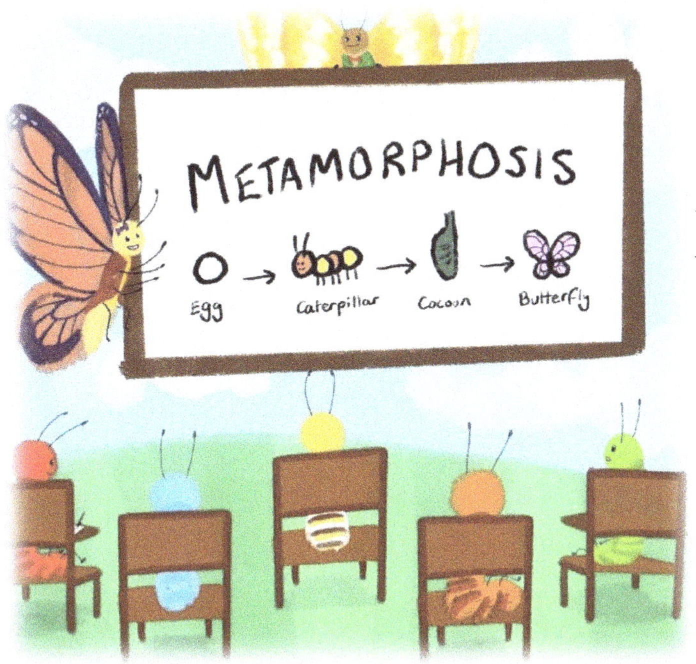

Metamorphosis—it's called—a very long word.

And, in *Butterfly Beauties and Magical Moths,* Fi did a super cute job sitting the little caterpillars in schools seats as they learn about themselves and teach a big word to the young reader as well – metamorphosis.

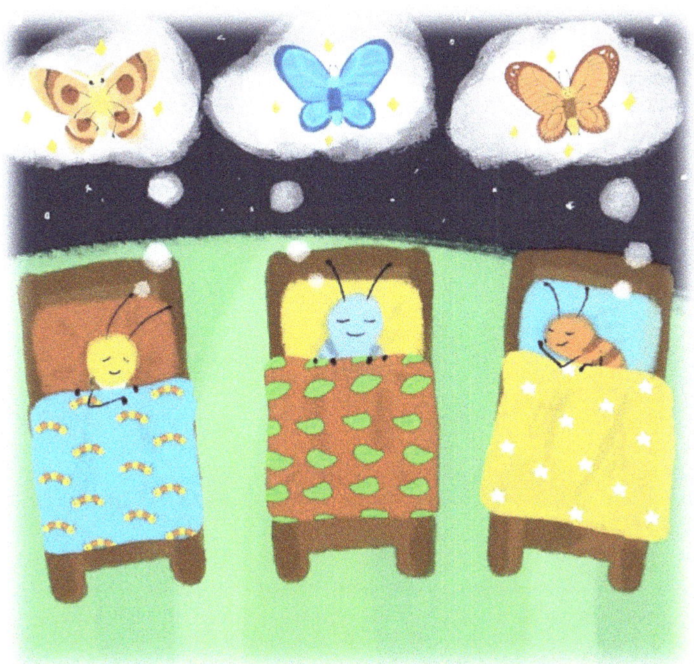

Youngster to adult - a new critter you'll see,
It's magical to find out what each one will be.

Also in the same book, Fi did a cute job of showing the little caterpillars in cute little beds dreaming of what they will one day be. Not only is this cute, it makes the information memorable for the young reader.

Fi was also hired to do my little Christmas book, *Chilly : The Lost Little Snowboy Ornament.* She did a wonderful job bringing Chilly to life in this little story as he accompanies his friend, Sally, to the mall but is lost. This little book shows Sally frantically looking for Chilly and Chilly frantically looking for Sally.

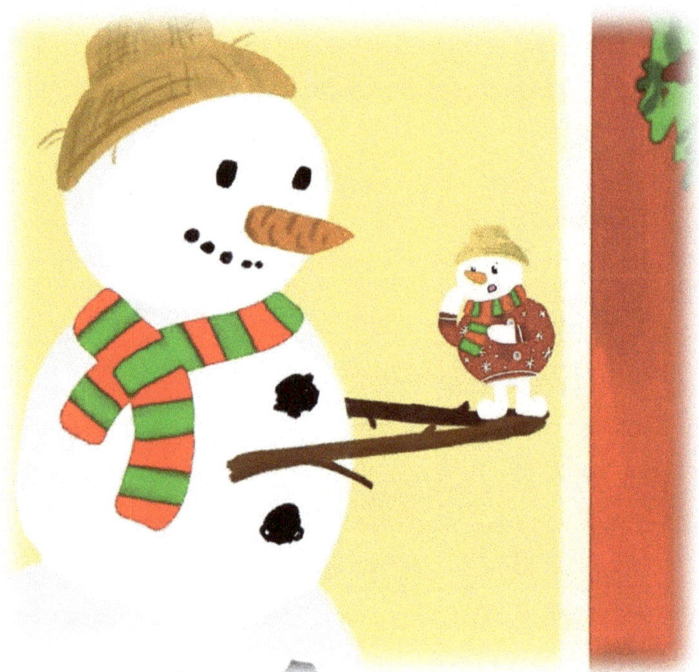

Mom called Sally as the snowman asked, "Do you want to be a snowman, Chilly?" "Oh, no," said Chilly. "It is much too cold outside for me. I want to be a snowboy and have adventures."

Juliya makes even slugs and snails seem cute. Ughhh, I say.

It's almost unbelievable because these are creatures I usually find -and think most others do as well – these creatures to be avoided. The truth is snails and slugs are important parts of our environment and David R Morgan makes us like things we thought we could never be interested in or appreciate.

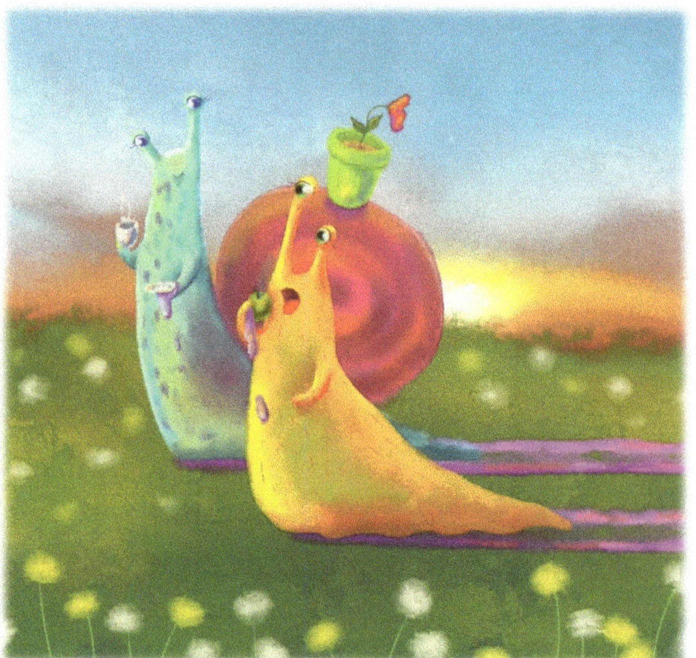

Across the lawns at dawn you'll see,
Our shimmering trails - like pearly poetry.

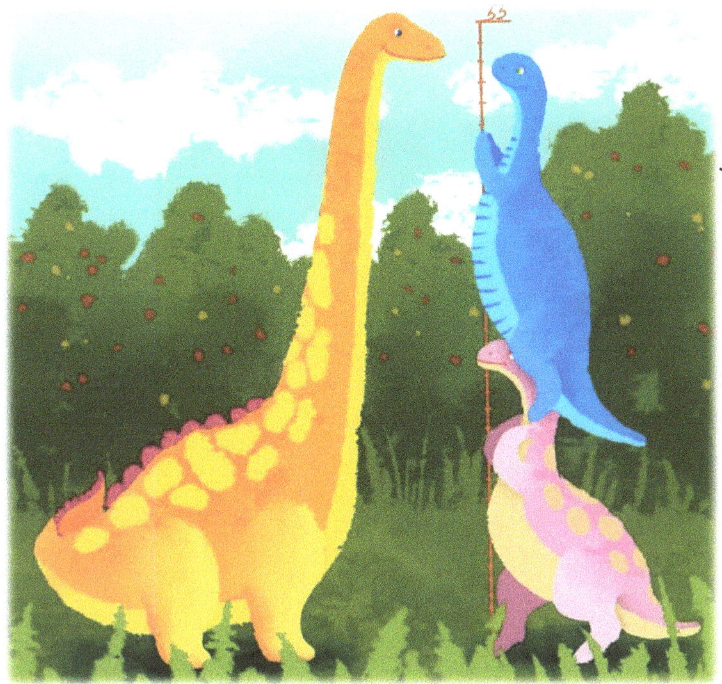

Juliya also illustrated a book about dinosaurs. When the line was about the height of some dinosaurs, she cleverly stacked other dinos to show the height. Creativity like this makes the children's books the treasures they are. Children find this amusing and it helps them to remember these facts.

.

The biggest dinosaurs were 100 feet long and 55 feet tall,

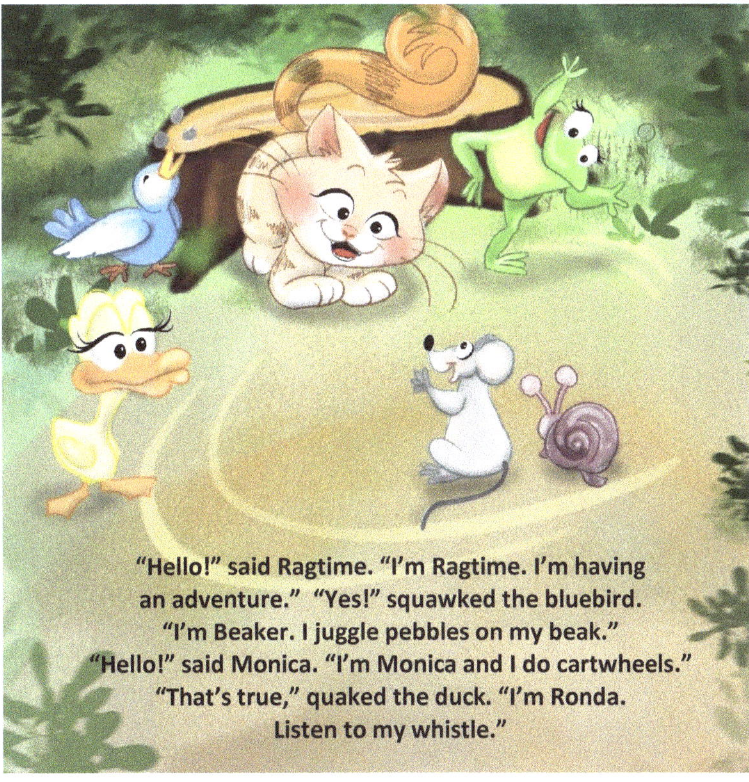

Denise is a versatile artist. She is the exception in that she has more than one style of art. She comes through in every project, but she is talented at making each project special. In *Runaway Ragtime,* her art brings this runaway cat and her friends come to life in a 'Disney-like' art style. The friends she finds along her way are cutely added as well.

Denise also did a great job illustrating a real-live pet that one author wanted to create a book about. This can be challenging because many authors have a preconceived idea of how the art should appear in the book. Denise is talented and this is what this little bulldog looks like.

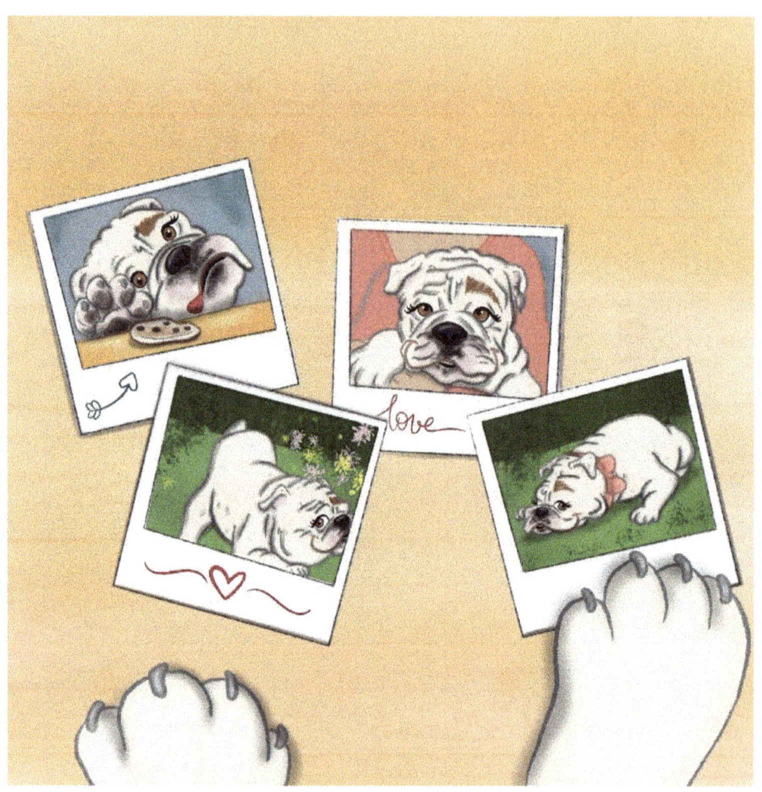

Denise illustrated *Belly Busters* - a small book about overweight cats and their need to slim down.

She used pencils and her art style is simple but cute and different from her other work. She adds all the fattening foods the new recruit thinks about all day and the fit and trim cat shows what are healthy foods. This is creative as well as cute.

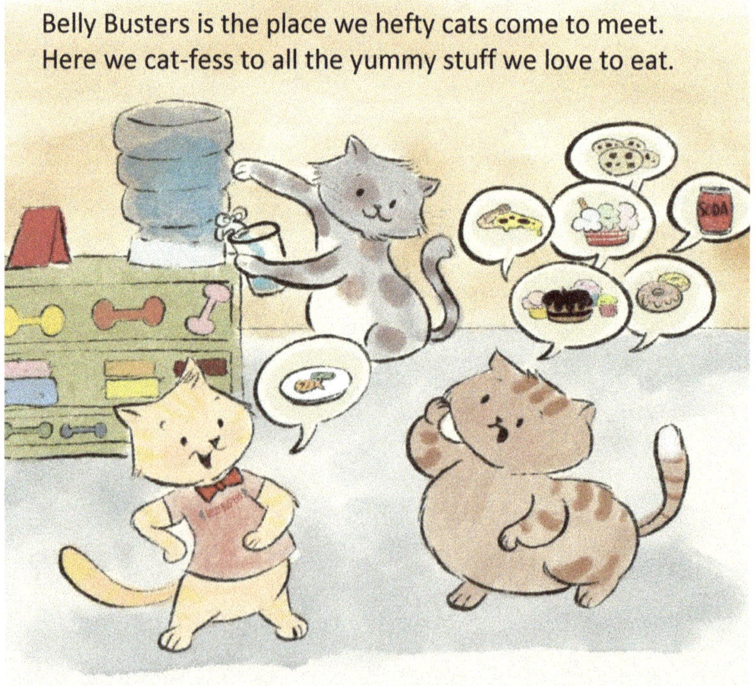

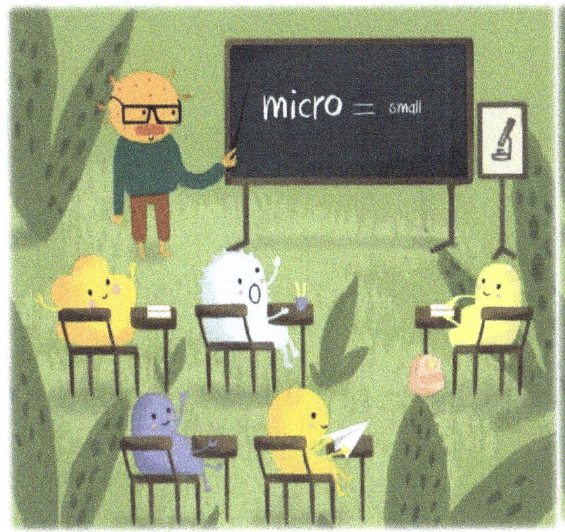
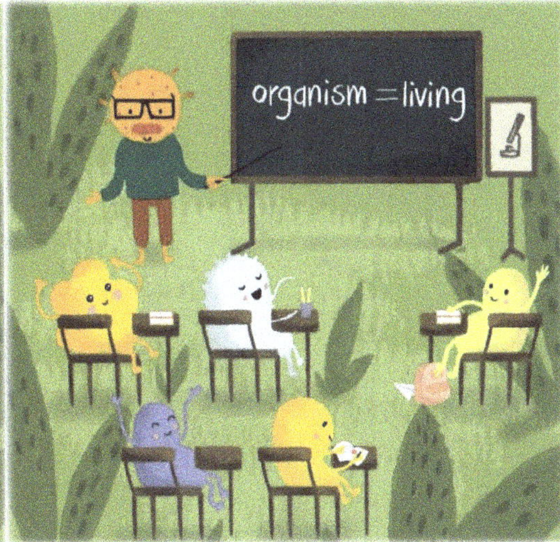

Micro means very, very small,

Organism means 'living' - that's all!

The art for the book titled *Single Celled Sensations* is an educational book about microbes. The artist not only had the challenge of making the one-celled organism life-like, she also needed to make them appear very small. Here the artist included cute things children do in class - like making paper airplanes and writing notes.

In *Deep-Sea Dazzlers* below, this artist helps bring another subject most children find boring interesting. The deep sea and the Midnight Zone are still a mystery to most scientists. The author hopes these books will inspire the young reader to want to learn more about the subjects of one-celled organisms all around us and the deep sea.

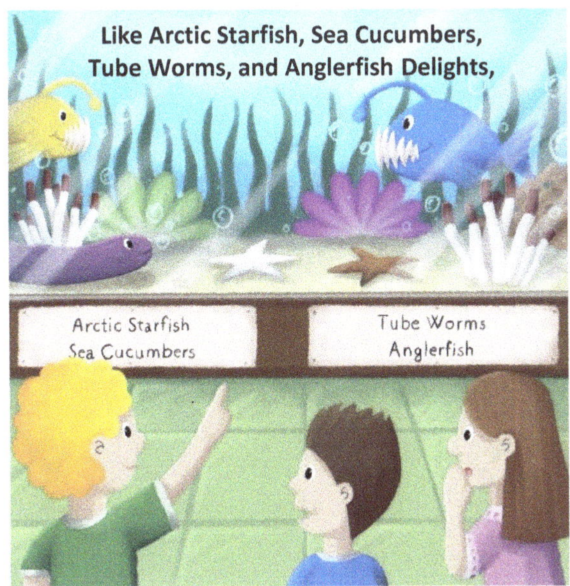

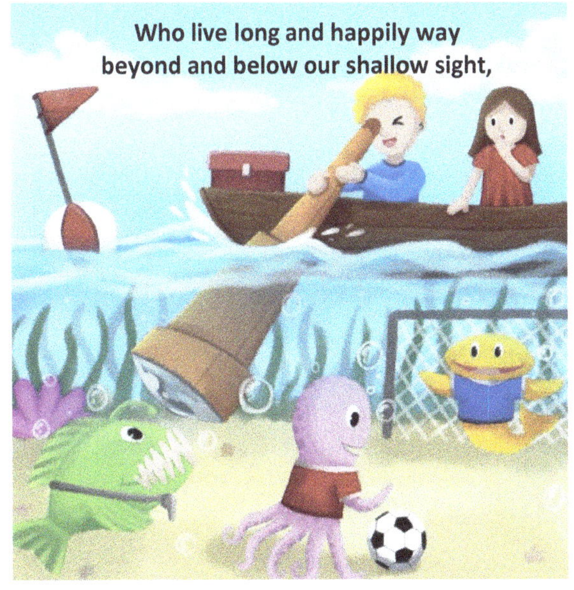

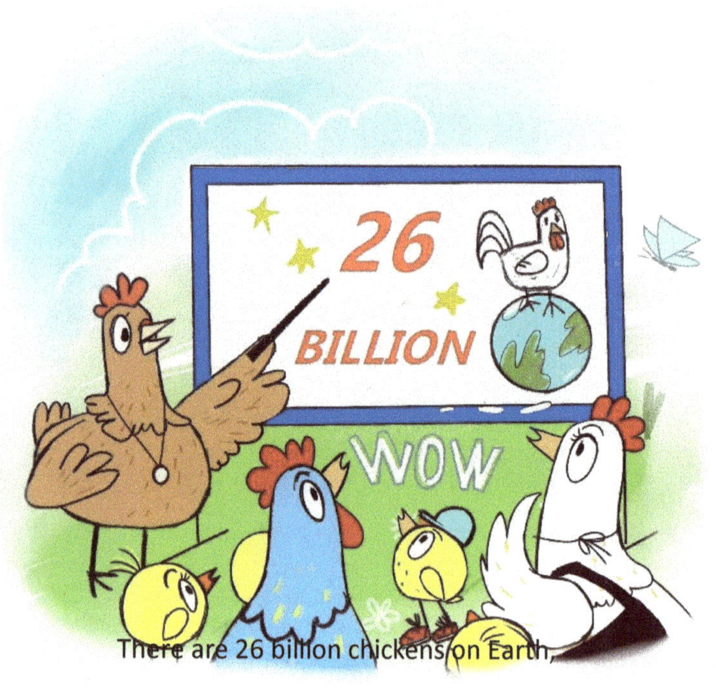

There are 26 billion chickens on Earth,

David also created children's books about the animals in the barnyard. This little book about chickens shares fun facts about them as well the egg-laying facts that are interesting as well as fun.

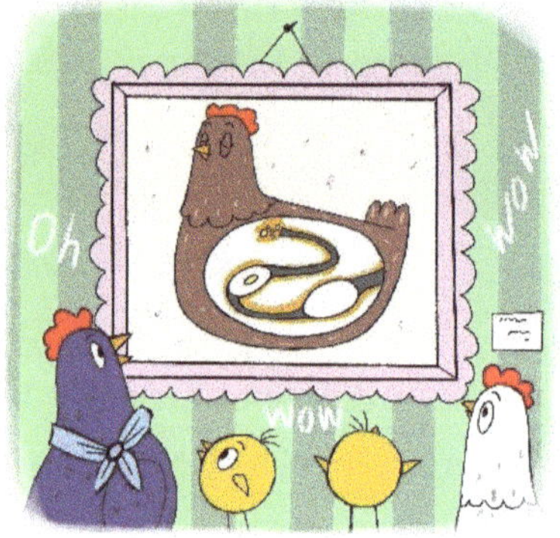

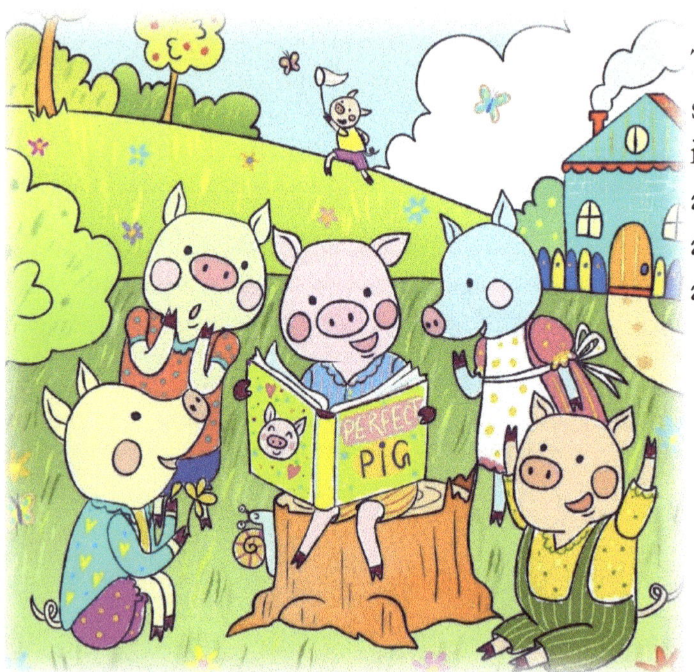

I hope that everyone will really dig,
This fun little book, "Perfectly Perky Pigs."

This little book about perky pigs has so many fun facts about pigs – including their great memories and ability to smell so many things and the amazing fact that they are very clean animals! Anna is the artist for both!

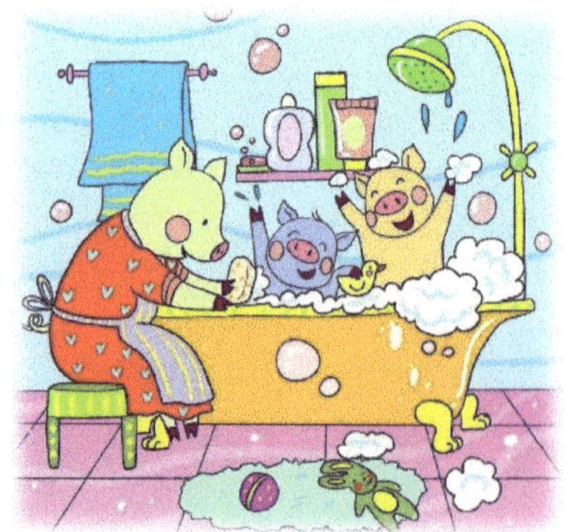

Now pigs are good and kind and rather clean,

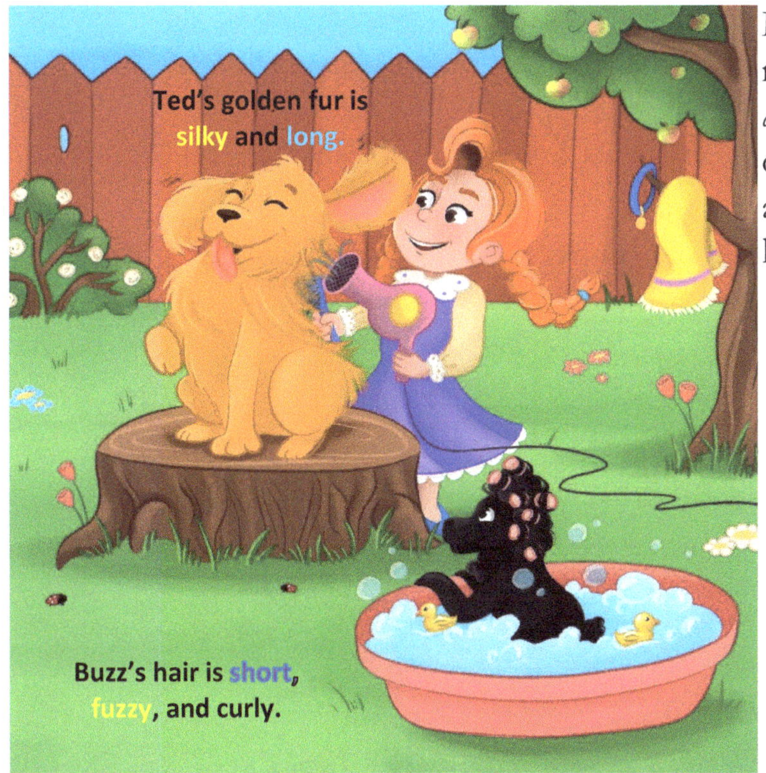

Marharyta did a lovely job making both dogs cute in *Buzz and Ted's World of Opposites* based on two real pets. I love the addition of the curlers in Buzz's hair.

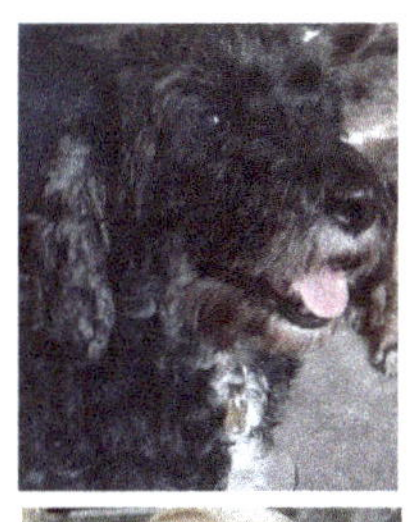

Buzz

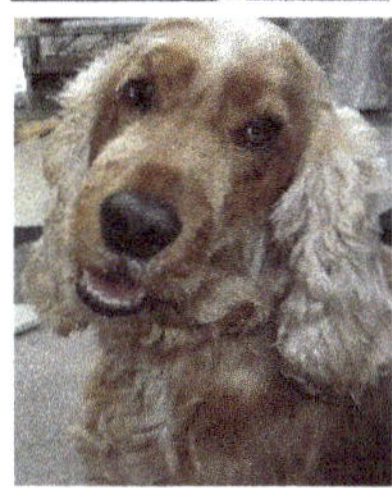

Ted

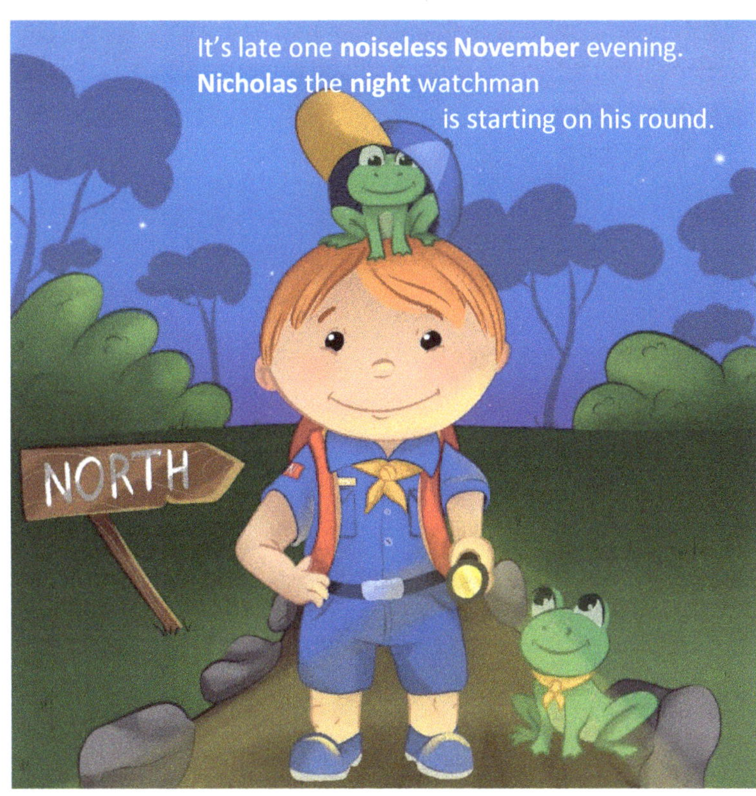

In *Finding N : The Great Alphabet Hunt*, Marharyta used her creative style on all the pages for this special little book with N words and Nicholas and his natterjack toads with him on all his night rounds.

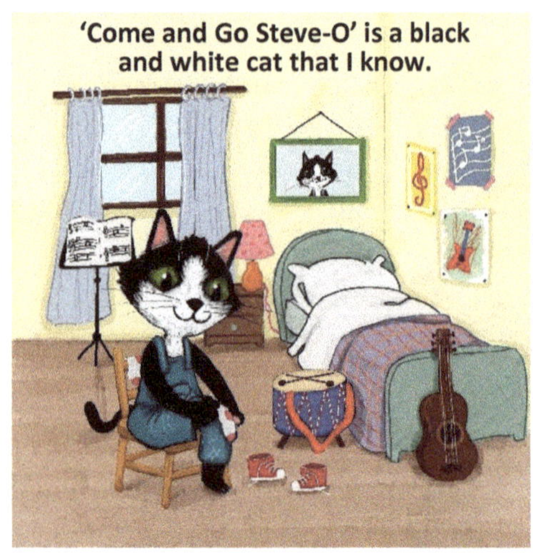

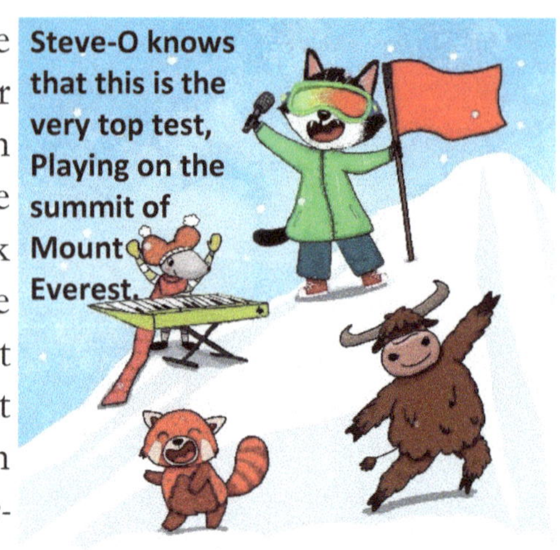

I usually don't like the colors black or grey or brown because they are drab and I think picture books are better in bright colors. So, what Zaida has done in *Come and Go Steeve-O* is add color to the black cat, Steve. She put him in a blue coverall and gave him red tennis shoes as well as changed up his look depending on where he is in the book. If he's on the waves, he has beach-wear or when he's looking at the sun, he shields his face.

It is not possible to add such detail to a storyboard, but the artists have added their creativity as can be seen here.

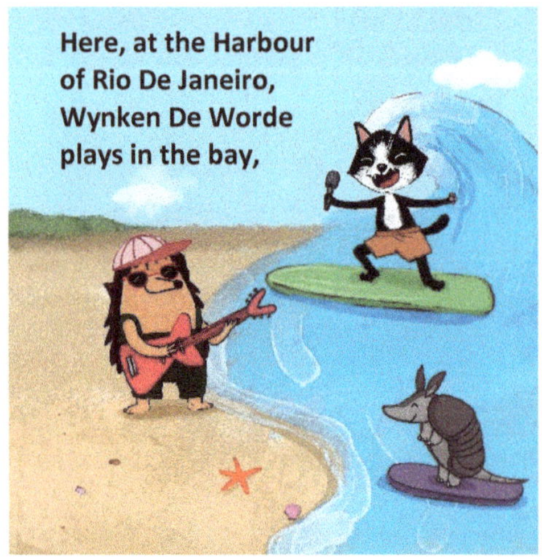

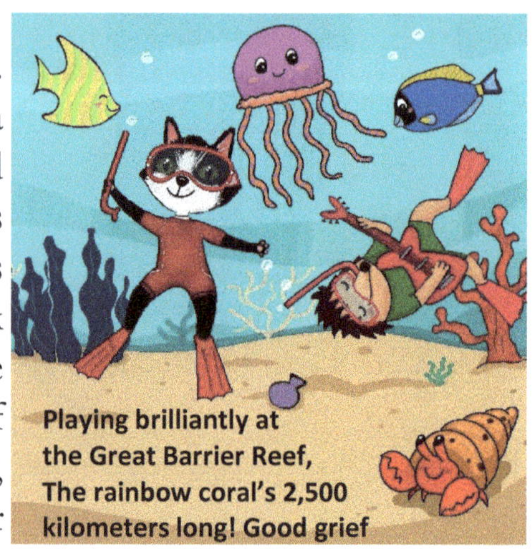

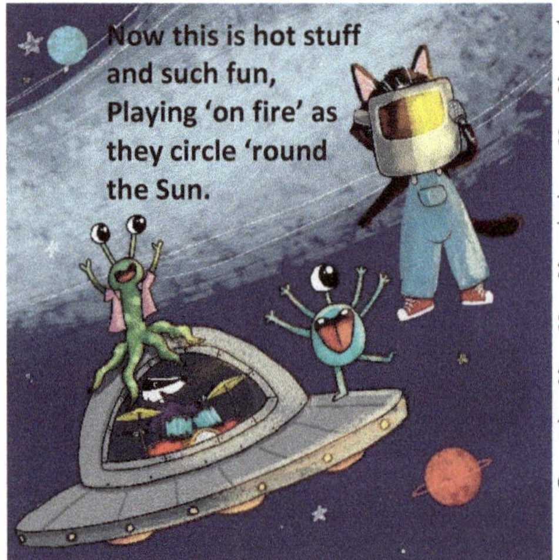

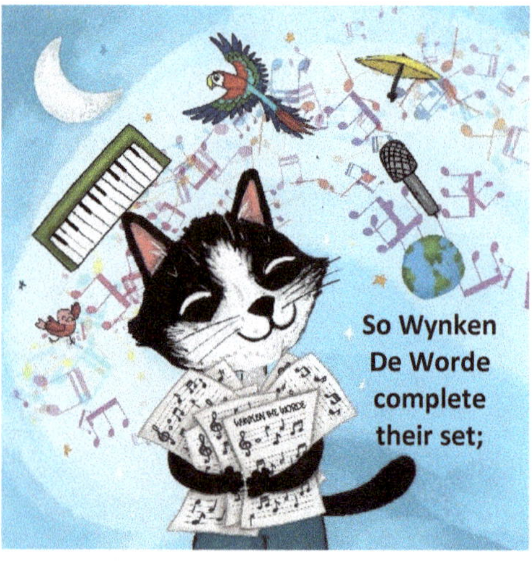

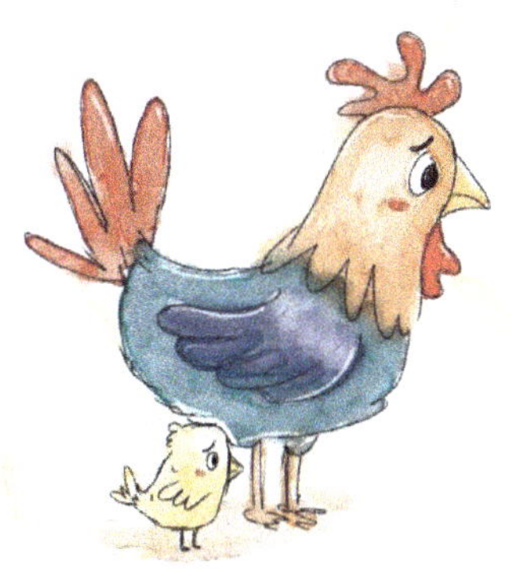

Talented Zaida also created art for David's book about social concerns today. Even simple illustrations can be special and cute.

Nadii is one of the best artists I have worked with. She creates the most amazing art! The spaghetti has a little mouse in the mix because he's *The TV Mouse* that is involved in every aspect of the television station – including pasta!

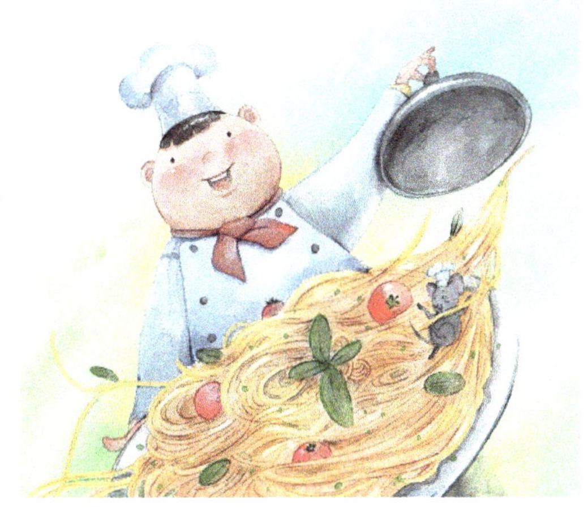

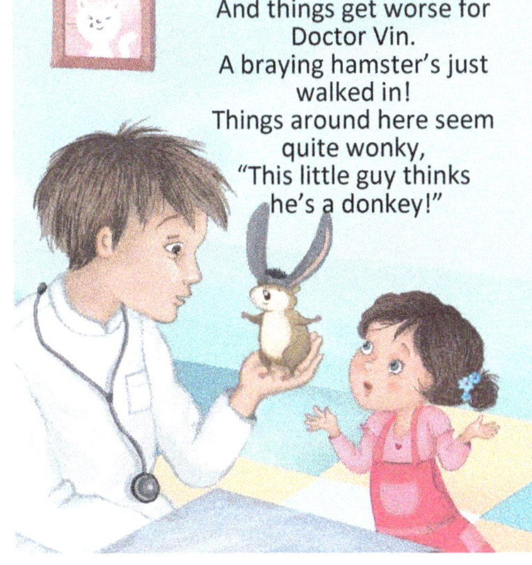

Alenka brought my award-winning book, *The Day the Cat Said MOO!* to life as she adds great expression and detail in the pictures as can be seen here. Each book I publish is different and a masterpiece in itself. Finding the best artist and the artist providing the best art is teamwork and the best part of creating the picture books.

Naomi Peña brought *A Thoroughly Modern Grandmama* by Moira Andrew to life with her unique style. I enjoy leaning from each artist and see how they use their creativity for my books. She really captures the boredom of the children in the book and adds a little drool from the young man's mouth and a bored bird on his head. Again, storyboards are great for general guidance, but creativity is a great

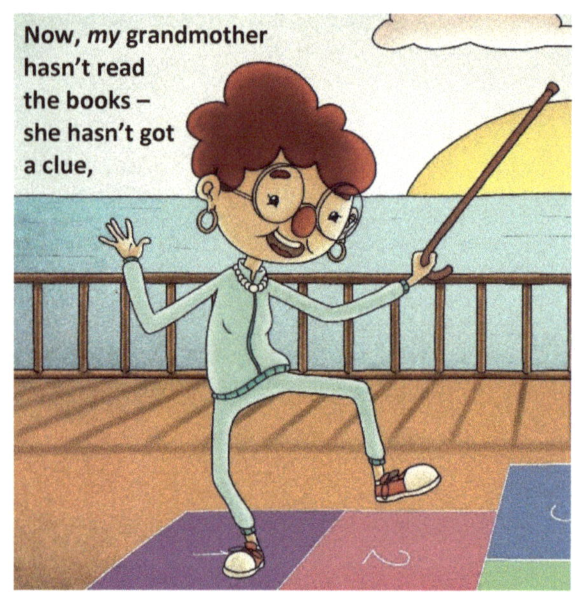

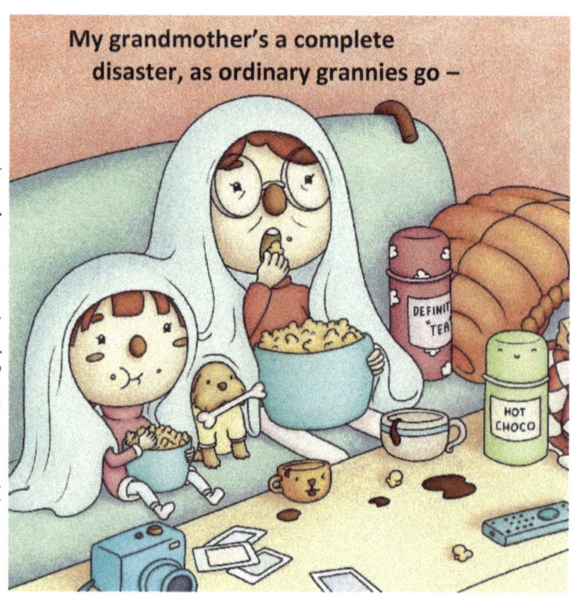

thing for each artist to tap into to make every book special. Moira is a grandmama herself and I speculate that she, herself, was the inspiration for this cute book about a Grandmama that is fun and exciting and does the most outrage things.

Naomi has a truly wonderfully creative ability to add fun detail to every book she creates for an author or publisher. This little book has grandmama riding a roller coaster, driving a fun car, hopscotching like above and watching scary movies live this picture. She adds the cute details of the pup also under covers and with a bone for his treat because he's not sharing the popcorn.

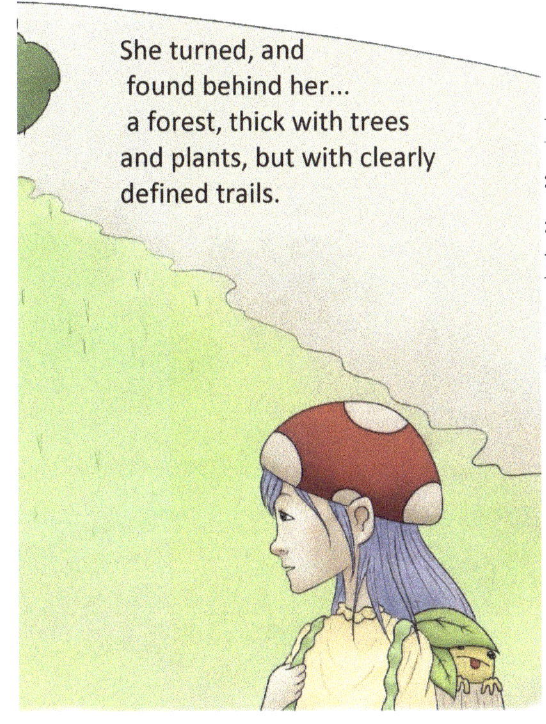

In *Poppy's Path*, Naomi creates a likeable 'Poppy' and in realistic detail. She adds a cute frog to accompany her on her journey in this book. The little frog in her back pack and peeping out is cute for children to see as they read along with the story

Children love animals and Naomi makes the frog as likeable as Poppy and cutely puts him on her head for some pictures as well as the little guy hops along in some of the illustrations.

Creative for sure. Ideas can be come to artists themselves as well as bouncing ideas off other artists and sometimes they adopt my suggestions for creative additions to illustrations.

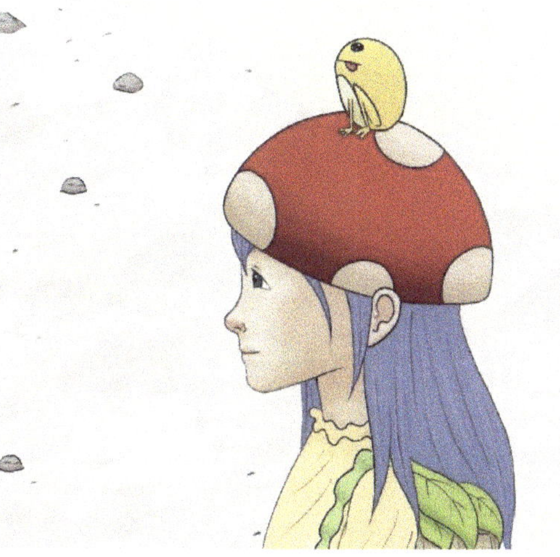

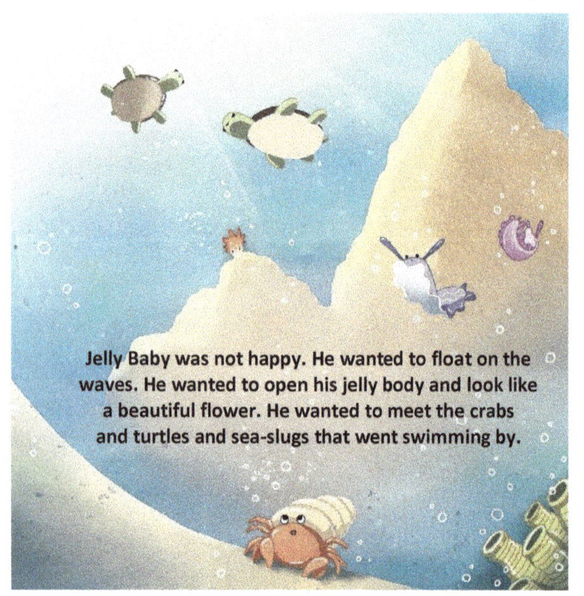

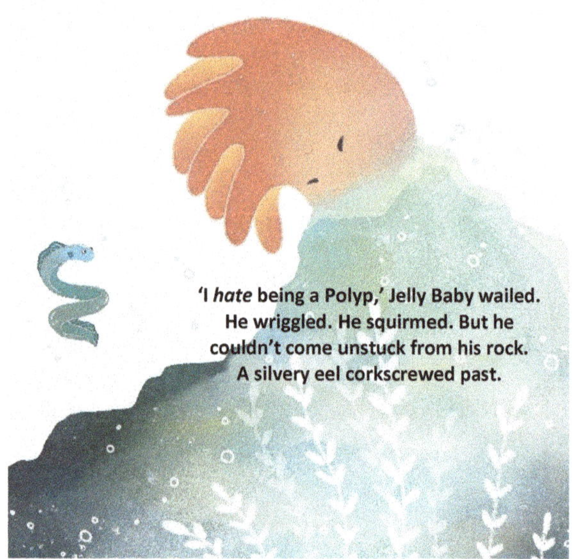

Illustration comes in all styles. Thank goodness for this. It would be very boring for the young reader to have only one style of picture books to enjoy. Above, in *Jelly Baby*, Caterina creates simple but special art that captures all the words and feel of the book and below, in *Thankful Me using my ABCs*, Nadii is very detailed. It fits here.

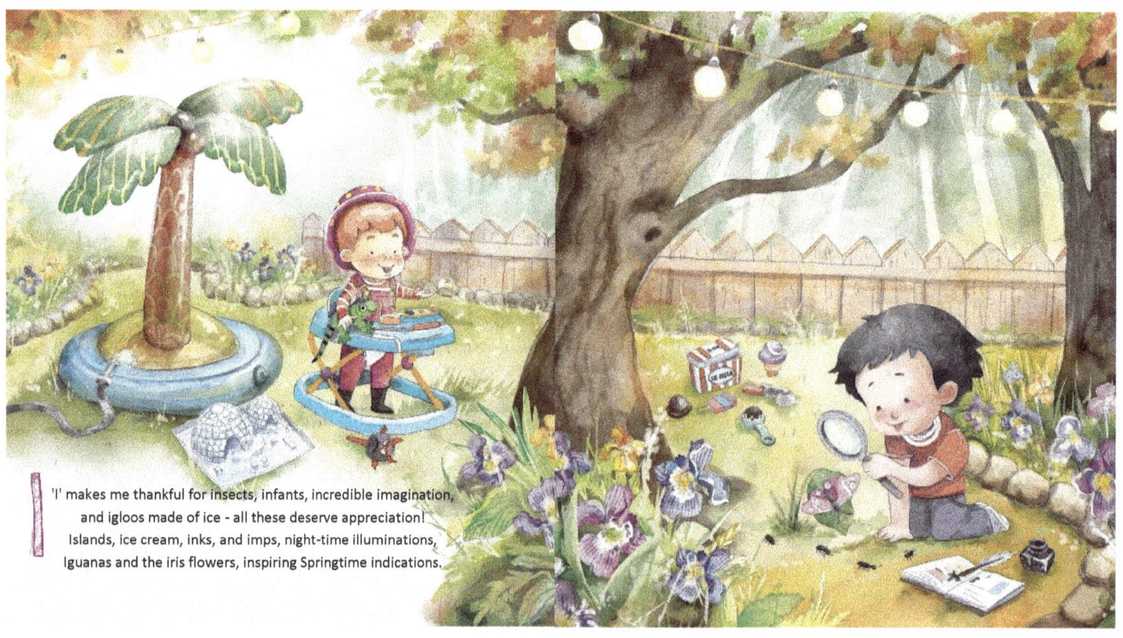

<h1 style="text-align:center">6</h1>

This or That

In addition to the aspect of creativity, I always make sure the overall illustrations are what I have in mind for a particular children's picture book. I look at color, facial expressions, focus, size of the picture and characters and more. I realize I can be 'fussy.' When artists tell me they are 'fussy' I am elated to work with them because they pay attention to every detail and I do too. Let's look at a few examples.

One aspect I consider when I'm creating a children's book is some small details. *The Little White Kitten and Her Little Red Mittens* is a story is about a little kitten who loves her red mittens. She loses them and is heartbroken, but she learns the lessons of giving and sharing despite loss and sadness. The artist, Fi initially drafted a small basket for her mittens. I asked her to create a BIG basket and feel it adds charm to the book.

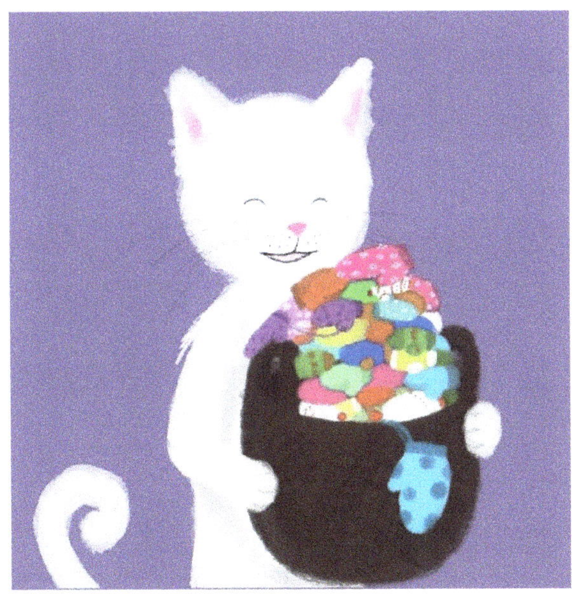 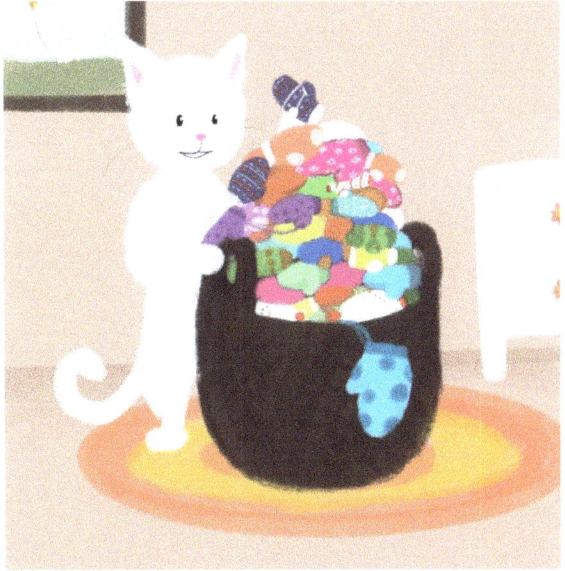

Another example of size in a children's picture book is in *Never 'TOO' Wonderful*,
Nina initially created an illustration with a red bike that I felt was small. I asked her to
make the red bike BIG because that's what the words are. The little bike isn't really too
big, it's his size. And I feel the young reader would *see* BIG in the bigger red bike. It's a
small detail, but I think this makes the book cute as well as the bird with a bike helmet
and his little bird wings motioning BIG as he repeats the wors TOOOOOO big.

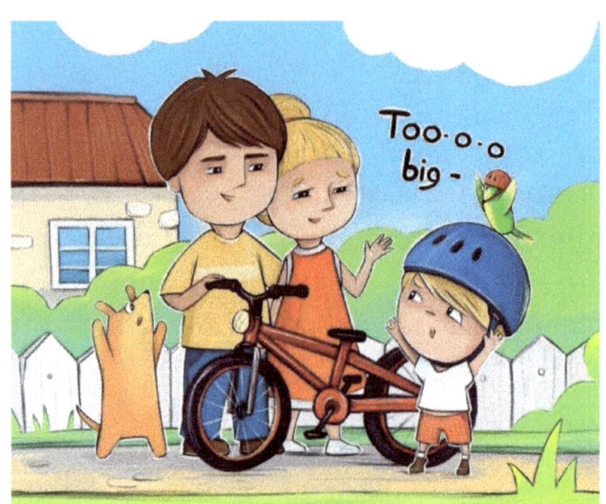

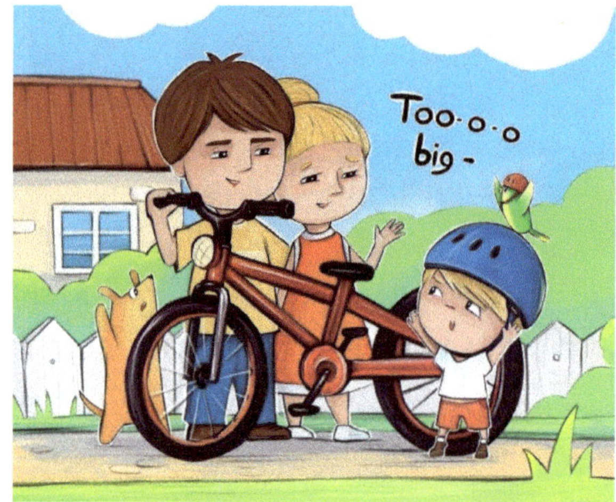

And that his bike is much 'TOO big and TOO red!'

Expression is something else I'm 'fussy' about. I think you will agree. In *Finding U : The
Great Alphabet Hunt*, I prefer a 'good' eye to a 'stern' eye in the narwal. The referee is
not 'angry,' he's just a ref.– this is how the artist made a better expression.

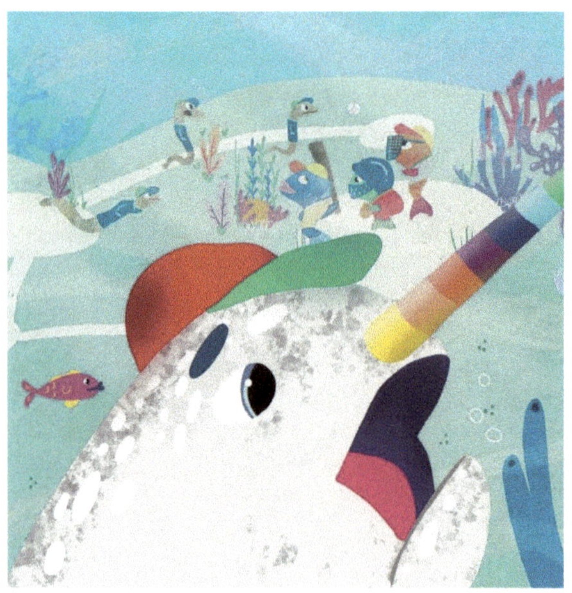
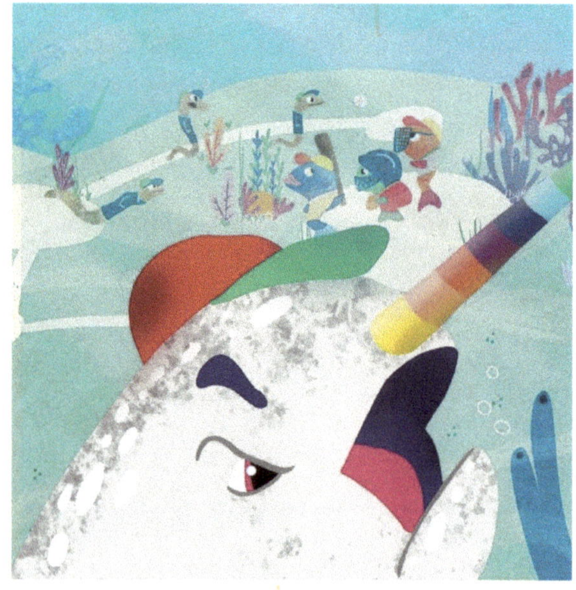

Another really important consideration in the illustrations is coloring – see in

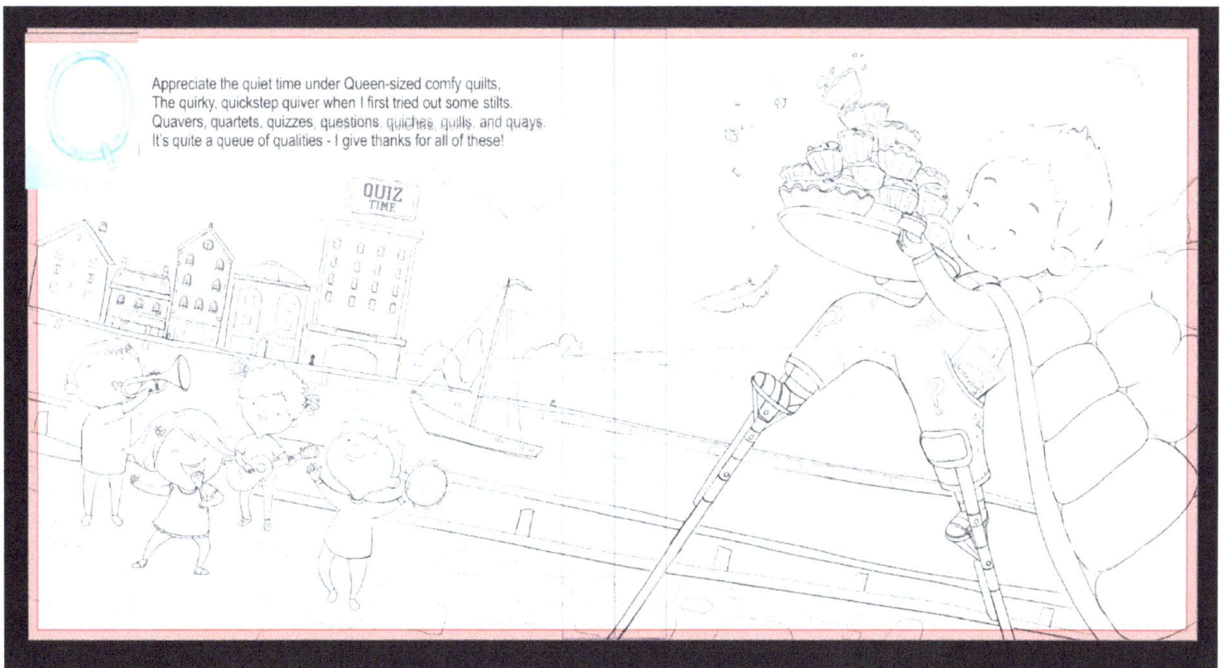

Thankful Me Using My ABCs – the artist sketched the Q pages – (not G) and she colored the quilt flowing behind the young man on stilts holding quiches with a plain brown color that was too plain for my liking – as seen here below -

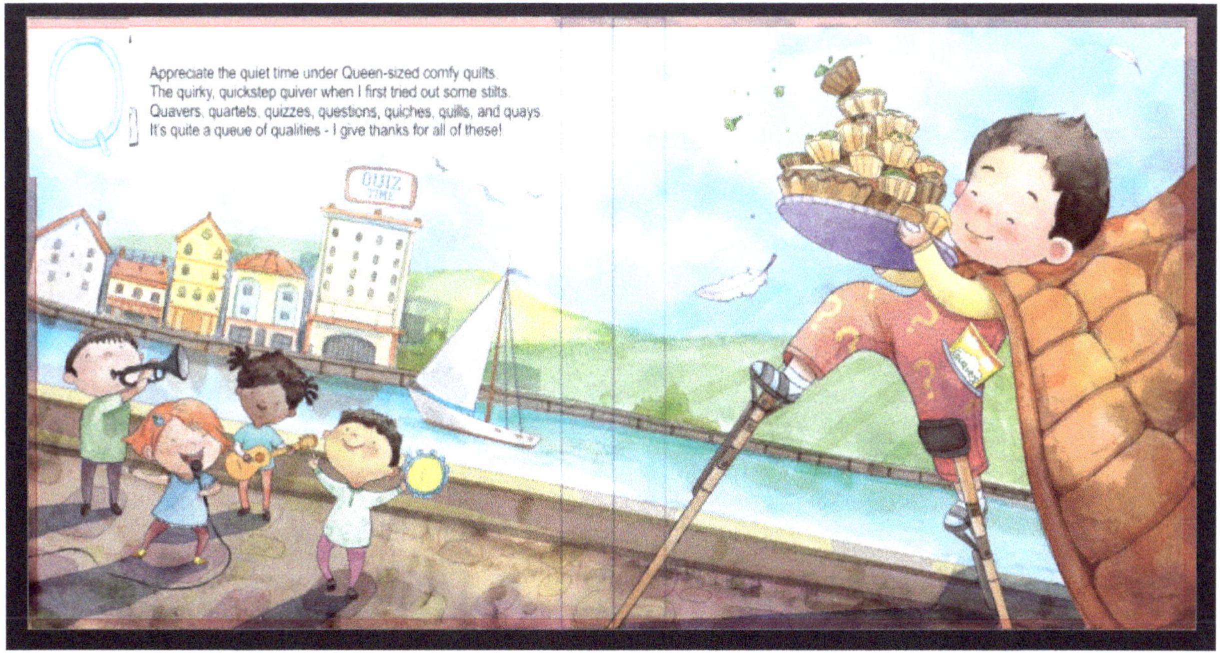

So, I asked her to make the quilt different colors and she did this lovely change-

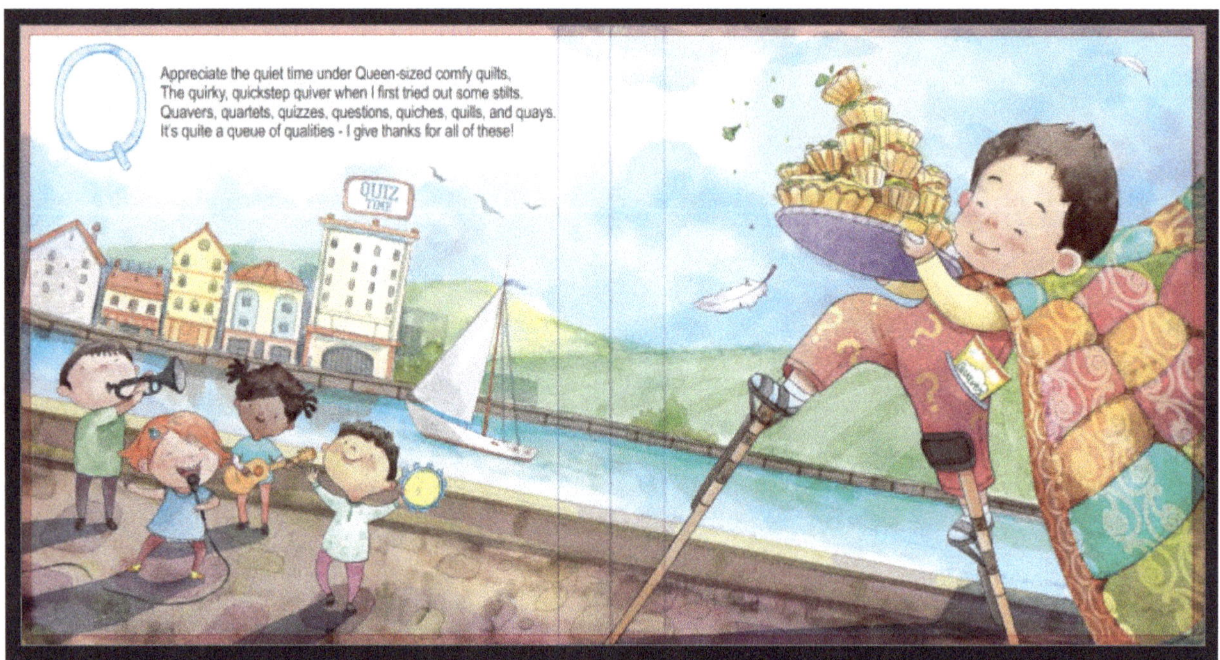

I think everyone agrees children's books should be colorful! Children love the colors. In addition, this artist always leaves an area where the words can be placed that isn't so dark it's difficult to see the words. Sometimes dark art is necessary because the words describe it being dark, as in *Finding N : The Great Alphabet Hunt.* The book is set at night. As can be seen, it's easier to see 'white' words than black on darker backgrounds.

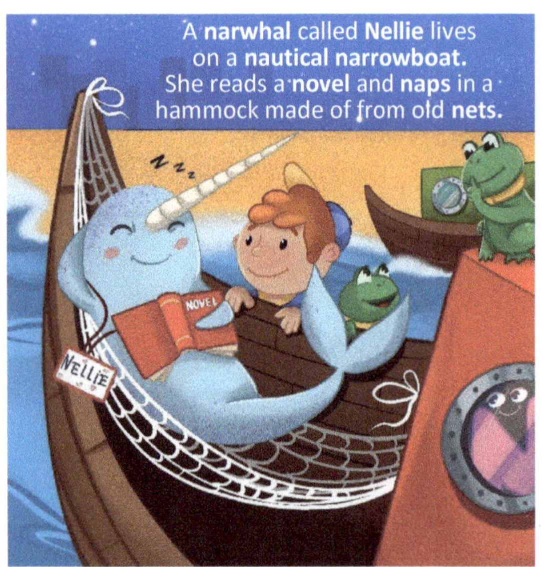

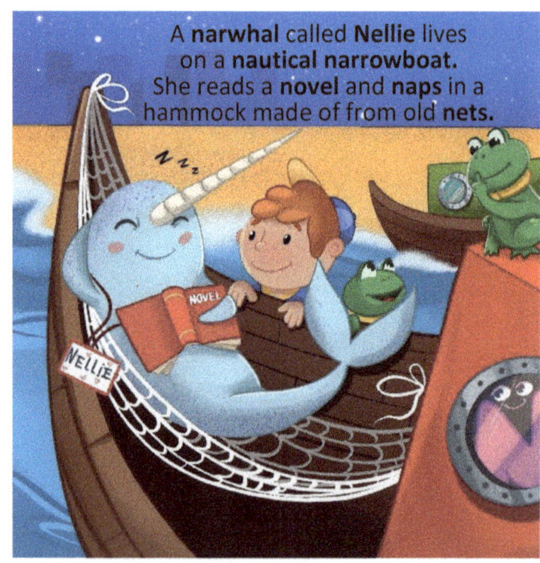

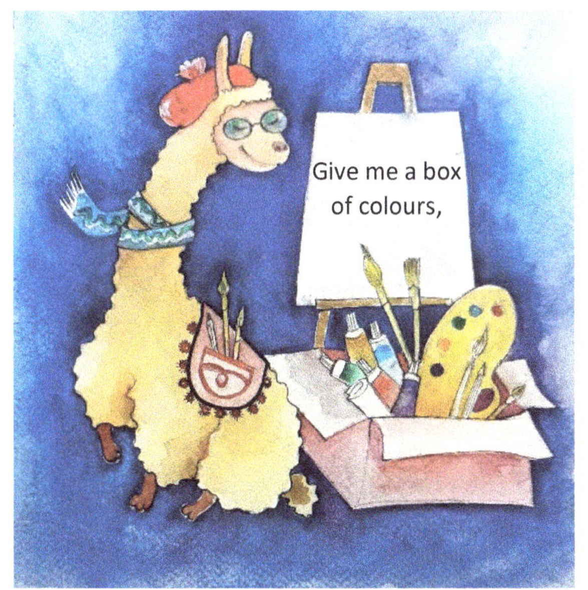

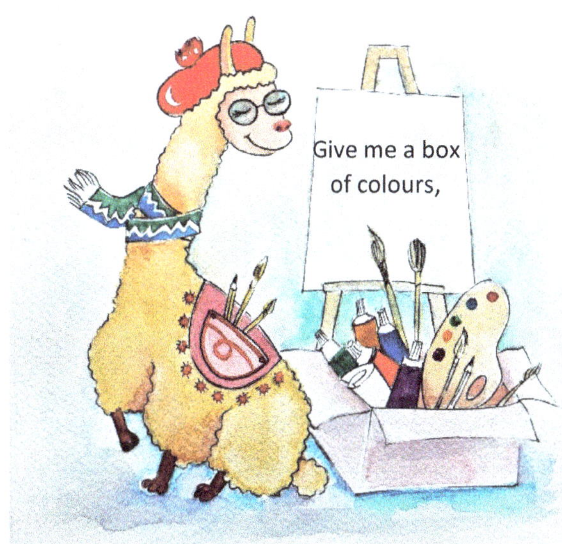

 As can be seen in the pictures above, I prefer the one on the right because it's lighter and even though the words can still be put in the canvas area and are easy to read, if they needed to be put on another part of the picture, the picture is way too dark to have the words easily seen. I run into this often with artists. And pics print darker.

In the picture below, there really isn't anywhere to put the words on this page easily as can be seen. On odd pages, the page is on the right side of the book so the words need to be placed to the right or center of the page. When words are placed to the left they can lost in the binding or can be difficult to read because of the binding.

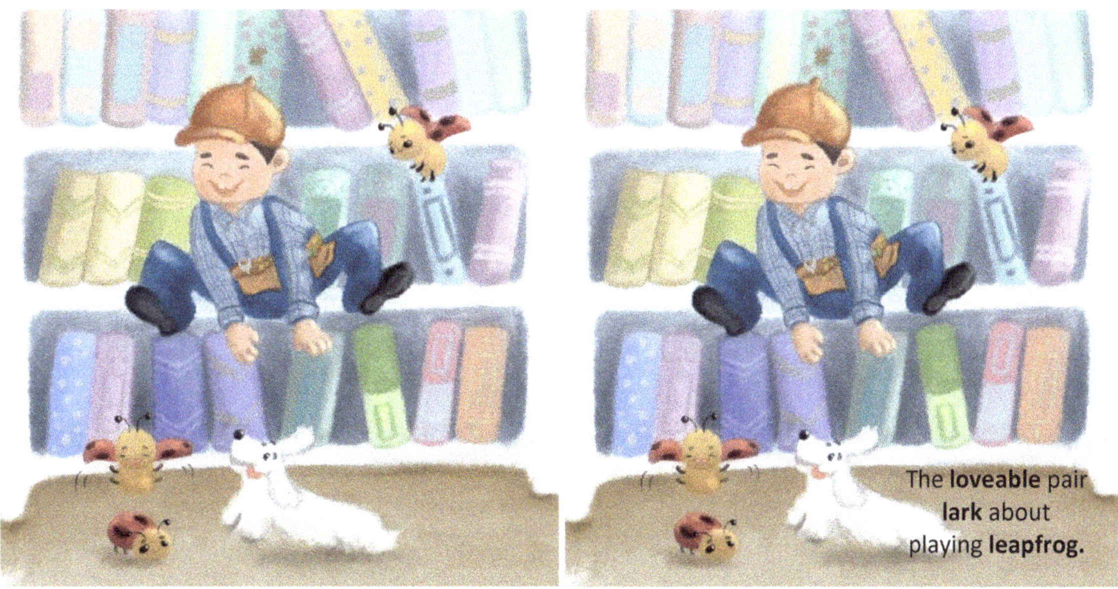

The same artist makes a larger area on the illustration to put the words on the left illustration but the illustration on the right is nice, but there is no place for words –

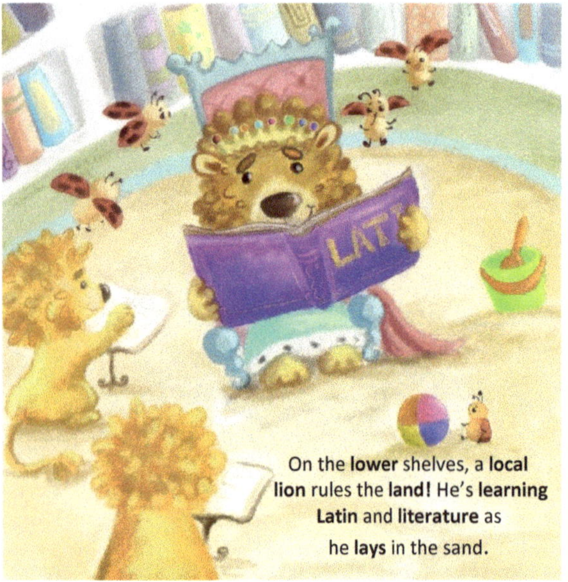

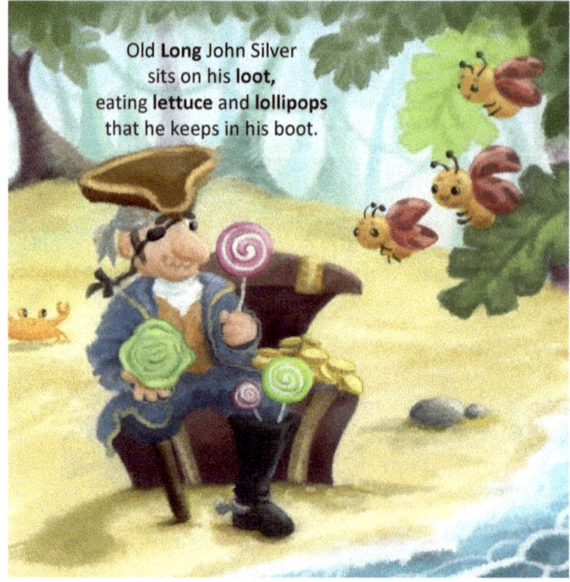

The color of the page where the words are placed as well as any busy art make a difference in the ease of reading the words. As has been seen in Nadii's illustrations of the letter Q above, she leaves sufficient space for the words and light areas behind them to make the words easy to read. Nadii does this very nicely – as can be seen here - lots of art – but the words are easily read.

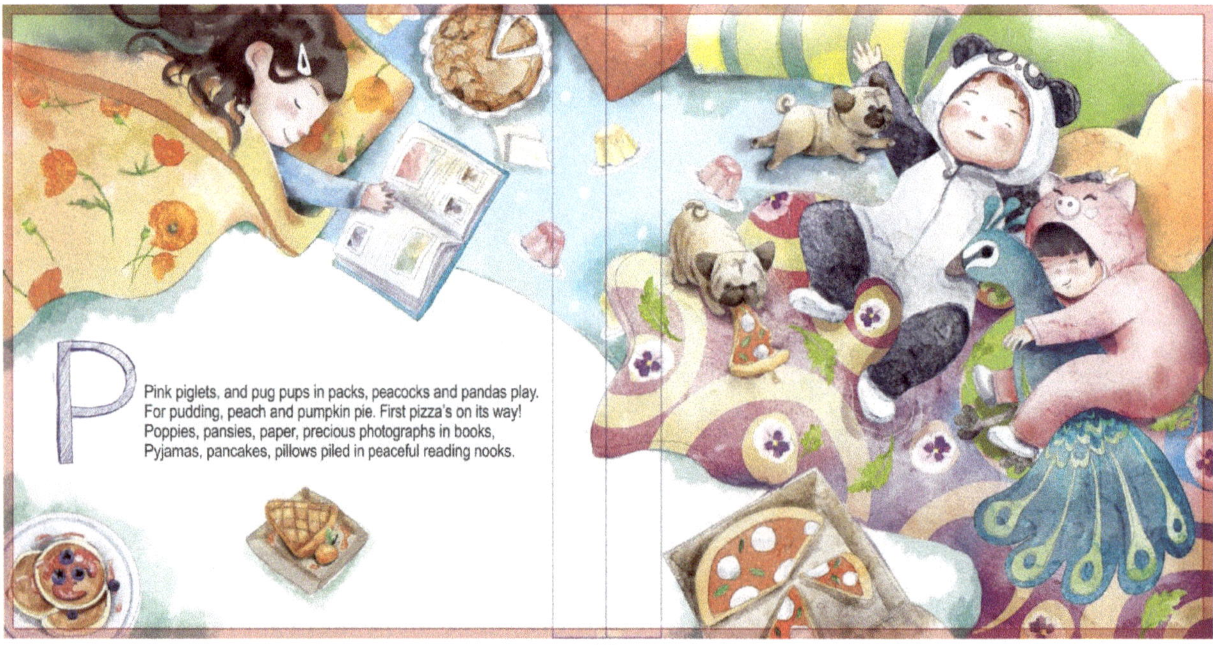

Perspective is something I consider as well – sometimes artists want to include more background than needed - for instance in *Finding R : The Great Alphabet Hunt,* Olesya sent this sketch. The individual details are alright on the left, however, I feel the main aspects of the picture are too small and this isn't something I think is a good fit for my picture books. I asked the artist to make the car the main focus larger as on the right.

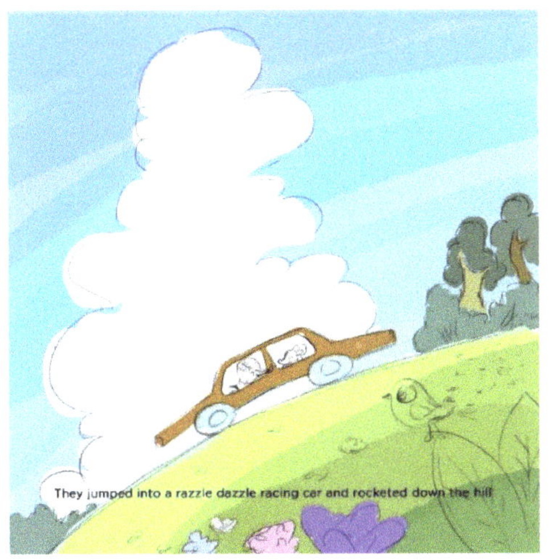

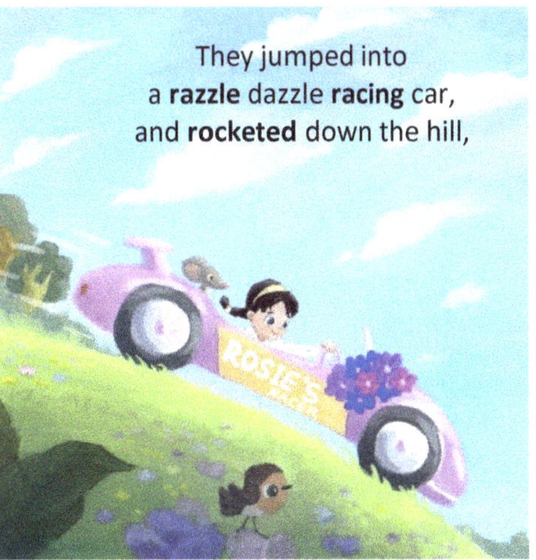

In addition, perspective also includes the angle of the picture. I realize sometimes the picture calls for an 'angle' where the reader is 'looking down' on a certain aspect of the picture as another picture below in *Fining R,* where Rosie climbs a tree, however the picture on the right is a 'downward' view that I prefer to avoid. Also, the art is busy under the words for Rosie and this makes them difficult to read sometimes.

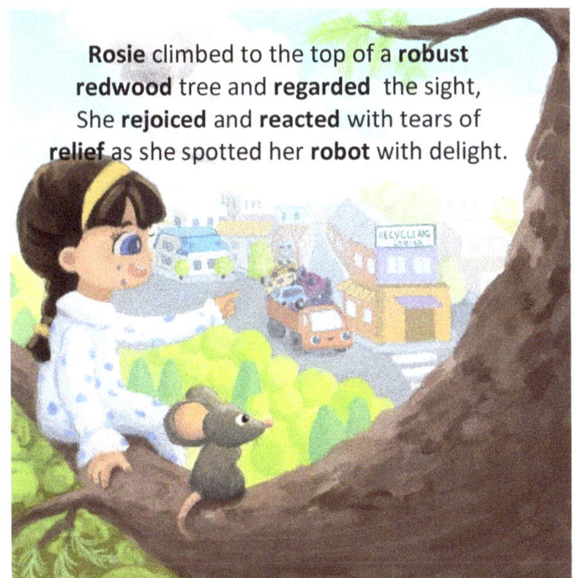

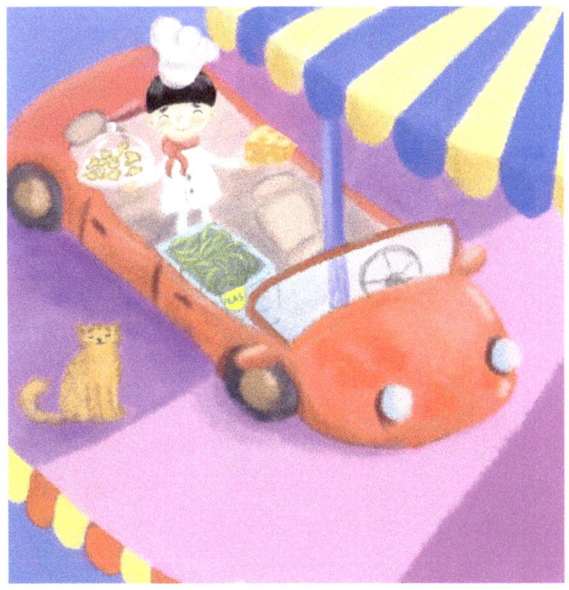

In the following pictures, the artists created nice illustrations, however, the EVEN page left and ODD page right – the even on the left and the odd on the right side of the book - the binding will be in the middle of the pages. There is not enough room for the main art to be comfortably on the page and easily seen by the young reader. There should be at least one inch where the binding will be on the right or left picture.

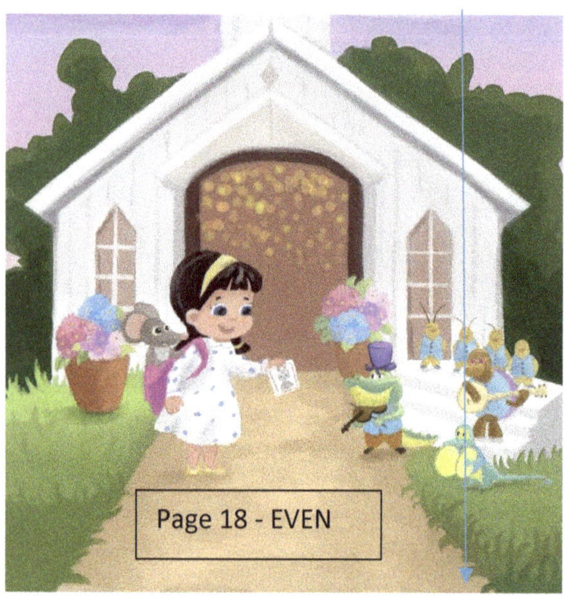

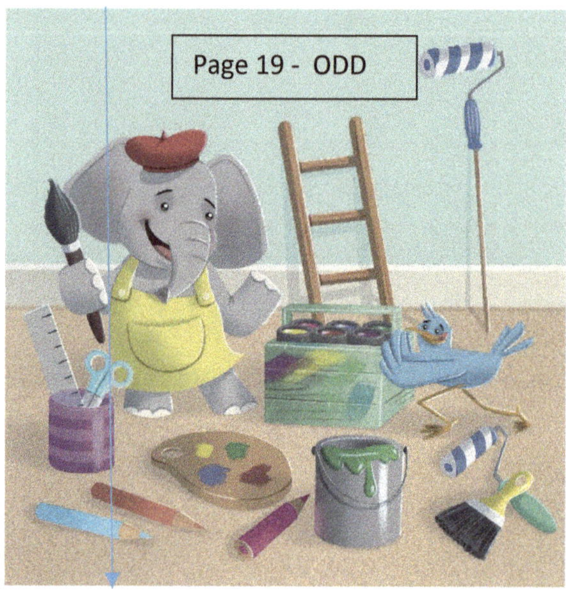

While I agree eyes should be closed when praying or sleeping and some other times like in these illustrations – like these below-

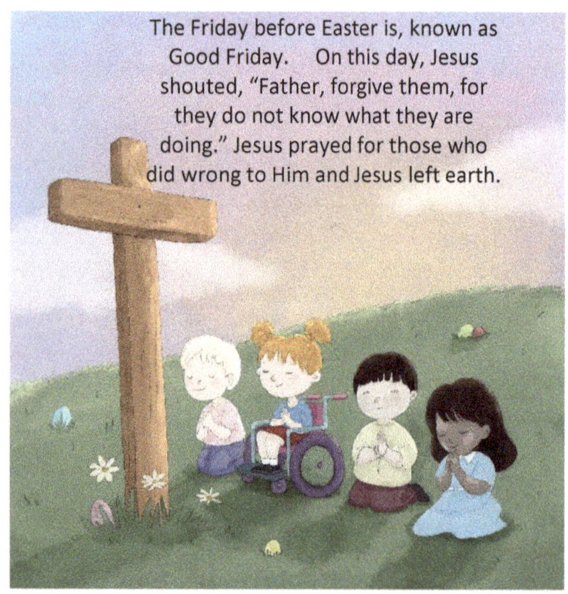

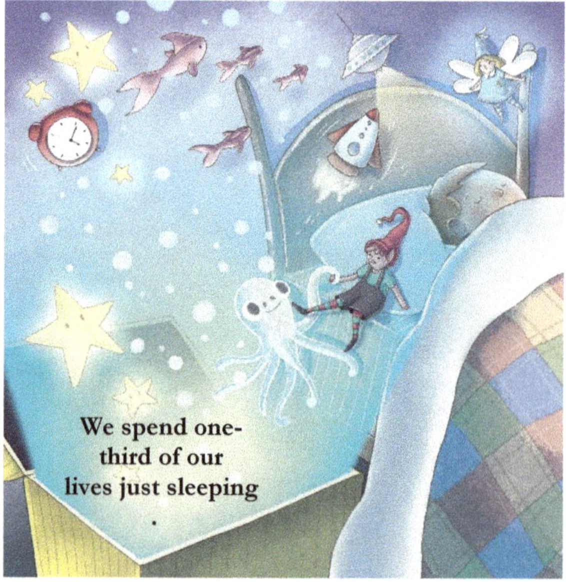

But in general, I prefer open eyes. I'm not sure why some artists like closed eyes, but always check on this. Most probably don't give it a second thought, but I like open eyes.

I imagine this is personal preference, but I like seeing the eyes. They are expressive.

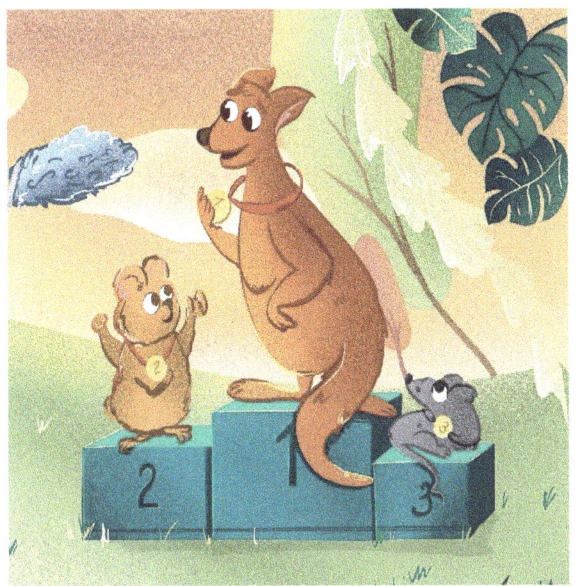 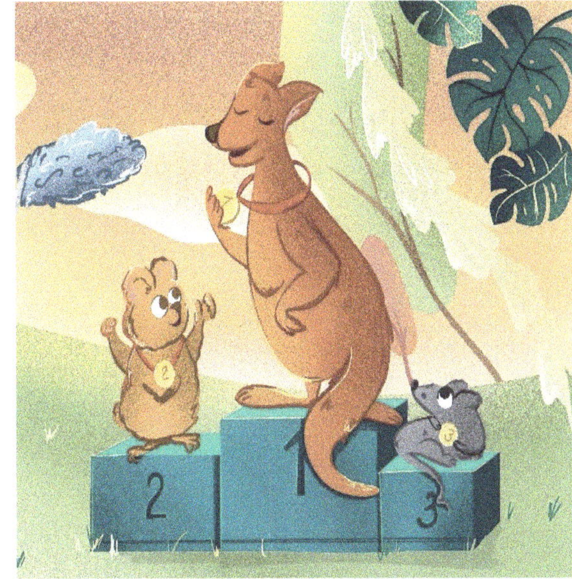

    This should go without saying, but the art needs to match the words. The words for this illustration are, '….with rainbows over purple mountains, green seas, and golden sands.' I love the art to be honest, but there are no purple mountains here and the rocks don't count as mountains I don't feel. Also, the waves may say 'seas' but not green seas

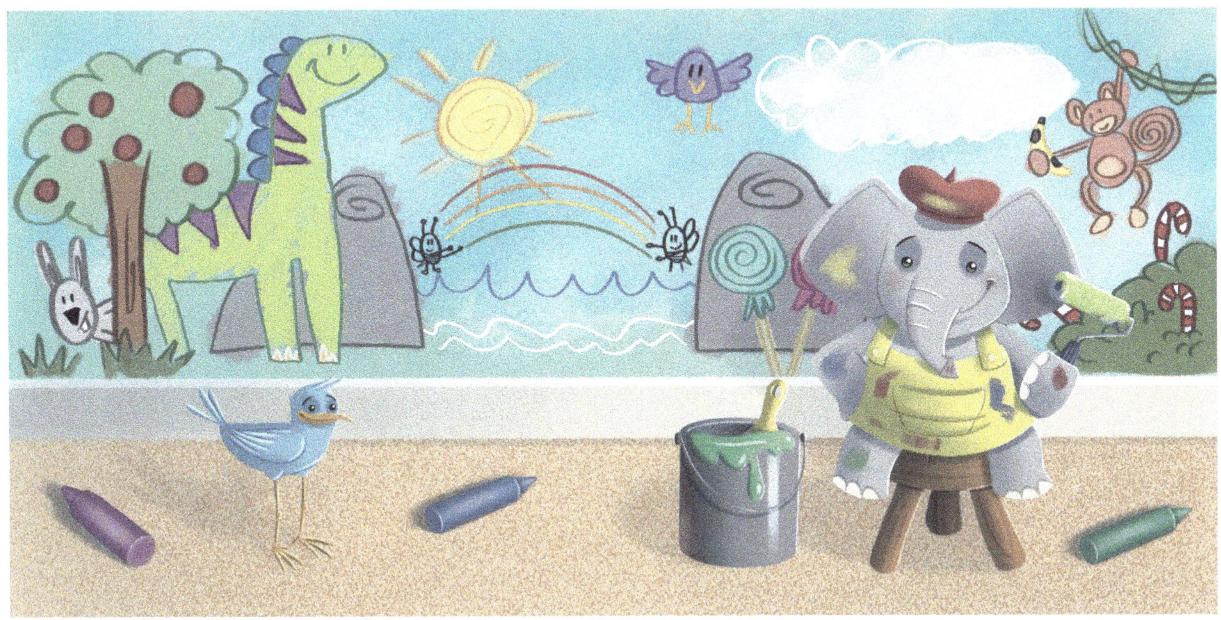

and I don't see golden sand. Even though I love the actual art, the art for the words is missing. Sometimes my artists are not English-speaking and translating causes some difficulties at times. This is overcome with patience, but they do much work before it's sorted out sometimes. The artist hired for this book and these pages did these –

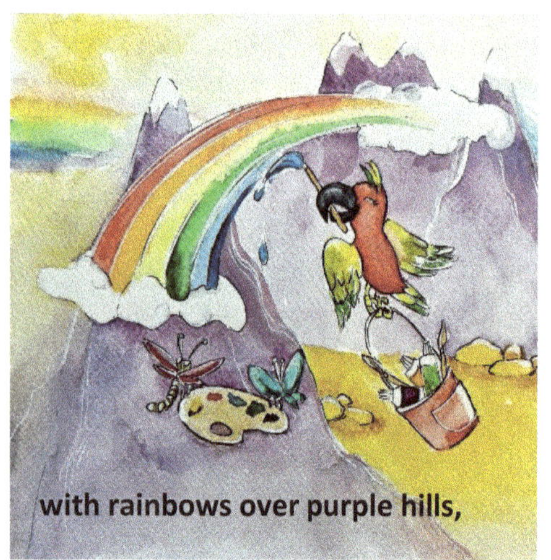

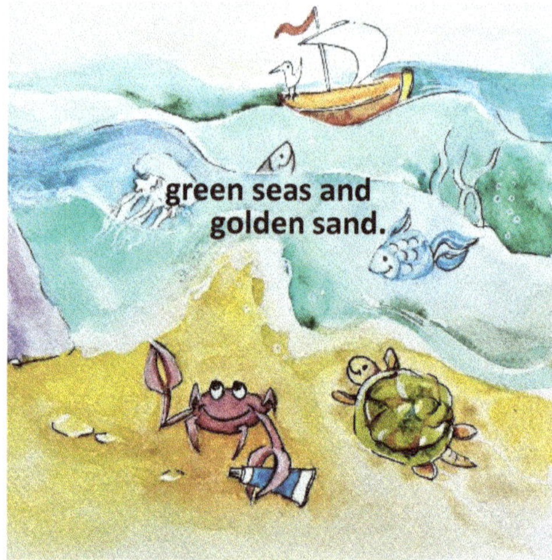

To add to the 'need for the illustrations to match the words,' in the story, in *Oscar's Truel Friends,* the artist was asked to make '2' Oscar. He was added to the second draft.

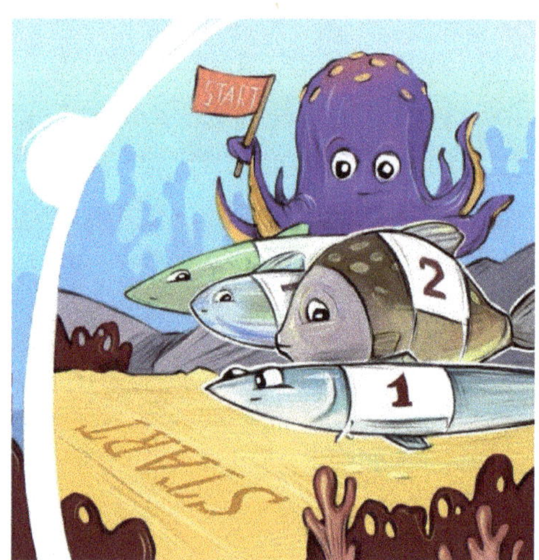

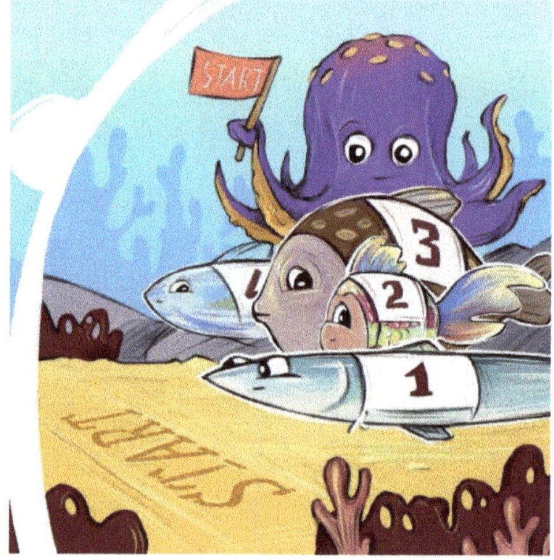

This better matched the words, 'While he was swimming home, Oscar thought and thought, and he came up with a plan. At school, there was a race. Everyone knew Dash was going to win. She was the fastest fish at school, but Oscar decided to join the race anyway.' Dash is #1 and in the first draft, Oscar is not in the first picture but he is #2 in the second draft of the illustration.

For an additional note on coloring, sometimes an illustrator uses the same colors over and over. Once this artist used quite a bit of pink and purple so I asked for a change,

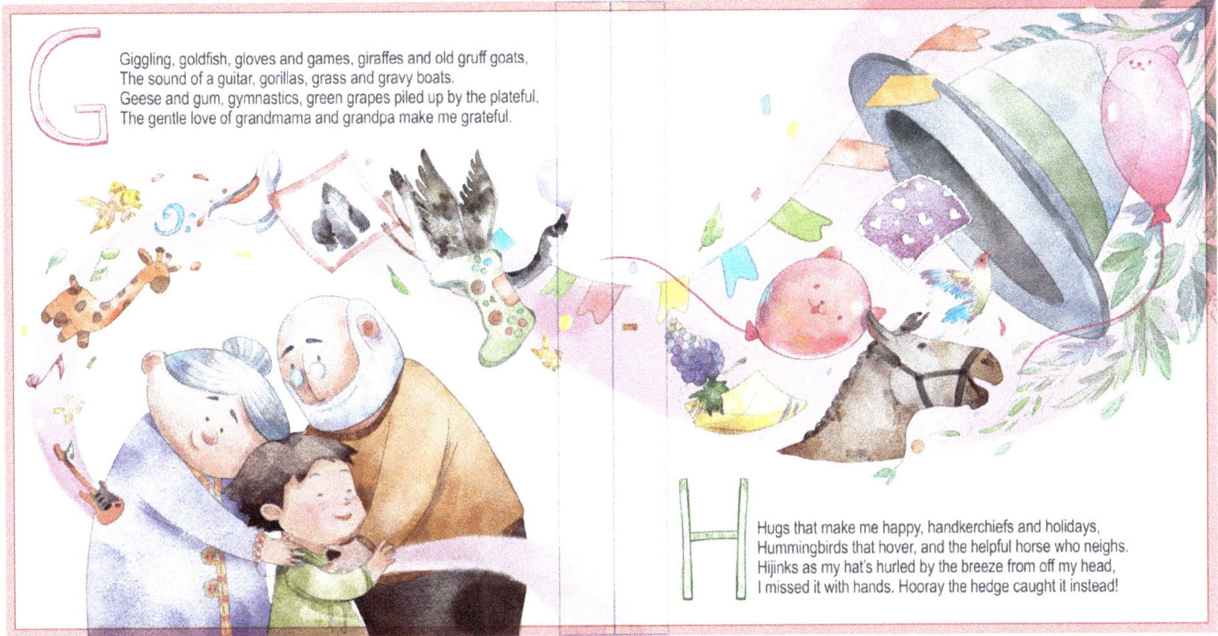

….and she changed the purple – so it's easier to do if you're working in photoshop. It makes a more interesting book to not have all the same color. I always say 'there are many colors in your palate! There are over six million different colors! Use them!

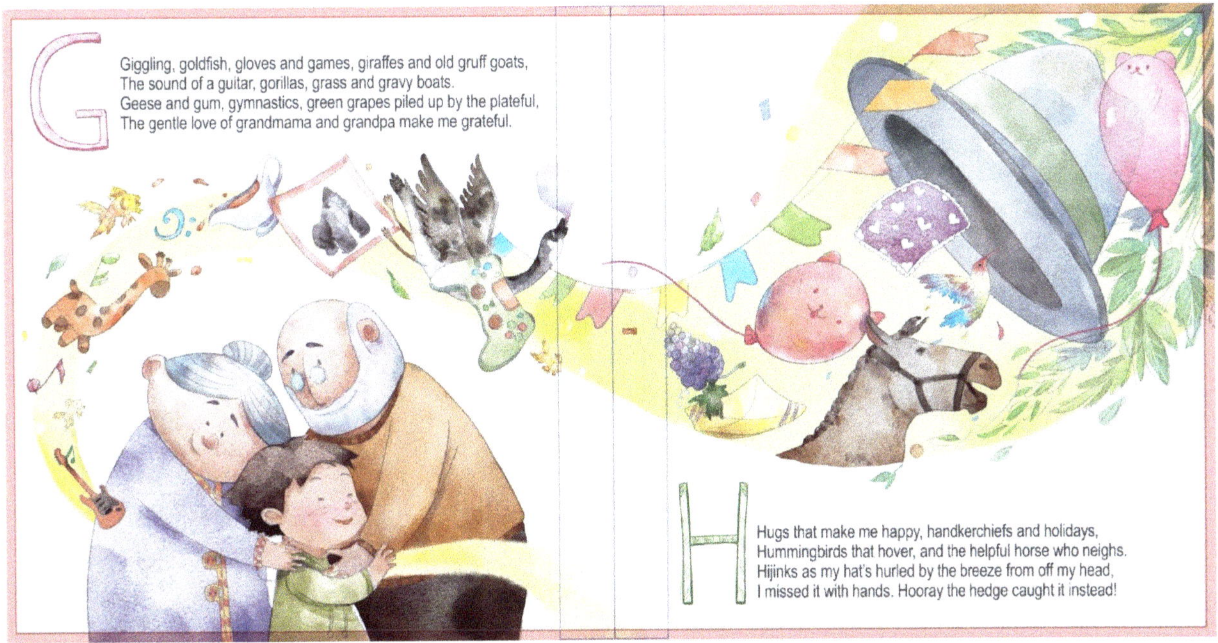

Sometimes artists are frustrated with me when they show me a sketch, I approve it, and they color it, and I am not happy with the illustration. This doesn't happen often, but it does happen and the reason is I don't always know what it will look like colored. For instance – this lovely sketch from *Roman is a BIGGER Brother* is lovely, however,

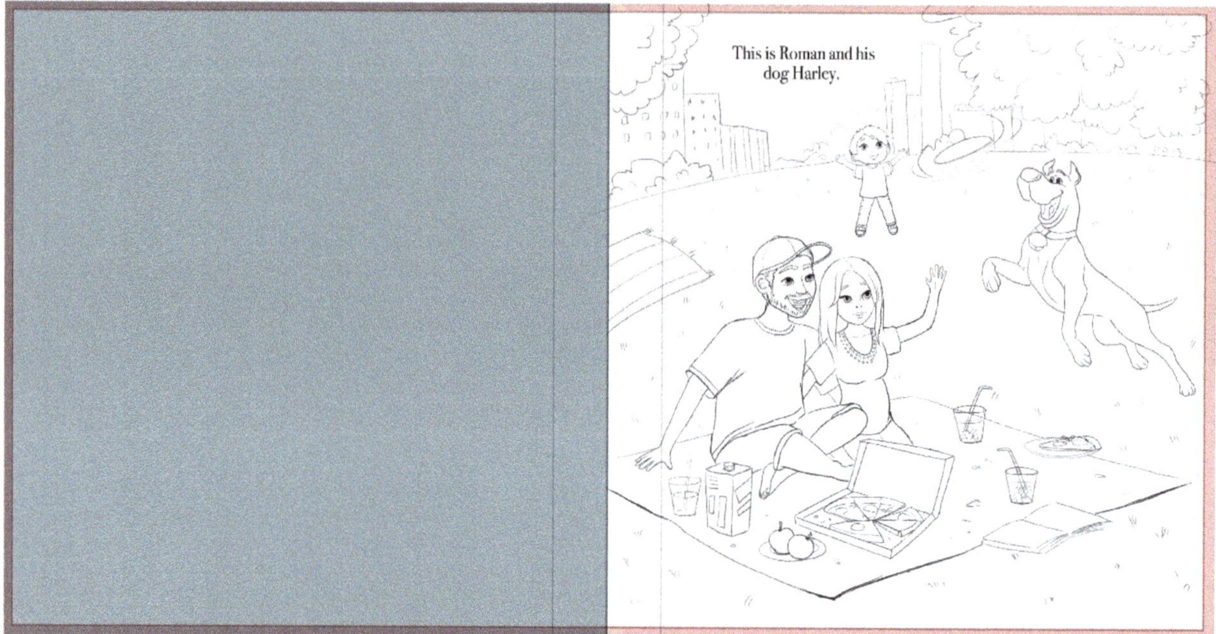

Was originally colored like this - I felt the white highlights on the mom's face appeared somewhat odd, so I asked for this to change. The whole picture didn't need altered….

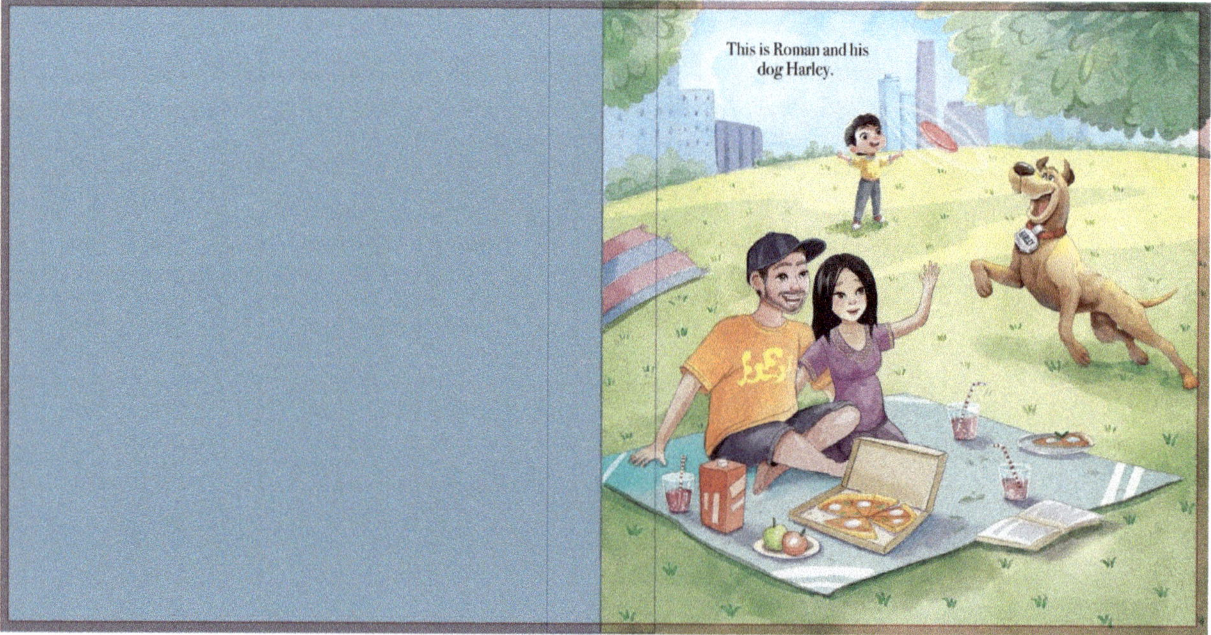

So she gave me this –

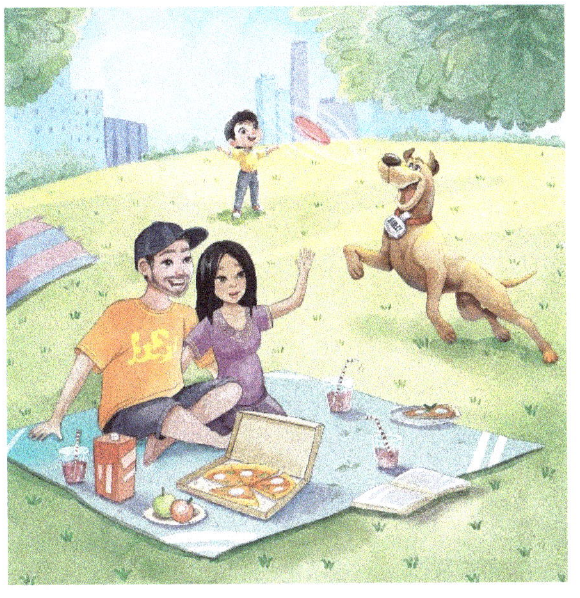

It's important to me that things look natural if they are meant to look natural. I could not have known until it was colored that I would request a change in the coloring.

In *Jesus is Risen A Bunny in the Room : An Easter Tradition*, Zaida submitted this sketch – which I initially liked

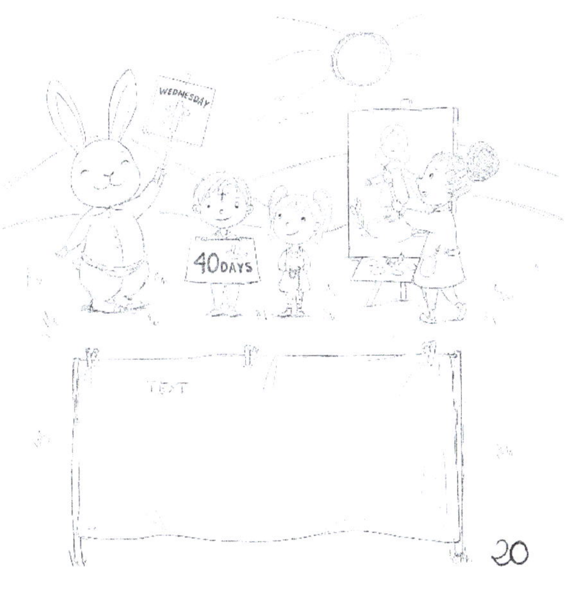

I addressed this above, and the sketch is light and difficult to see I realize…. but it was approved by myself and the author…

However, I also realize how much time and effort each artist spends creating a design. In defense of all 'fussy' people like myself, I am not able to tell how this will appear when colored. Zaida is lovely to work with because even though this was approved…..

I actually liked the one of the left, but the author didn't so we created the right…

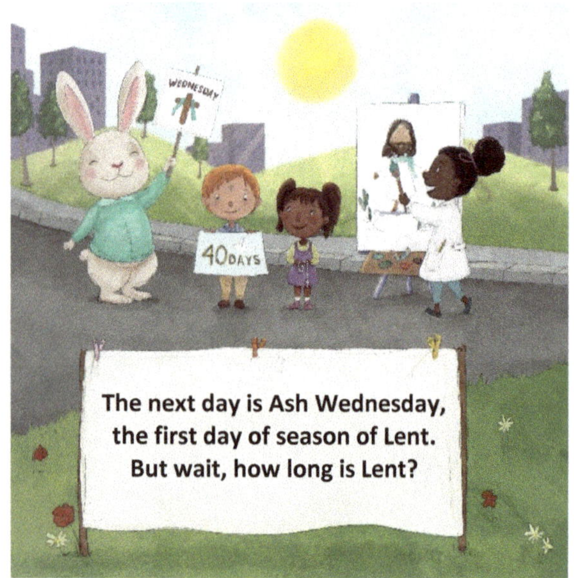

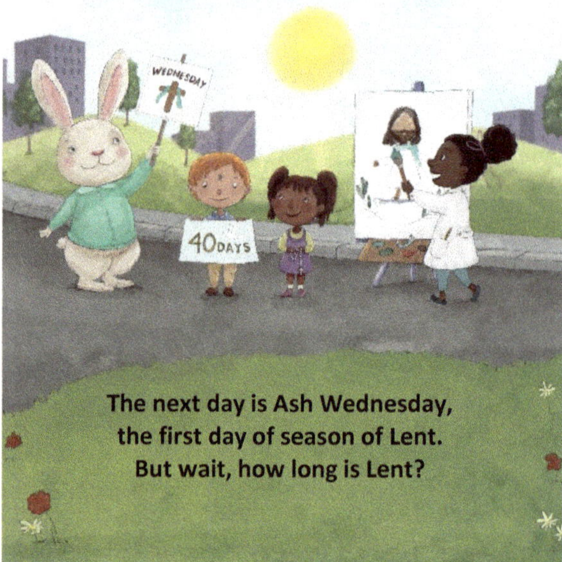

I admit I like the white area, but I try to accommodate the wishes of my authors.

Sometimes I receive a great deal of detail for an illustration – like this – there's quite a lot going on in this illustration spread. The cost increases with this much detail, but some books are really nice if they have this much detail and the story lines are detailed.

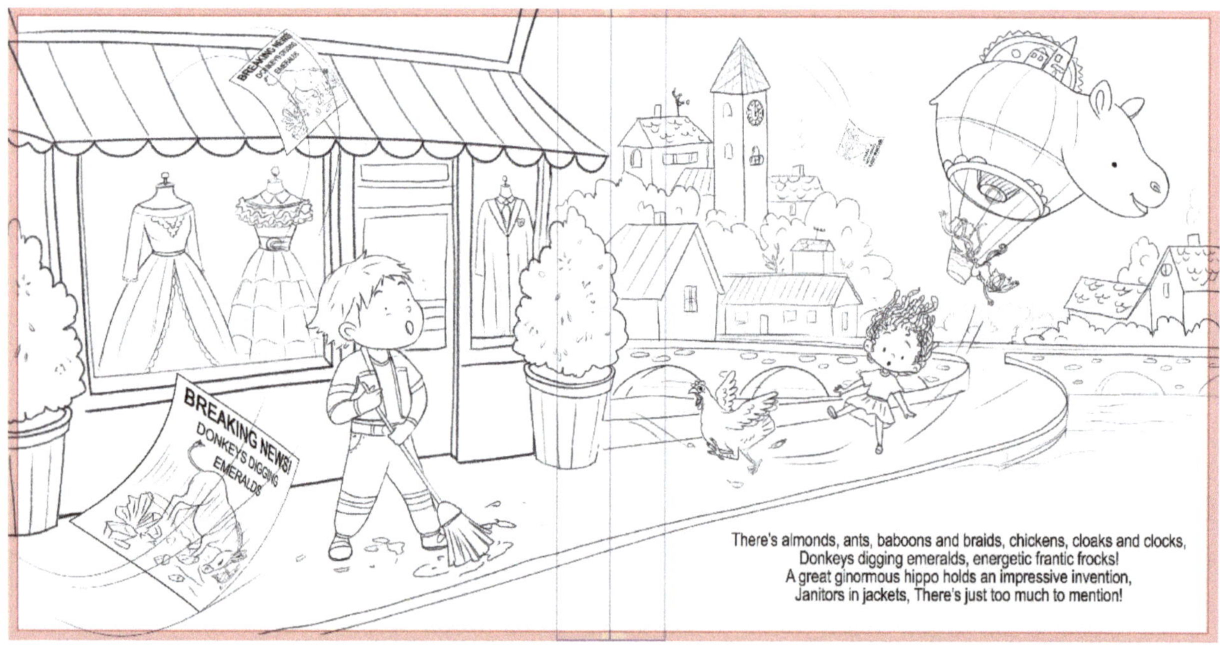

But, when the budget is not as flexible, simpler illustrations do the trick -

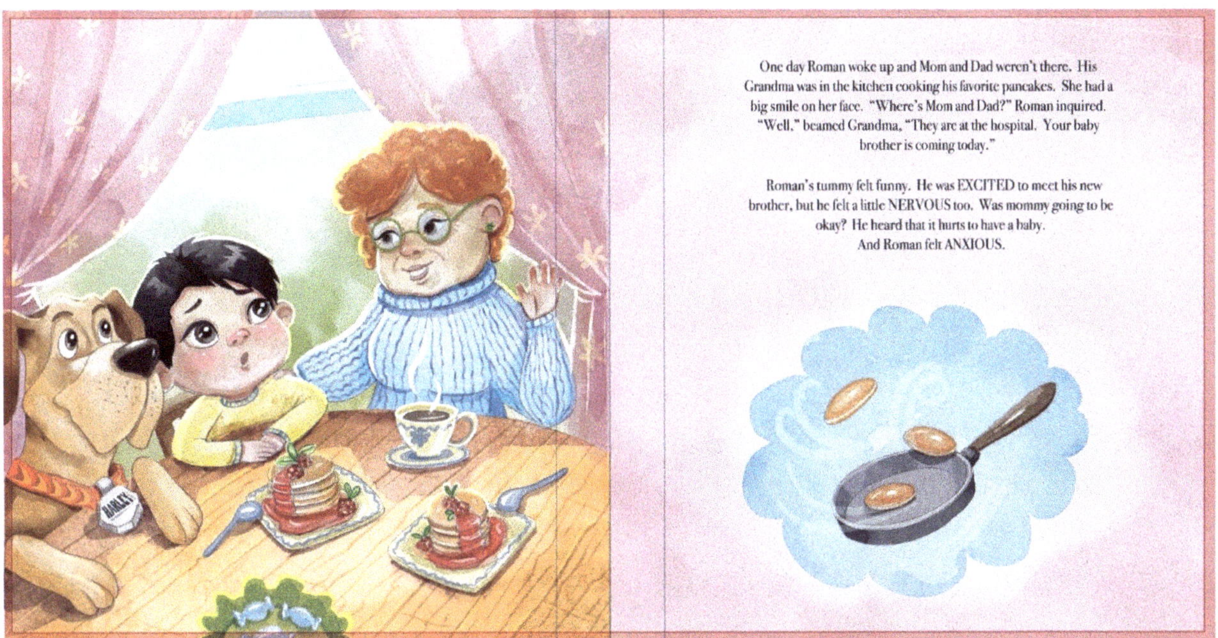

Some artists save the author or publisher money by making part of the spread simple.

As I think everyone can see, I love colorful things. I always tell my artists that I am not a huge fan of brown, grey, and black colors because I find them drabby, there are many animals that are these colors. What I learned from Beatrix Potter and other artists is that – never fear – there's a way to spice up blah colors!

So, Anna dressed all the mice up in *Finding M : The Great Alphabet Hunt* -

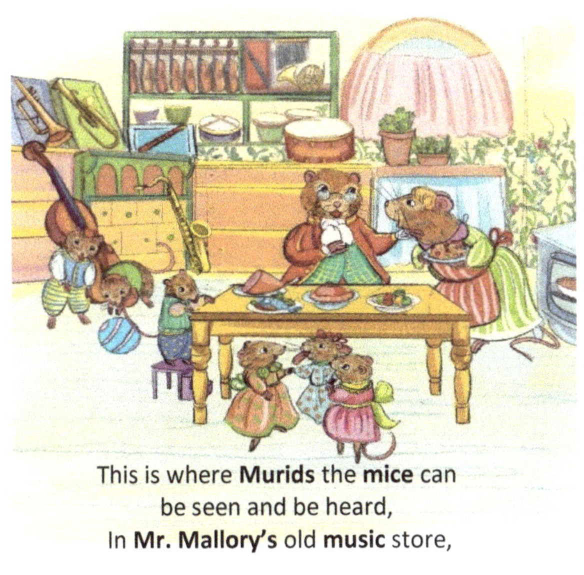

This is where **Murids** the **mice** can
be seen and be heard,
In **Mr. Mallory's** old **music** store,

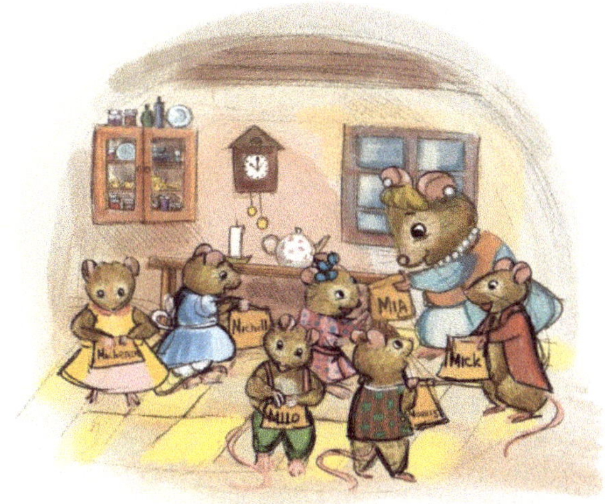

There's **Michelle, Morris,** and **Milo,**
Mackenzie, Mia, and **Mick,**

And the last THIS or THAT I would like to mention is diversity. One of my books was criticized for not having sufficient diversity, however, this was not intentional and I add different children to each book. Artists are very good at helping with this –

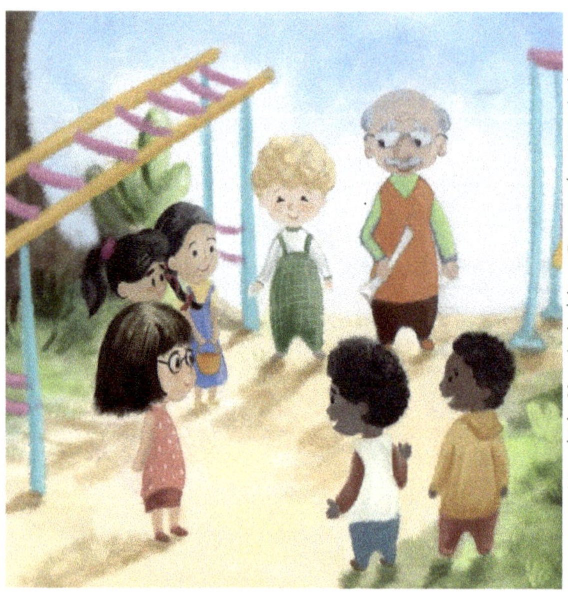

In *Just Right*, a Caucasian young boy, Eddie, has several friends he meets on the playground when he and his Grandpa visit the playground.

One of his friends is a Hispanic boy, another is an African American boy, another is a Native American girl, and India Indian girl, and an Asian girl. The cheerful message in this little book is that no matter what we think are faults, we are *Just Right!*

In *Jesus is Risen! A Bunny in the Room : An Easter Tradition,* Zaida sweetly adds children of different nationalities and some with disabilities to help every young reader know they are included in the reading experience and life experiences.

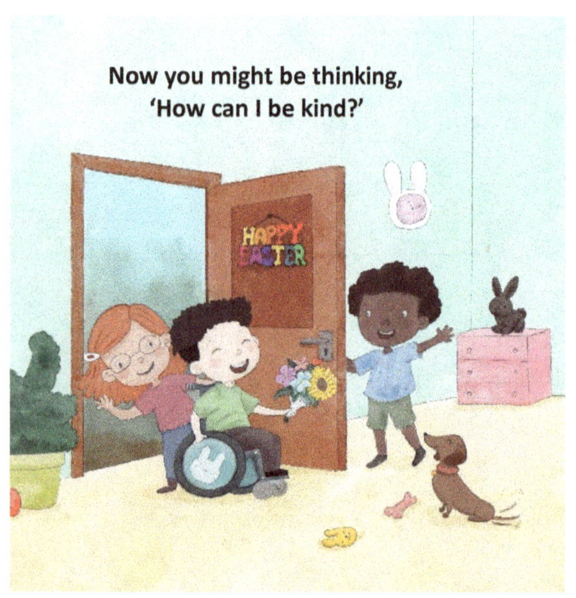

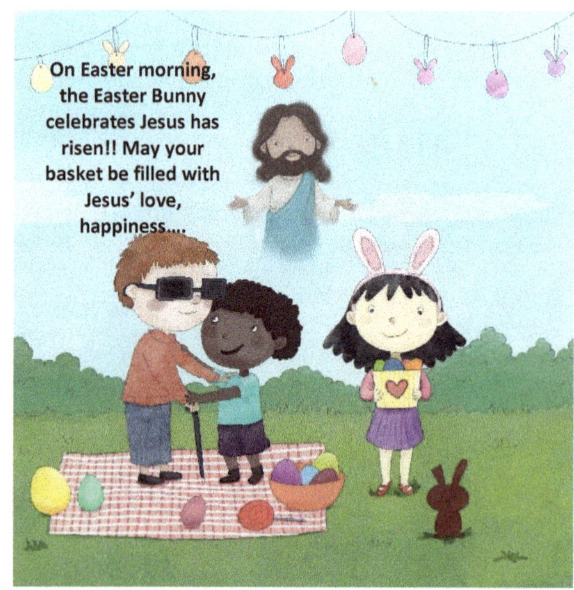

7

Great Benefits : Literacy and Language Development

Everyone knows literacy is the ability to read and write. The average age for a child to learn to read is between the ages of 6 and 7, however, many children learn at an earlier age and some at a later age. There is no 'one-size' fits all when it comes to learning. Children learn to read by hearing words and seeing pictures.

Pre-school children – ages 3-5 – develop pre-reading skills such as recognizing letters and sounds. They are able to understand printed words and can begin to develop a vocabulary.

Kindergarten aged children – ages 5-6 – is when most formal reading skills develop.

Early elementary children – ages 6-7 – begin to read fluently and develop reading comprehension skills. Again, there are no 'set-in-stone' rules for development.

Speech, however, develops at a much younger age. Children 'babble,' making sounds, at about six months of age. Soon, they are talking to their friends and family.

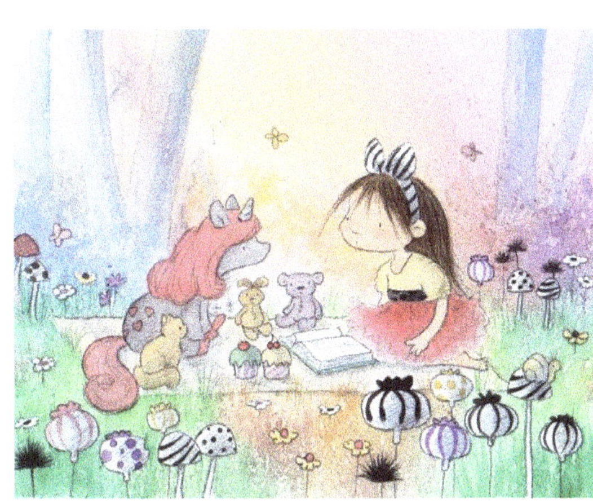

First words arrive at about ten to fourteen months of age. Children are able to make these sounds because they have *heard* these sounds.

At eighteen months to 2 years of age, children learn to make sentences.

Talking to children comes naturally and is important for children to learn language and talk themselves. Even though infants cannot respond verbally, adults, siblings, friends, and relatives are always talking to and around the young child. Television and other audio devices contribute to an infant's exposure to words and sounds. Sound is an important aspect to speech development and then reading and learning skills. Obviously, additional teaching and learning techniques are required for hearing or visually impaired children.

So, how do picture books help children develop speech and language skill? Glad you asked. Picture books are worth their weight in gold!

Children love stories. They love art and time spent with the important people in their lives. What great time spent – reading to our little ones! This starts learning.

Some picture books are simple with few words but lovely pictures. For example, Moira Andrew is a well-known poet in England and has published over 100 titles! She partnered with me on several projects and her story *August Weather* is simple – take a look. The cute and clever art engages the young reader as they hear the words.

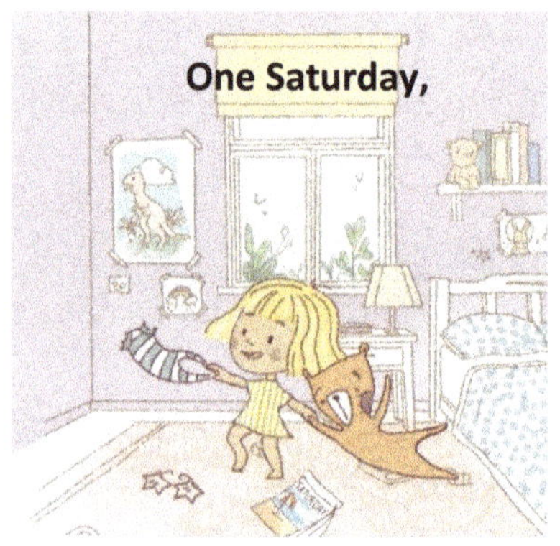

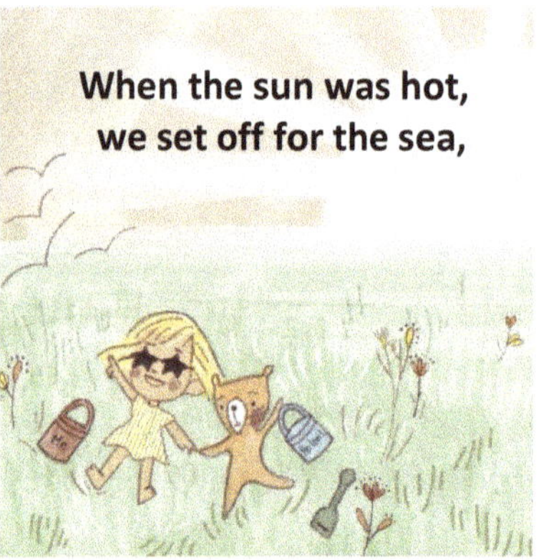

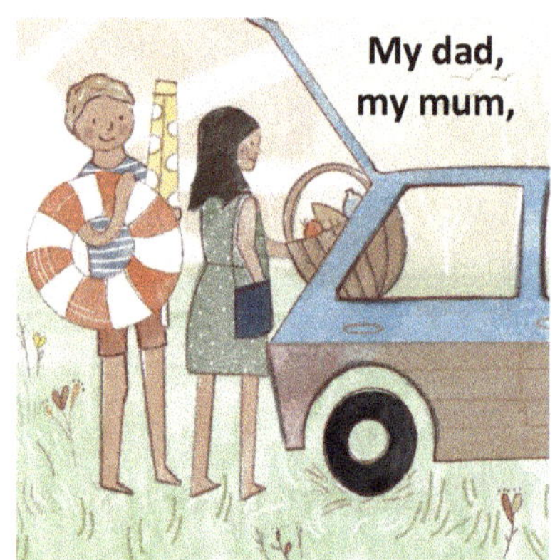

Moira has cute lines that are matched with cute pictures. Easy for the youngest reader.

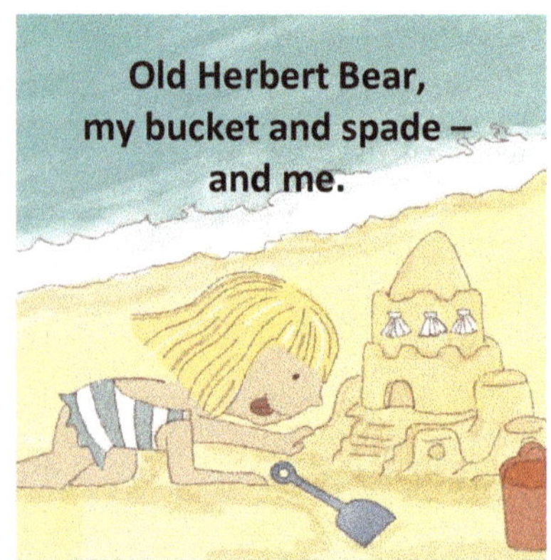

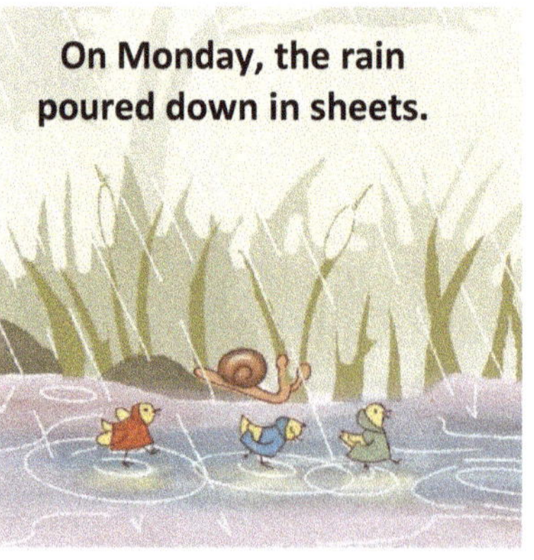

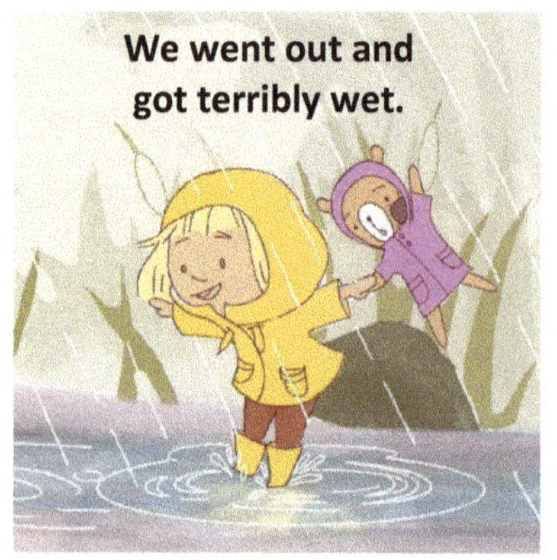

August Weather teaches the days of the week and the words are easily associated with the illustrations. Moira steps it up a notch in another picture book we partnered publishing to bring something special to the young readers. Moving from simpler texts to more complicated texts as in *Portrait of a Dragon* that is about a little girl who is an artist herself and has a vision to paint a dragon. The words are easily associated with objects, actions, and expressions in the illustrations. Let's take a look –

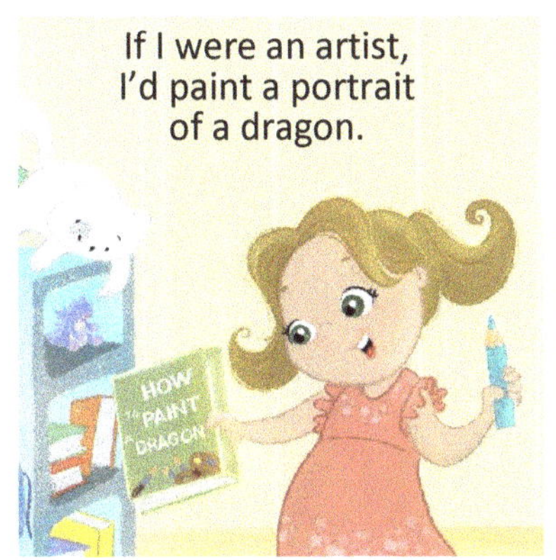

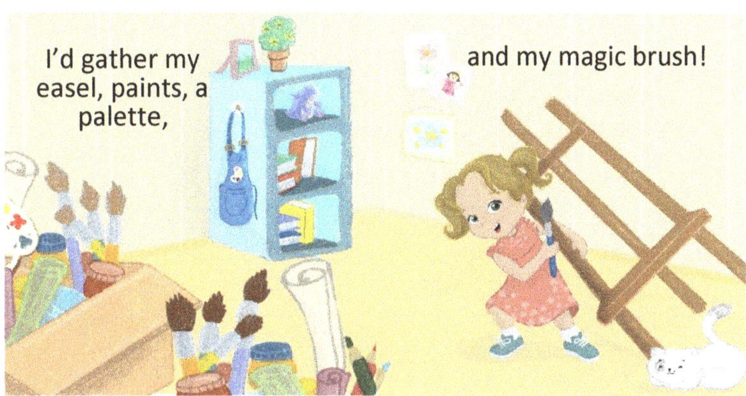

The illustrator did a nice job of matching the activity in the illustrations with the words.

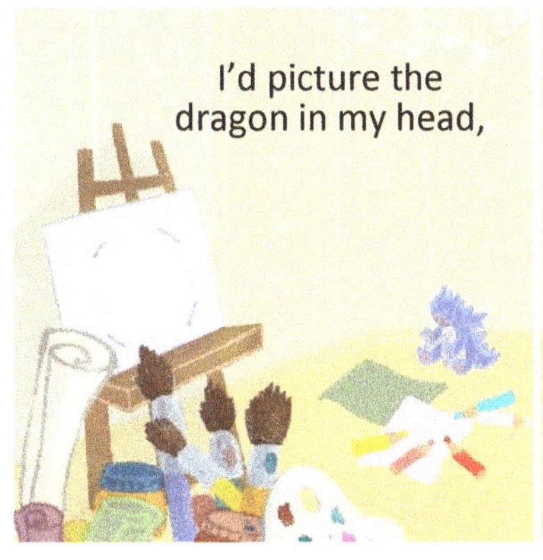

Moira's words are brought to life as the young reader sees how this little artist gathers her supplies and has her 'HOW TO PAINT A DRAGON' book on hand. Each word can be identified in the illustration. As can be seen here and here -

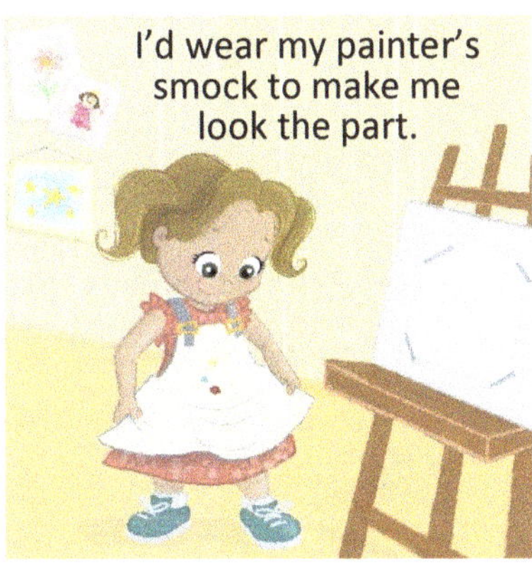

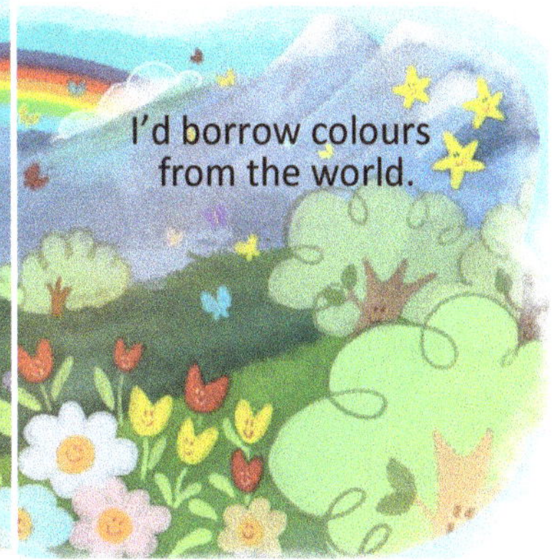

Hearing words – whether simple or more challenging - builds vocabulary and creates an understanding of language. This is the groundwork for learning to read and recognizing letters and their association to sounds. Picture books are ideal for introducing language to young readers. Another example of advancing vocabulary is David's fun and educational book about woodlice and isopods. Most young children have no idea what a woodlouse or an isopod is, but David is clever and Oksana is my creative artist who makes the information and picture book engaging. Take a look-

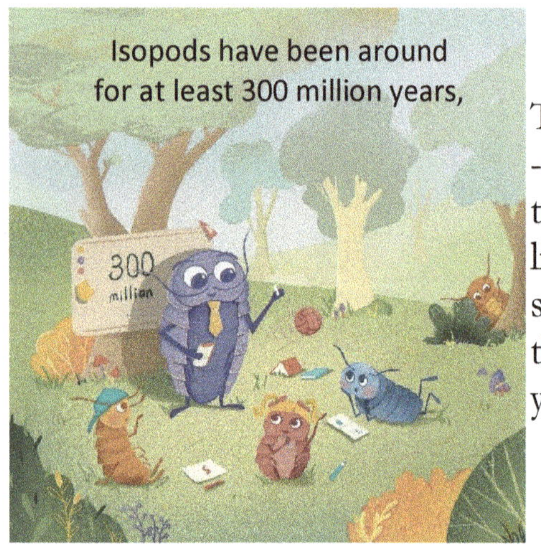

This may be a little advanced for a three or four–year -old, however, the cute pictures may make them want to know more about the world around them. These little 'bugs' are easy to find in most climates. Five to seven-year-olds may be fascinated by a story about these bugs and illustrators really do help engage the young reader. New words are also introduced here.

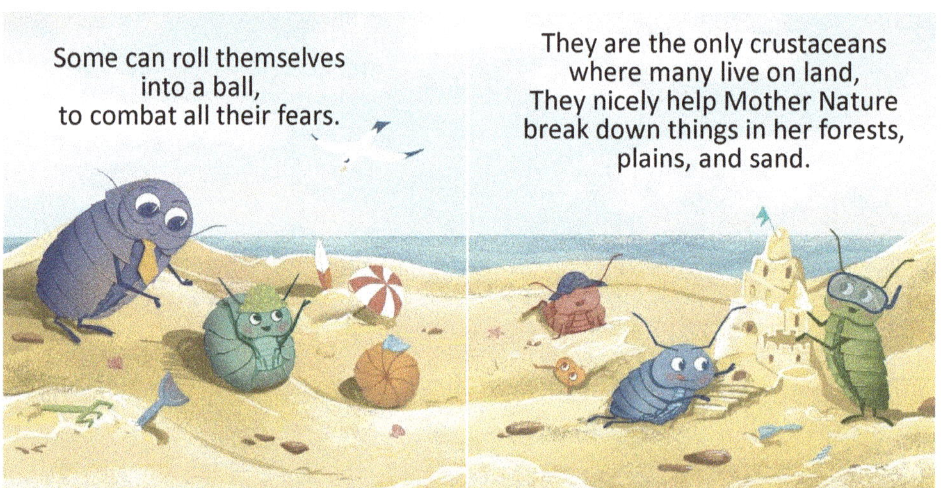

Yes, the words 'combat,' 'crustacean,' and 'plains' may not be in a four-year-old vocabulary, but reading the words to them and exposing them to the words as they see the crustaceans rolling their bodies in the picture and having fun in the sand helps them remember the words. As children hear words over and over, they grow vocabulary.

When I first began working with David, I felt his books were written mainly for boys, but girls can learn much from his little stories as well as his stories encourage youngsters to look around their world and understand it and not be afraid of things they don't know about. This is because they become acquainted with nature when reading David's books. See how cute the art is to reinforce the learning about worms!

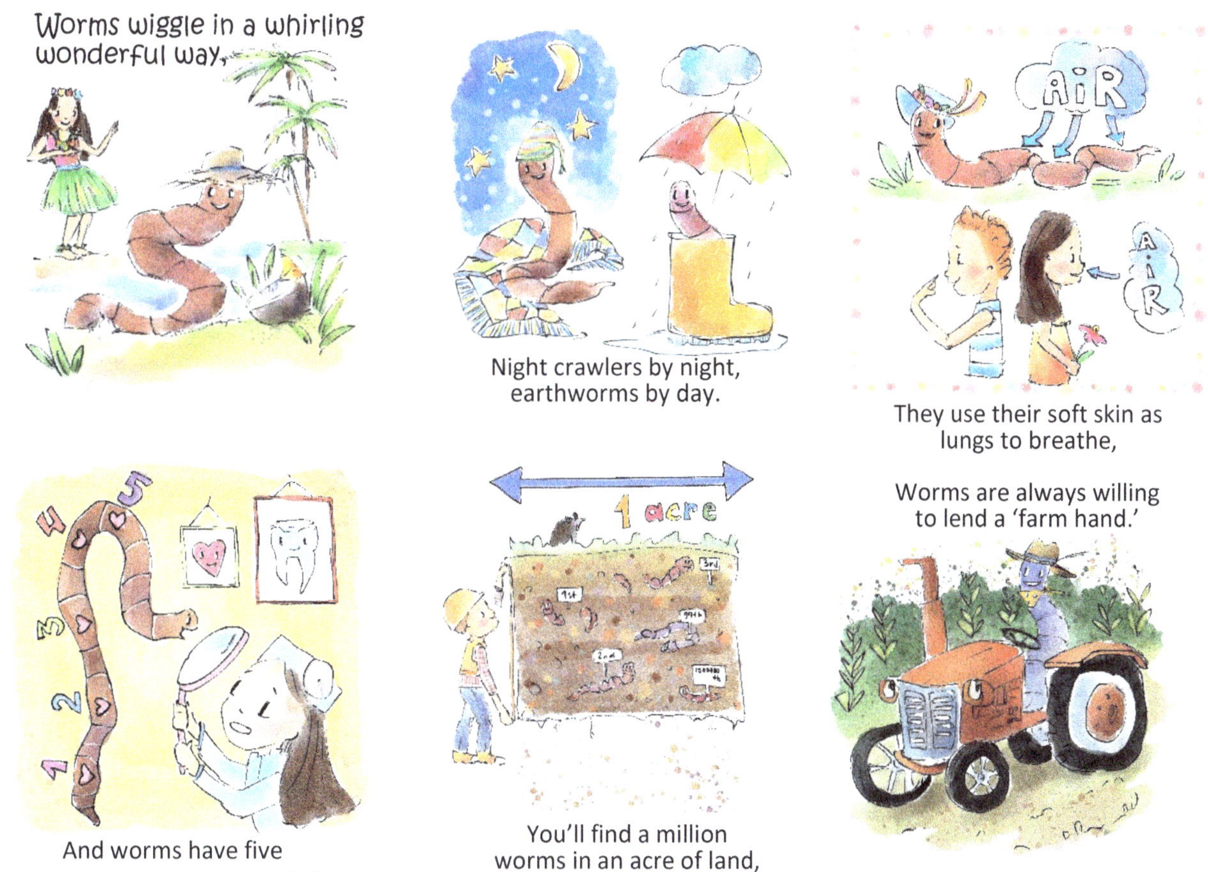

Night crawlers by night, earthworms by day.

They use their soft skin as lungs to breathe,

Worms are always willing to lend a 'farm hand.'

And worms have five hearts, but, sadly, no teeth !

You'll find a million worms in an acre of land,

Worms don't drive tractors, but Alexsandra does a cute job of making worms interesting. I don't find worms appealing, however, they have much to contribute to our ecosystem and 'boys' really seem to like worms. As mentioned, many of David's books seem appealing to a boy audience, but I enjoyed reading them and creating the books that allow the young reader to benefit from new words, interesting topics, and hopefully want to read and know more about things in the world around all of us.

David uses rhyming and alliteration to help the young reader enjoy the sounds and begin to learn how words relate to other words. David's other topics include turtles, crabs, owls, bats, trees, the marvels of sleep and more!!

While many picture books are simple and have basic language, Paula Curtis-Taylorson has created unique and sensational alphabet books to challenge young readers with simple and advanced vocabulary. I mentioned her A-XYZ book series in chapter 1 but will highlight one in more depth here. Paula uses many 'grown-up' words in this book series, however, I find these words common words children hear the adults in their lives use as well as on television or radio. Words are all around us all day long and these books may be for the older 'young reader' but are for any age that a parent wants to read to their little ones. Let's take a look at the words and illustrations in Paula's book *Finding F : The Great Alphabet Hunt.* -

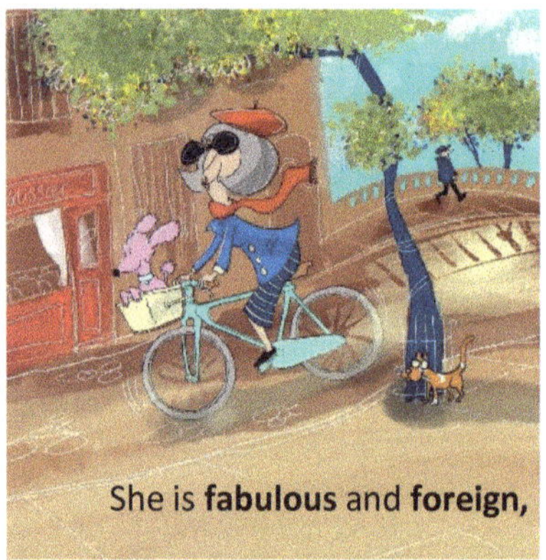

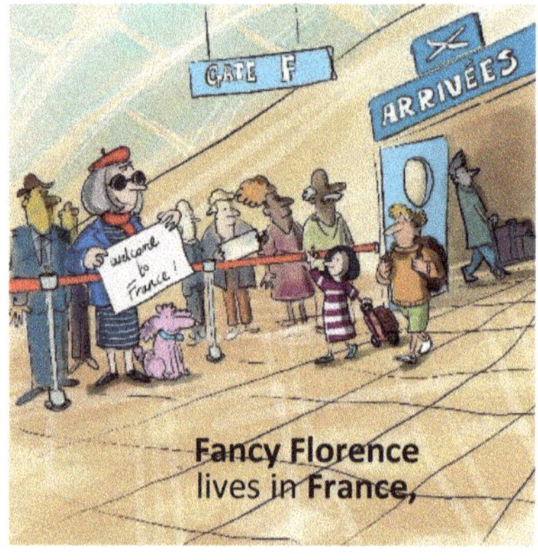

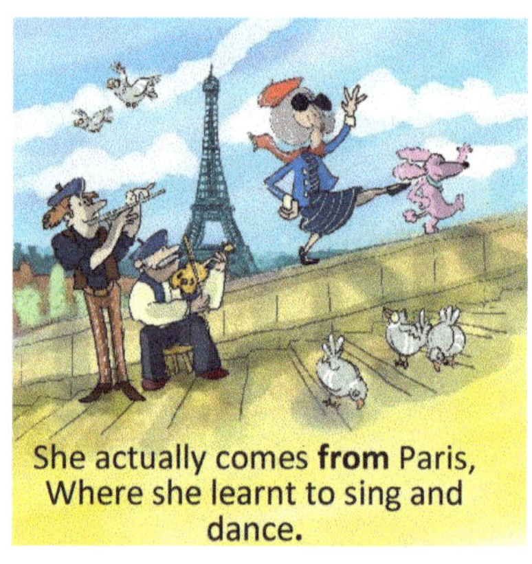

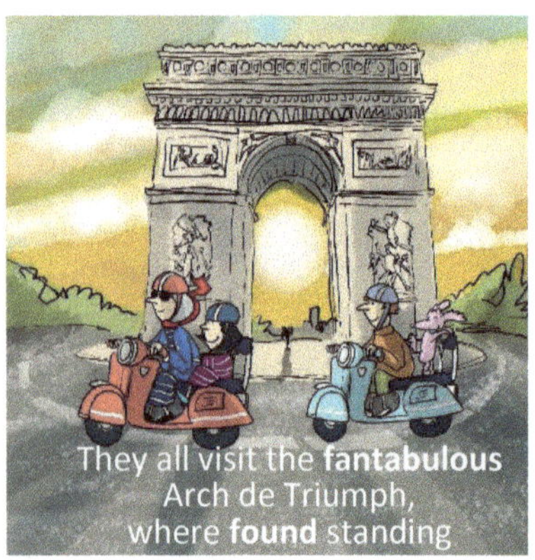

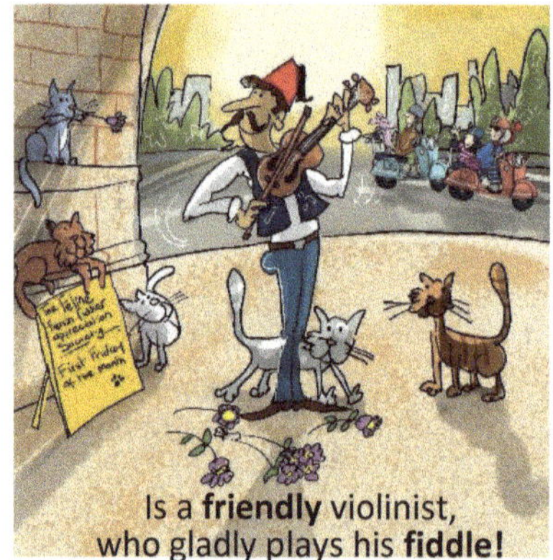

Timm does a lovely job of having the characters on the scooters around the famous monument. Then nicely has felines and other 'f' words in the sign in the picture. Cute. And Paula uses the word 'fantabulous' for the Arch.

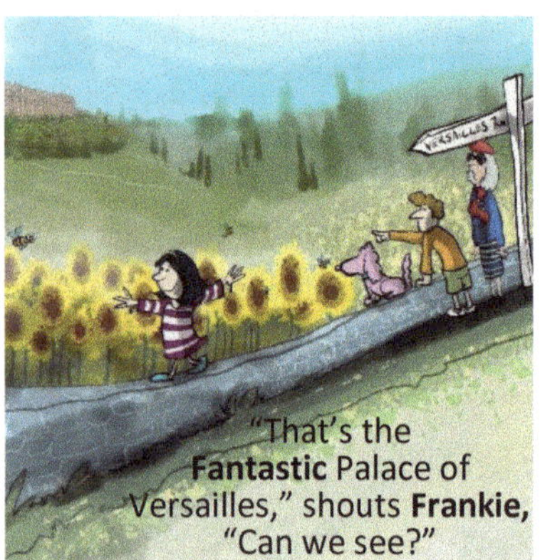

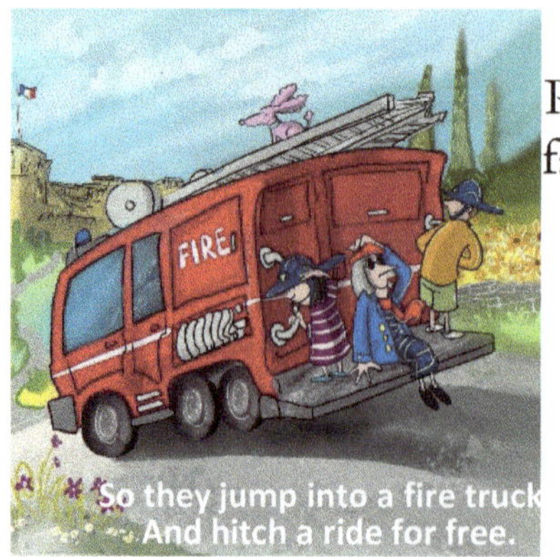

Paula also references another famous monument –
The Palace of Versailles.

Not only does a young learn the 'f' words, they are introduced to famous landmarks as well.

As can be seen in these little 'quips' from the books my company has published, not all children's books are the same. Each has their value for the reasons I listed and for different levels of learning, but the art is very important in each picture book.

As an educator myself, I feel choosing the correct book for the correct age is important, however, I never sell children short. Reading to children is a passive undertaking and children absorb words and sounds they are hearing.

The reader can make the book fun just by the way they read the words. Making much over the pictures and what is in the pictures helps children begin to understand the meaning of the words.

This is a benefit no matter how complex the topic of the picture book is. Sometimes it's difficult to hold a child's attention when material is over their ability to understand, but books can be utilized for years and some of the advanced ones may be reintroduced as children grow and develop. It's great fun to see children grow in their ability to read and understand. So, whether you read about Joe's going to Mars –

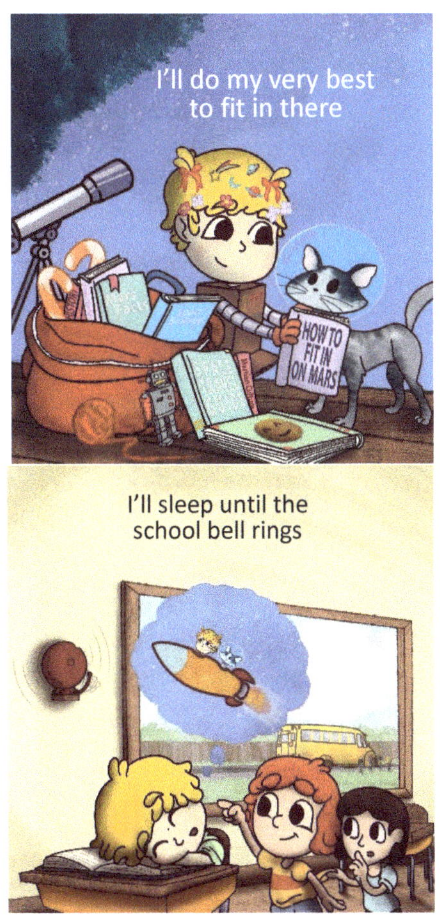

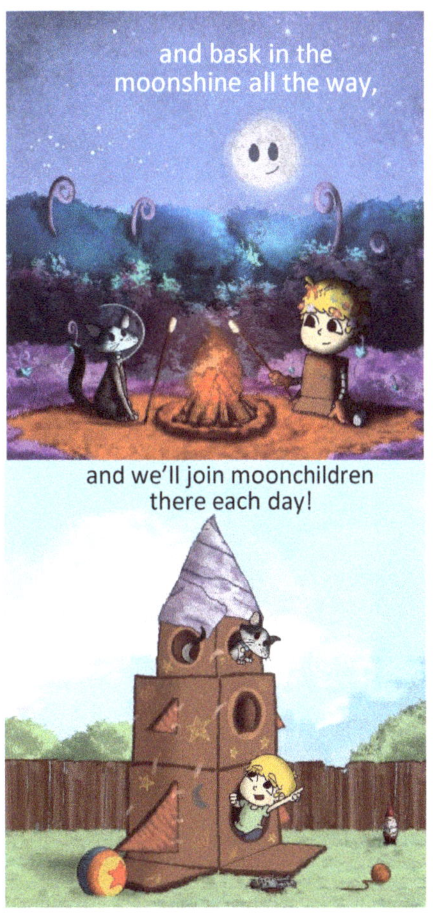

….or your child enjoys stories like *In Search of Christmas* about three search and rescue dogs, there's a story for every child and new words to learn with each new story.

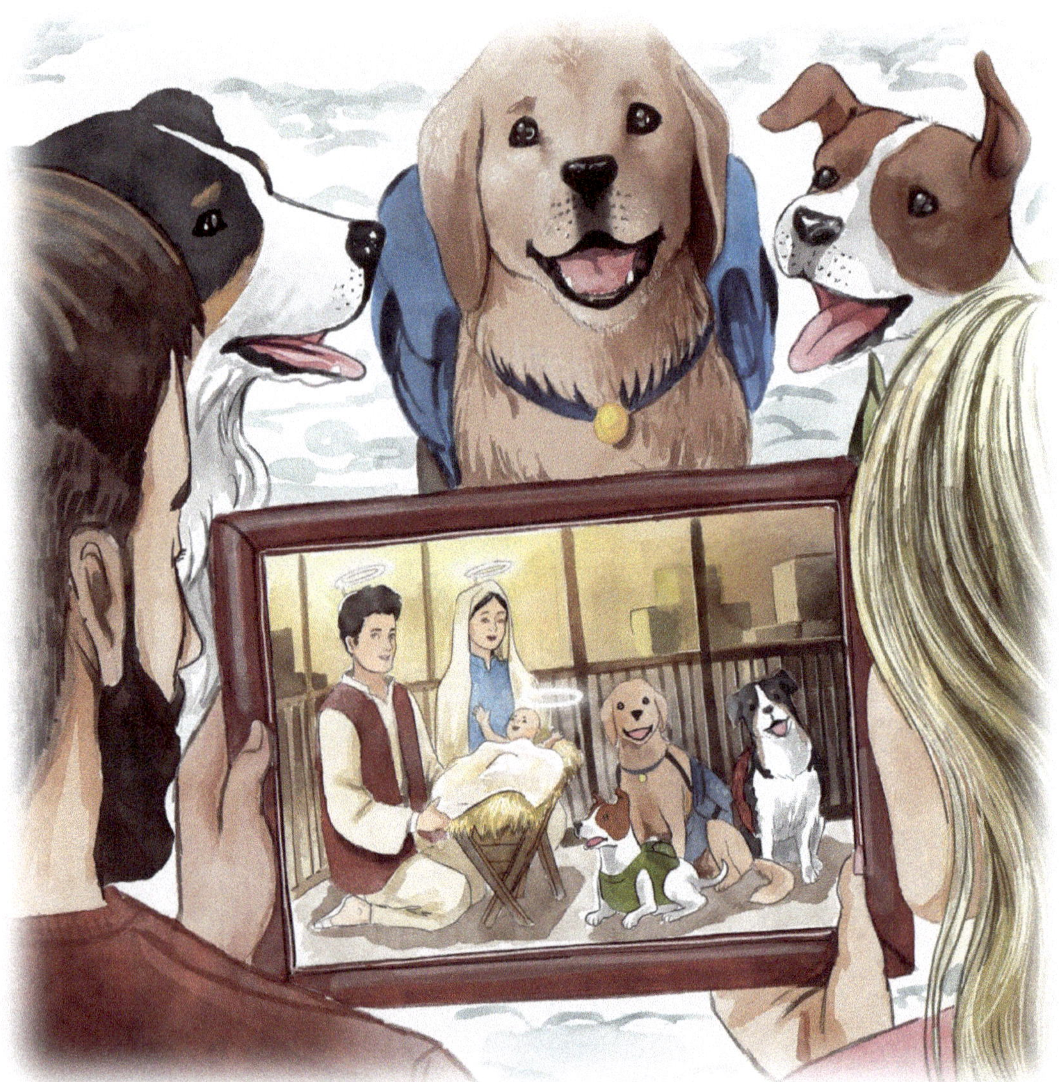

The entire town welcomed us home. We were as thrilled
to be reunited with Mark and Jenny as they were us.
We wanted Jenny to know we found Christmas!

8

Great Benefits : Comprehension

The illustrations in picture books help children develop their comprehension skills – the ability to understand and remember stories. Picture books have the basic elements of storytelling – so children learn to understand the sequence of a story – the beginning, middle and ending or resolution of a story.

The illustrations allow the young reader to analyze the story. If a child is having difficulty with words, the illustrations help them figure out the meaning of what they are reading or hearing someone read to them.

Let's take an example to see how illustrations help guide young readers through a story's flow. *Hopalong Hopscotch* was written by David R. Morgan and illustrated by Alexsandra This story was written with words, but I think it's easily understood by the pictures. See what you think -

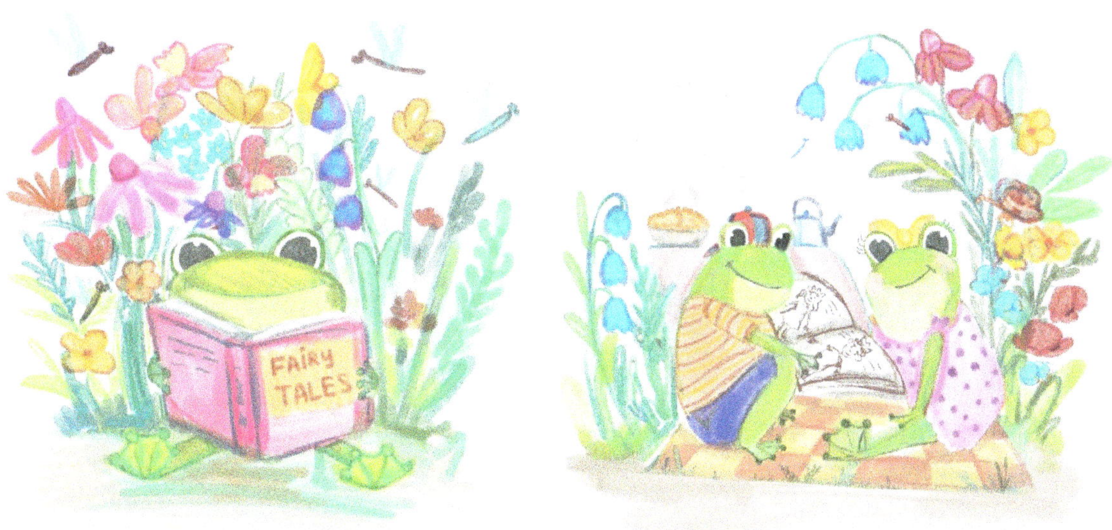

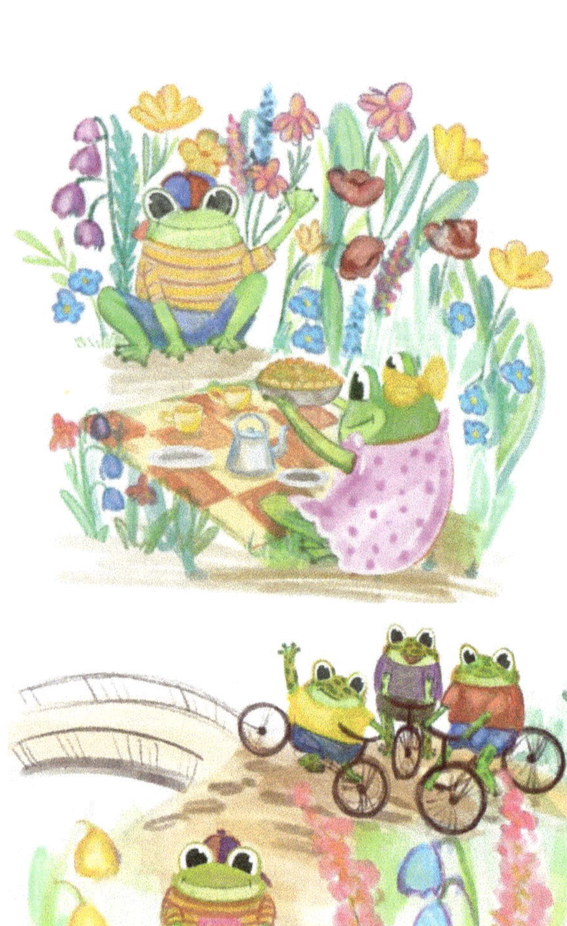

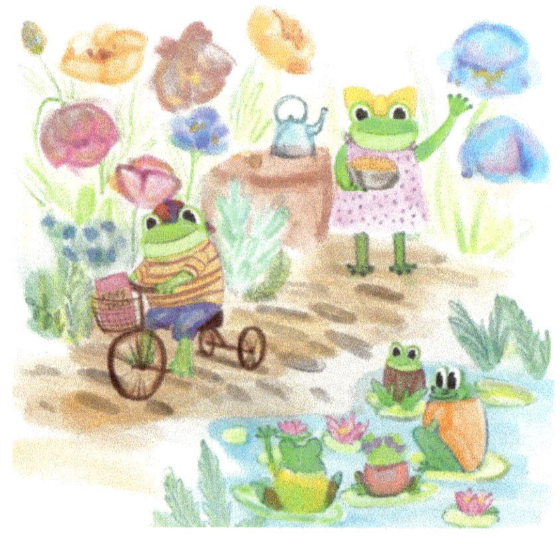

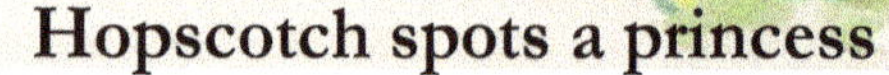

Hopscotch spots a princess

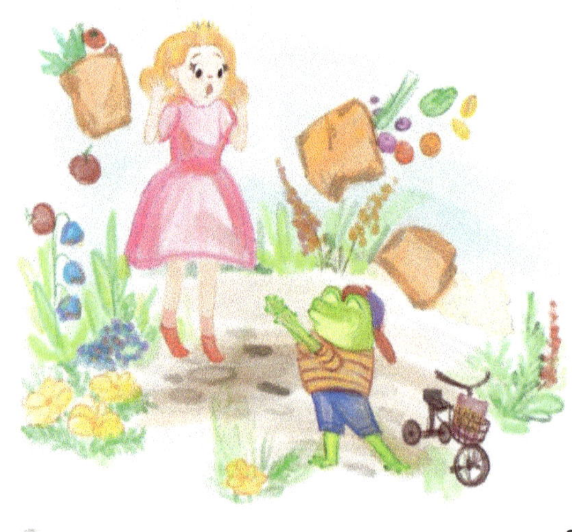

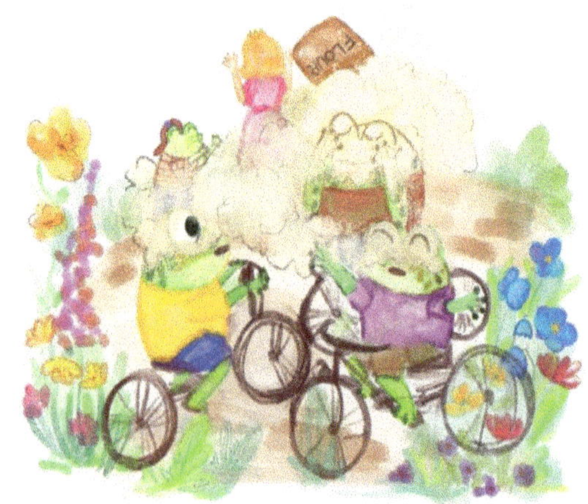

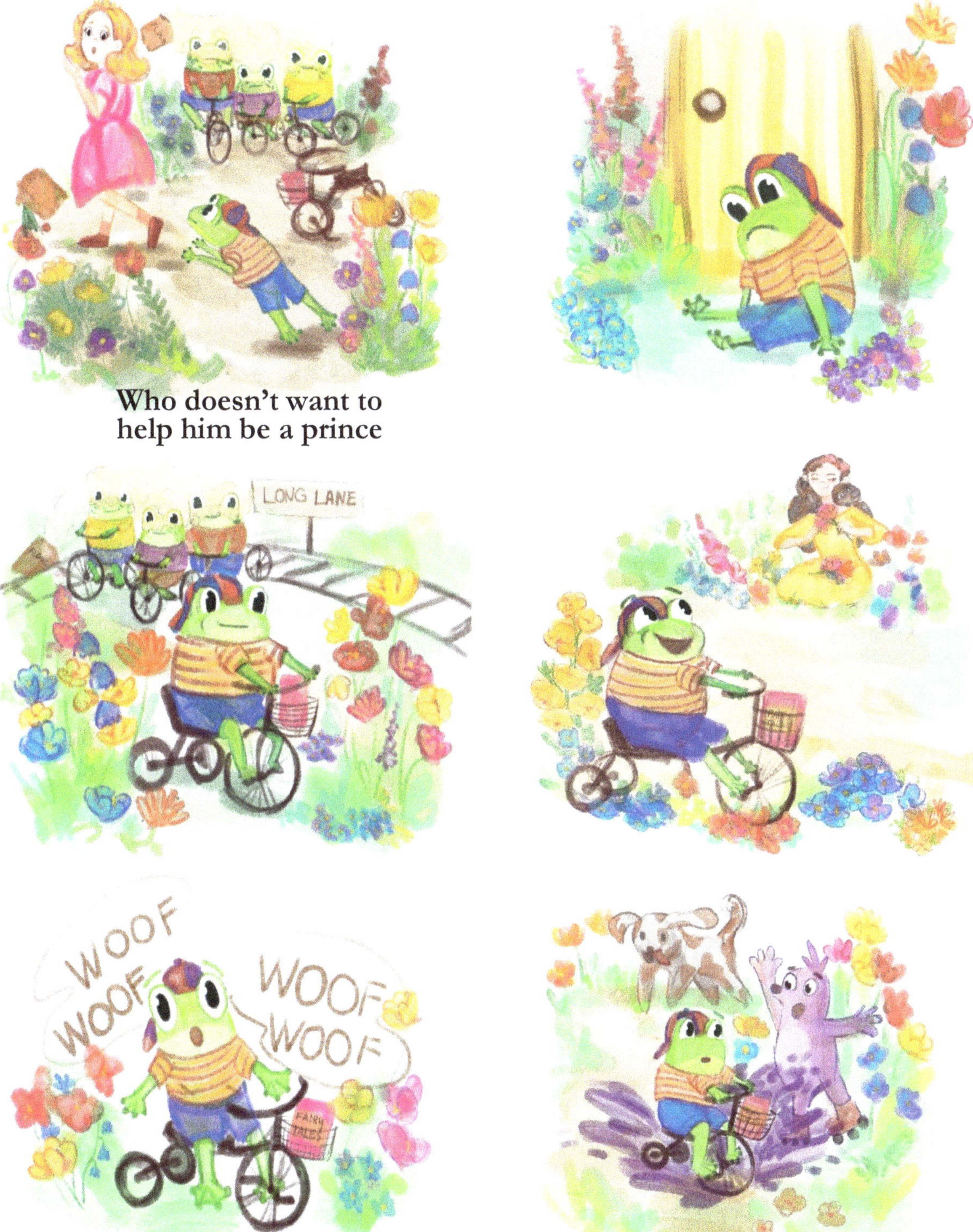

Who doesn't want to
help him be a prince

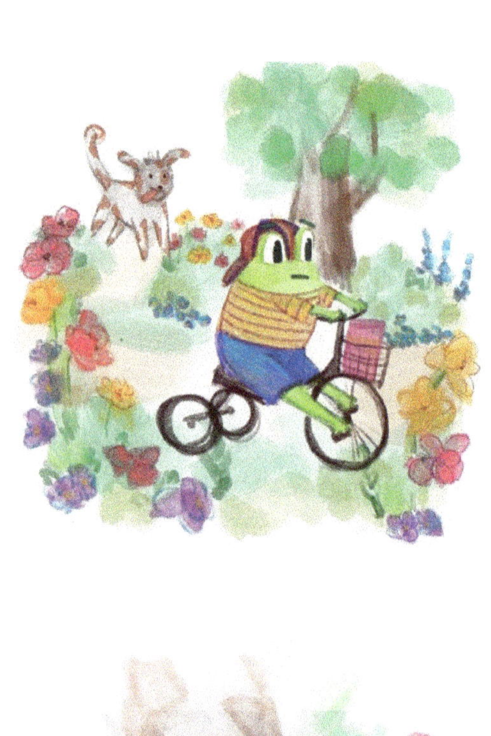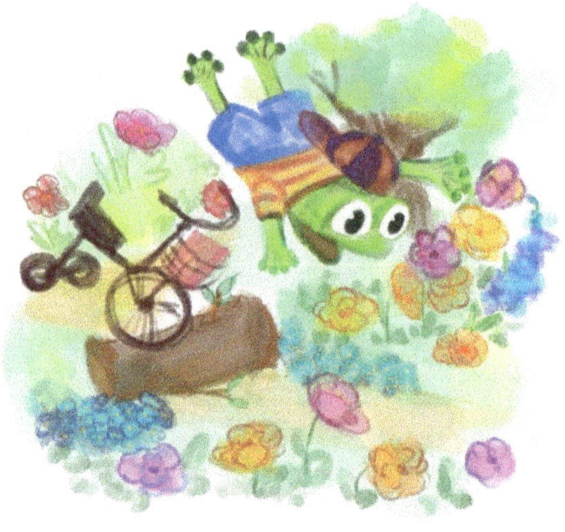

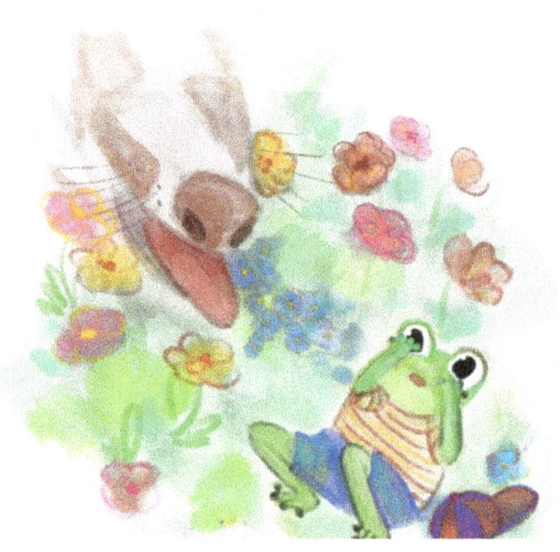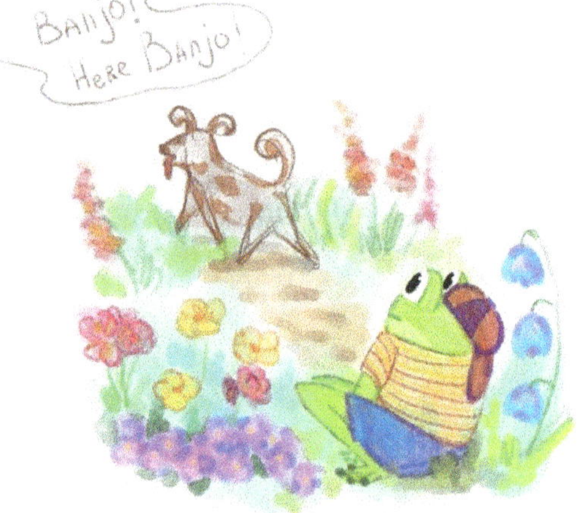
Banjo! Here Banjo!

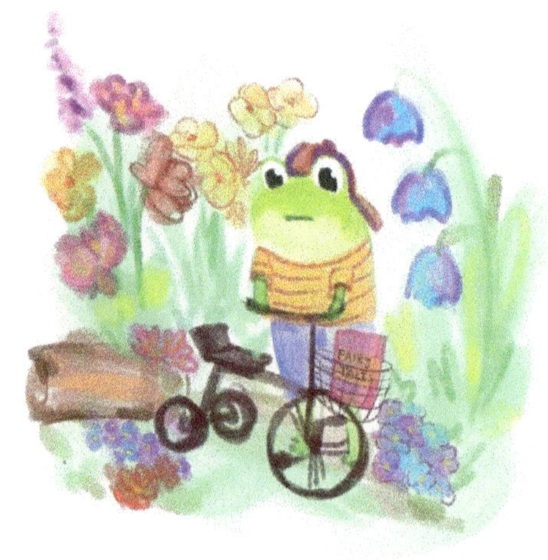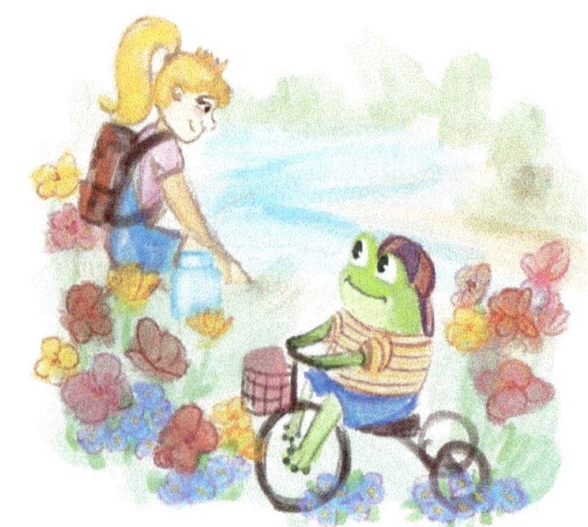

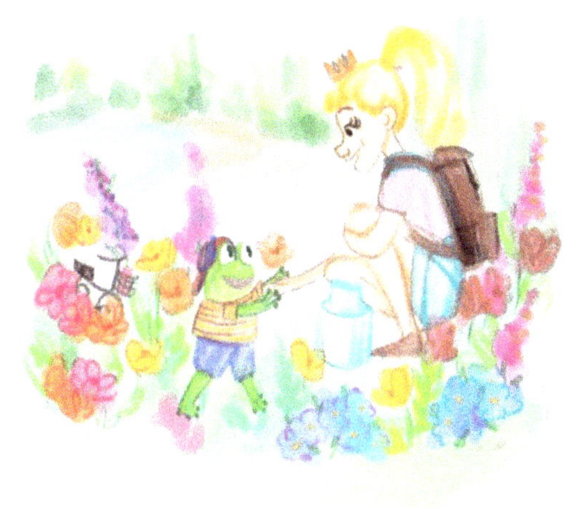

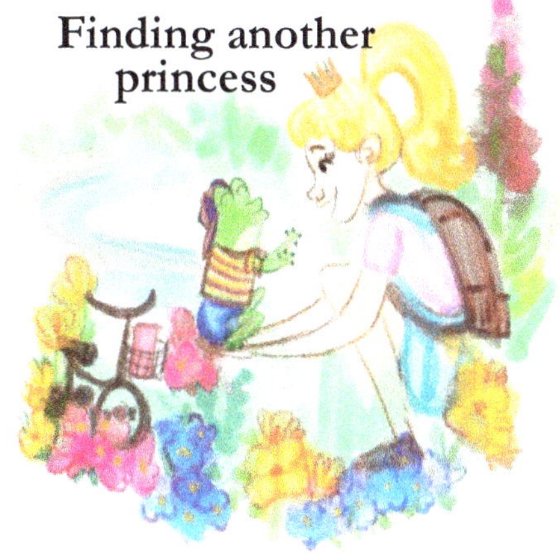

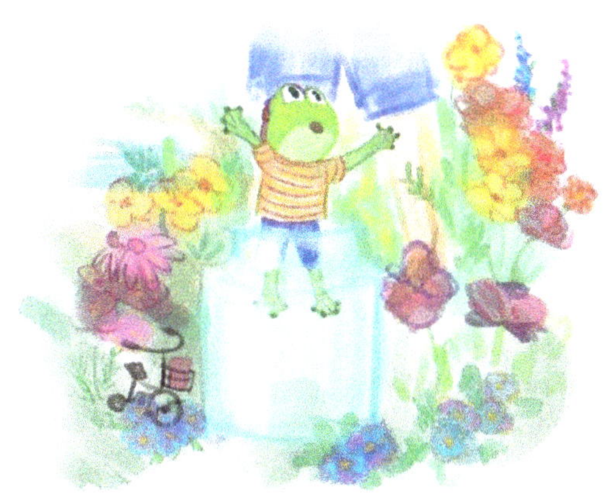

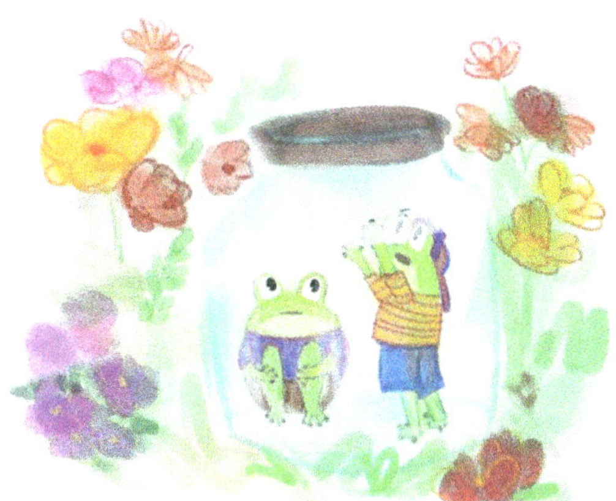

Also doesn't go so well

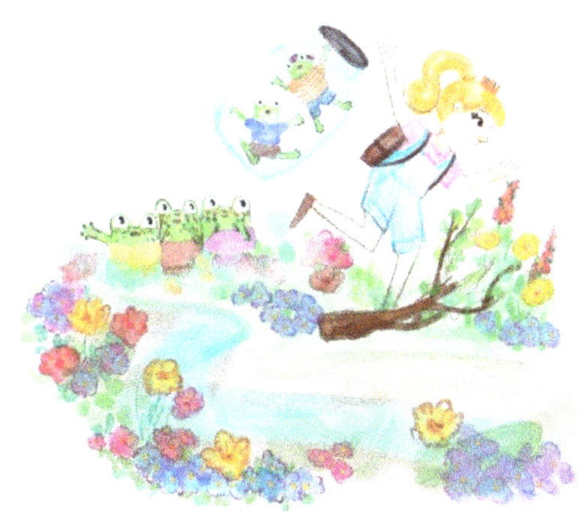

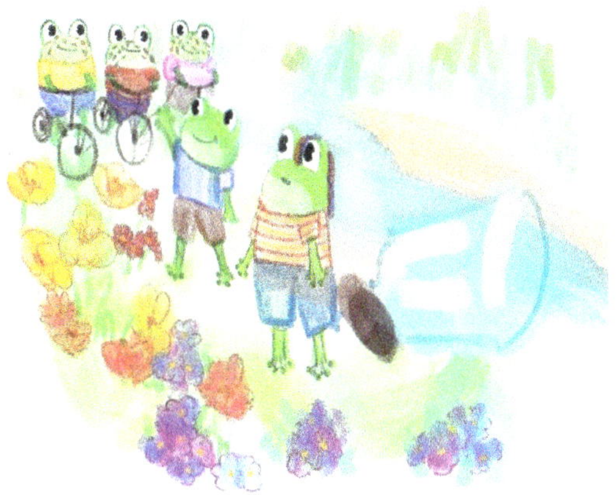

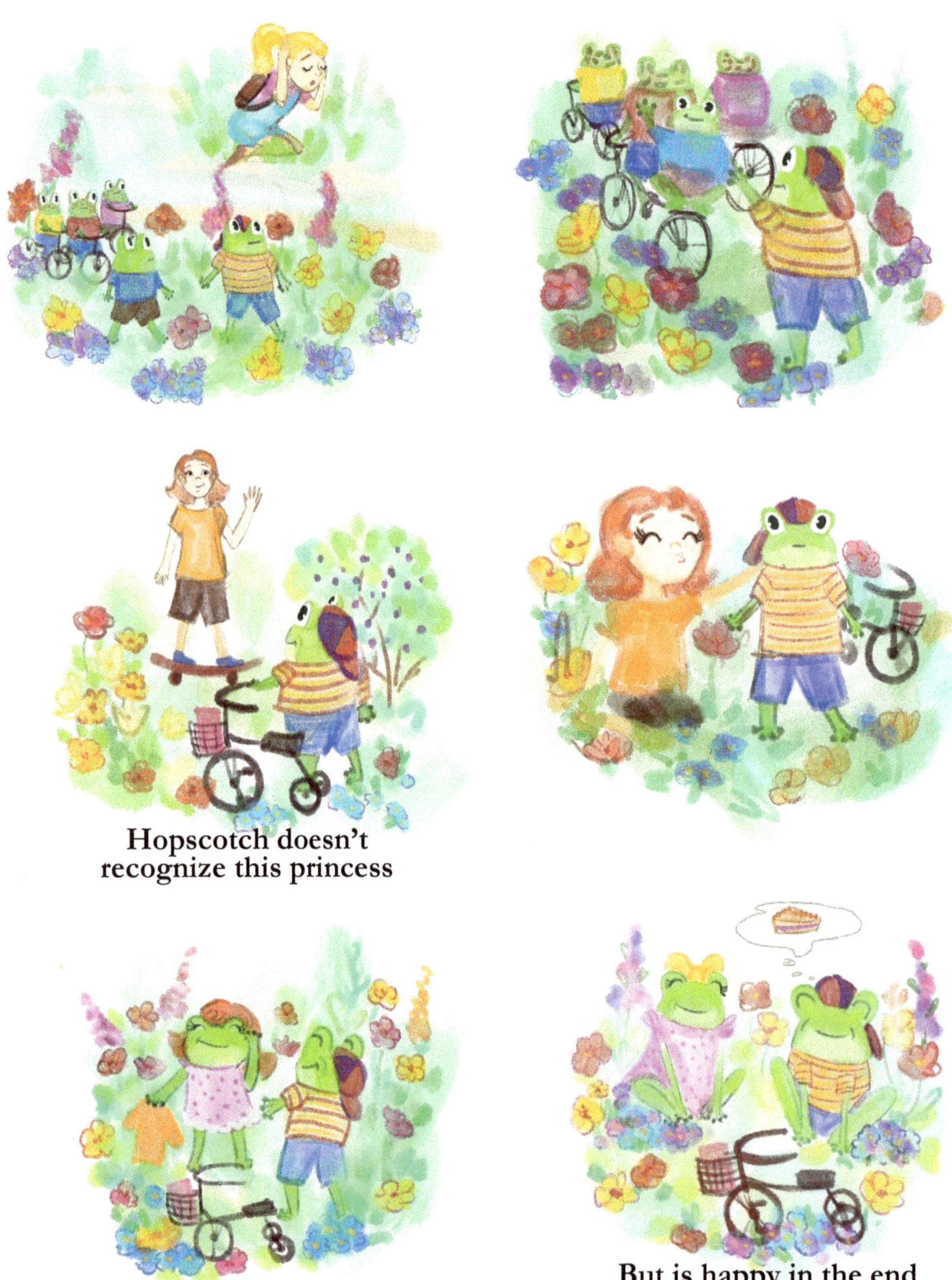

Hopscotch doesn't
recognize this princess

But is happy in the end

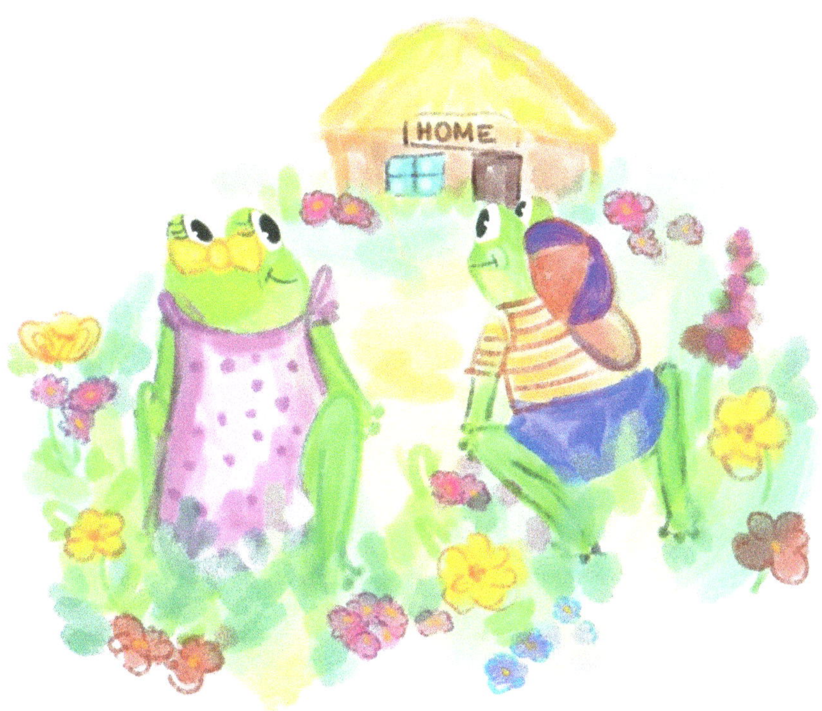

And together they hopped happily ever after.

I hope the story is clear that Hopscotch is a frog that is looking to kiss a princess so he can turn into a prince – something other than he is, a frog. The story starts with him reading a fairy tale book and having a frog girlfriend who makes him pie.

Then, he sets out to find a princess. The princess is not as excited to kiss a frog as a frog is to kiss her. Hopscotch is bummed.

Then he has some terrorizing experience with a dog and then finds another 'princess' who traps him in jar. He escapes to find a princess who does want to kiss him so he can turn into a prince but to his surprise, this princess is really his frog girlfriend who turns back into a frog when she kisses a frog!

And, the moral of the story is to be yourself – who you are meant to be.

After learning the flow of stories, children learn to create stories of their own –

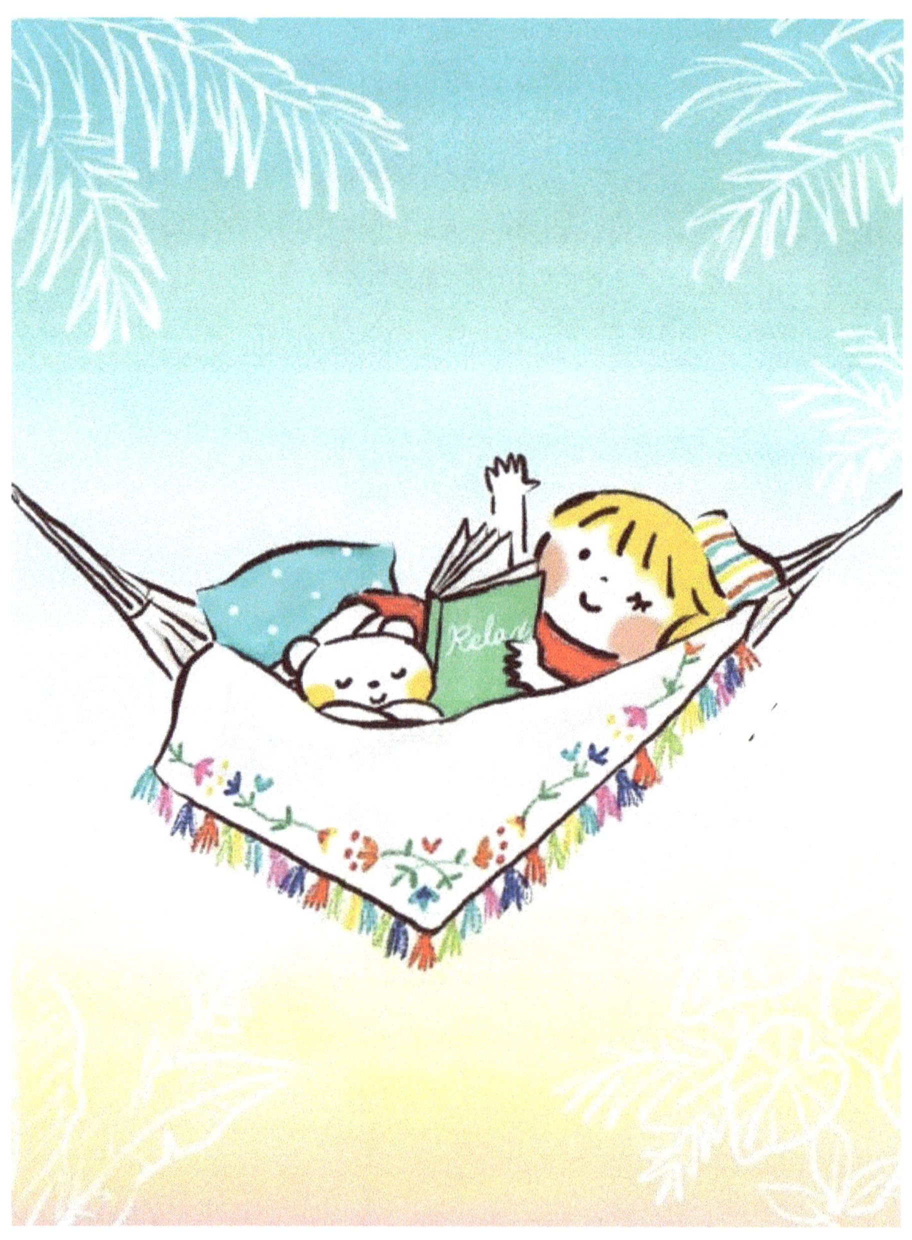

9

Great Benefits : Inspiring Imagination and Creativity

Picture books and fun stories help develop a child's imagination and creativity because children have a natural love for art. Children see the pictures and how the words connect to these pictures to real things in the world around them and in their imagination.

Illustrations are great conversation starters. Research shows that having conversation with your child helps them in school later on as well as presently. Illustrations spark imagination and inspire other activities like wanting to draw, coloring, counting, alphabet learning, and other forms of creative expression.

Moira's *Imagine the World* lets children think about writing and drawing and music and cooking and crafting and more - take a look —

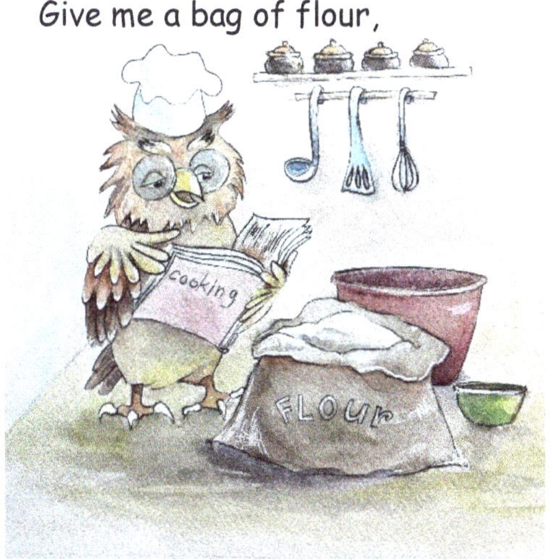

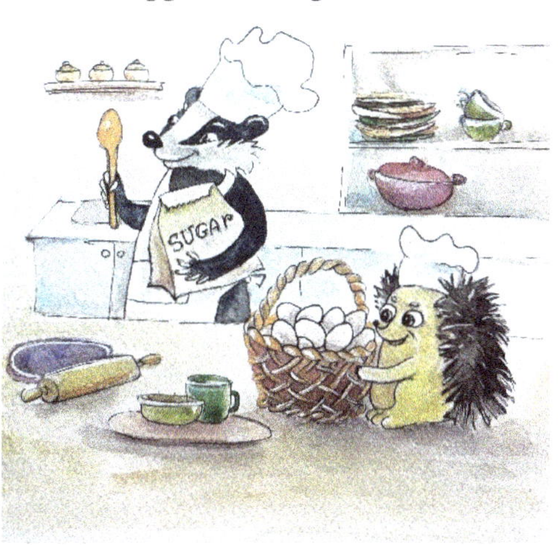

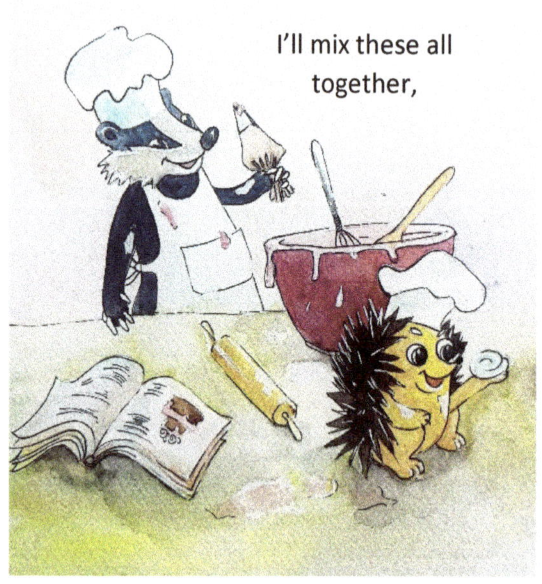

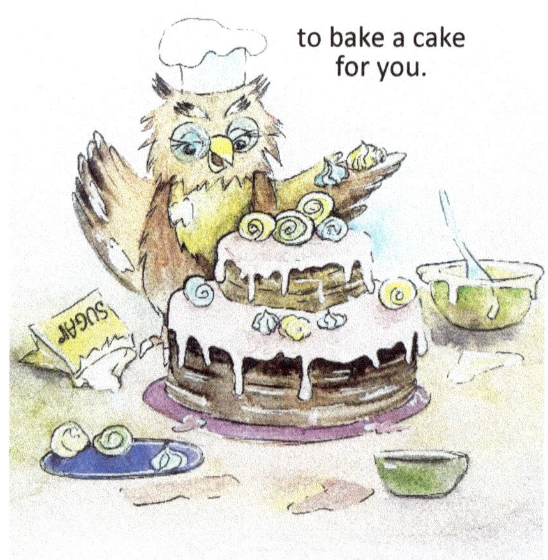

Don't you just want to get in the kitchen and bake? Please do not leave young readers alone in the kitchen. The pics also inspire planting flower or vegetable gardens as well as writing letters and words and making music and more! As children read the pages of her book, they are inspired to be creative themselves and experience the world around them. Natalie provided these beautiful pictures for this little book.

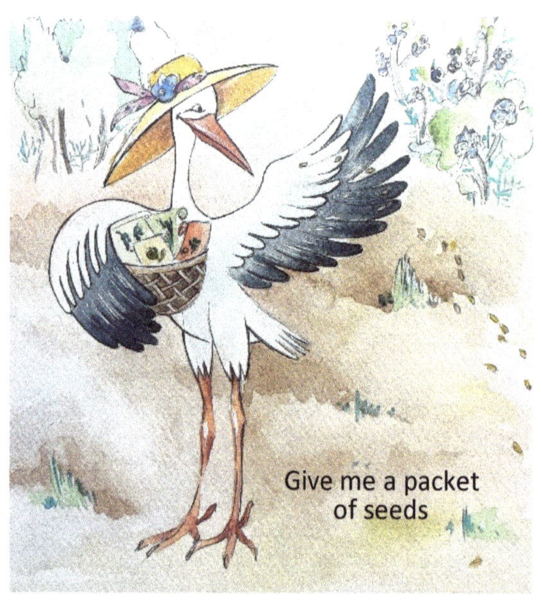

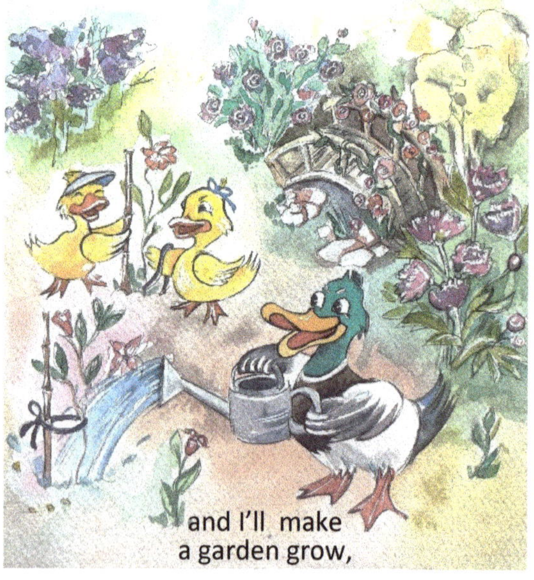

Joy McKay wrote a darling book to inspire young girls who feel they are not 'perfect' to continue to pursue their dreams – even if they want to dance but don't fit the 'mold' of a dancer. Let's see how the illustrations bring *Joy Outside the Box* to life -

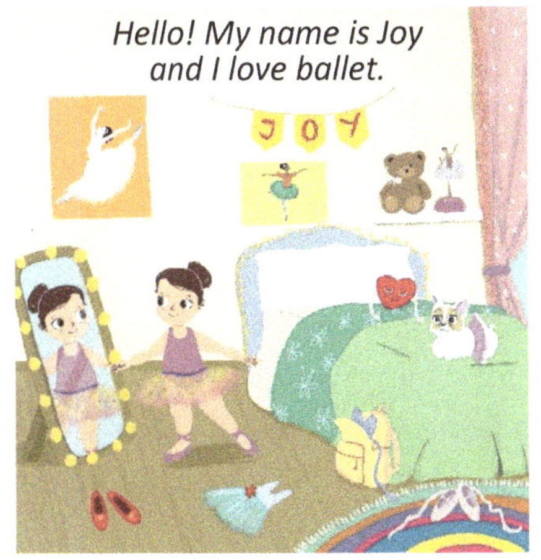

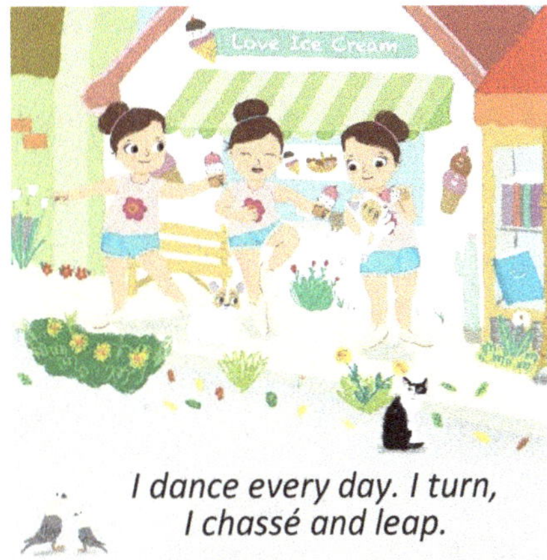

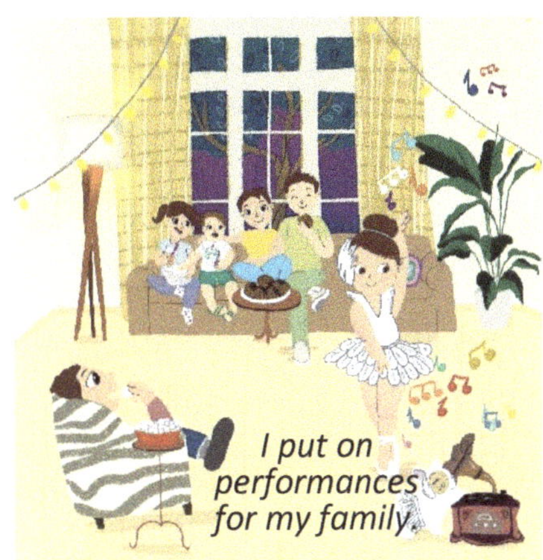

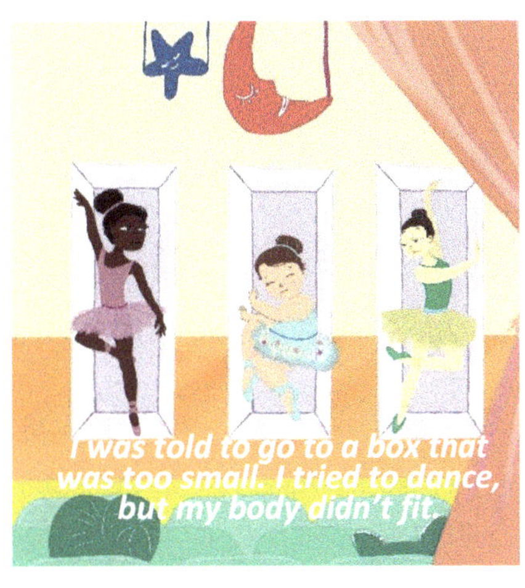

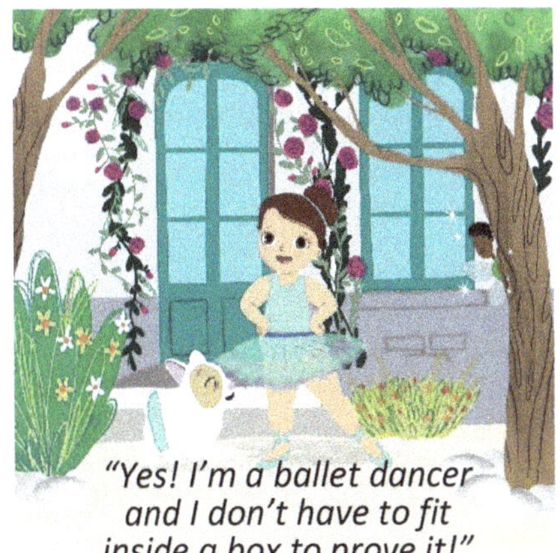

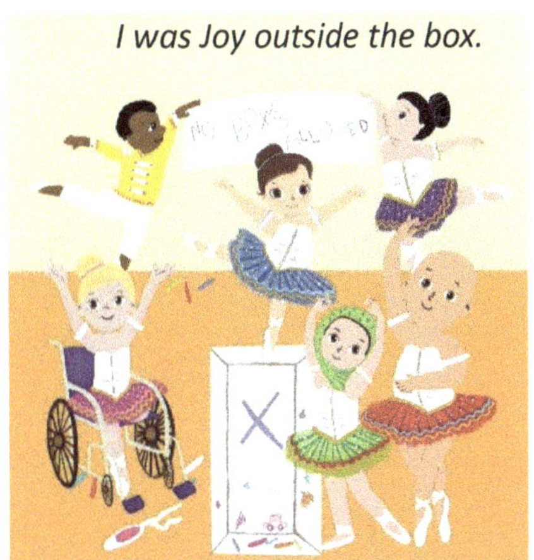

Joy wants every girl who loves to dance, to dance!!!! And dream.

One small book I created for the young reader is *My I Can Draw Book* with pages for the reader to draw and inspiring art to give the young reader and artist ideas –

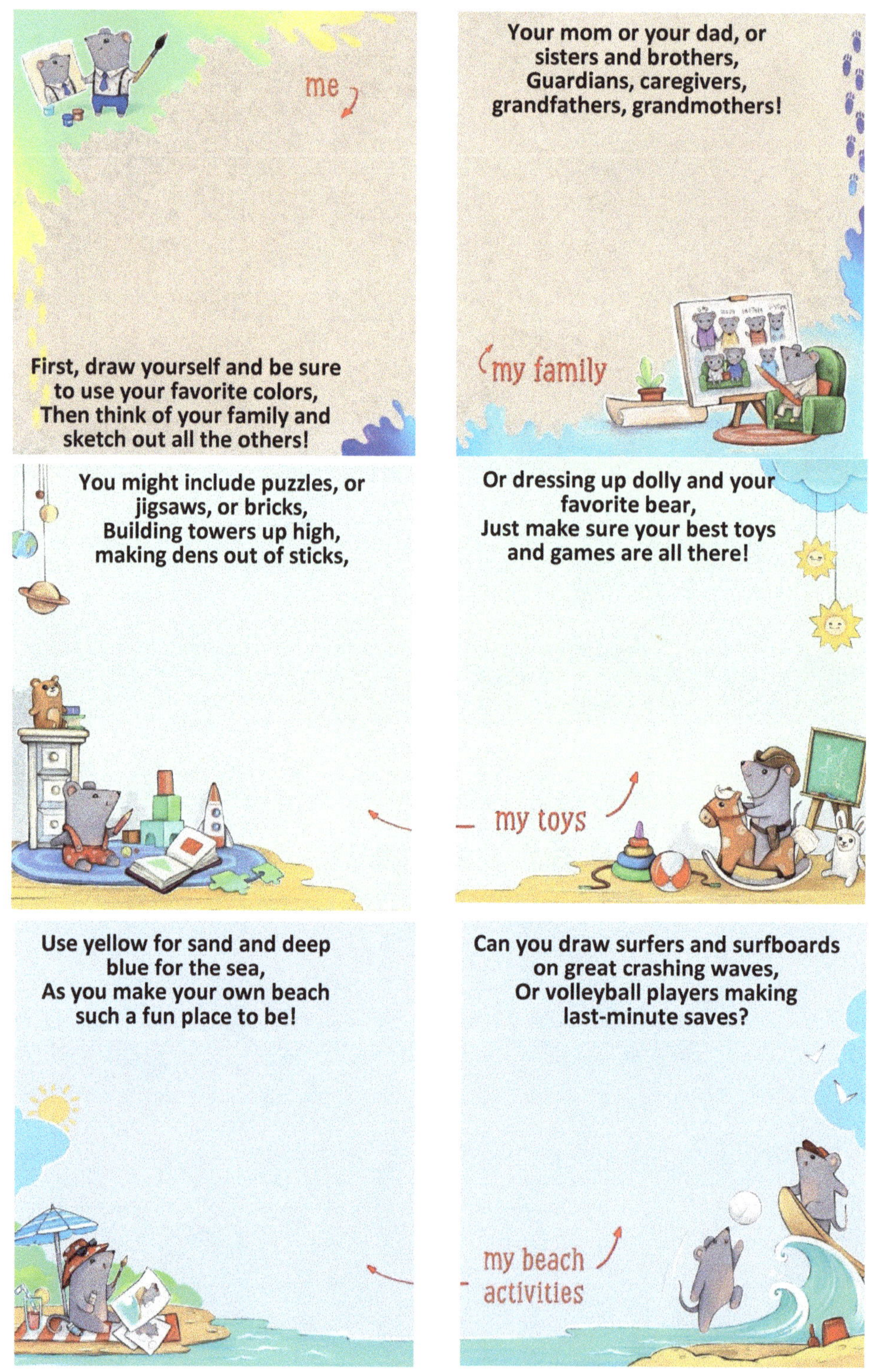

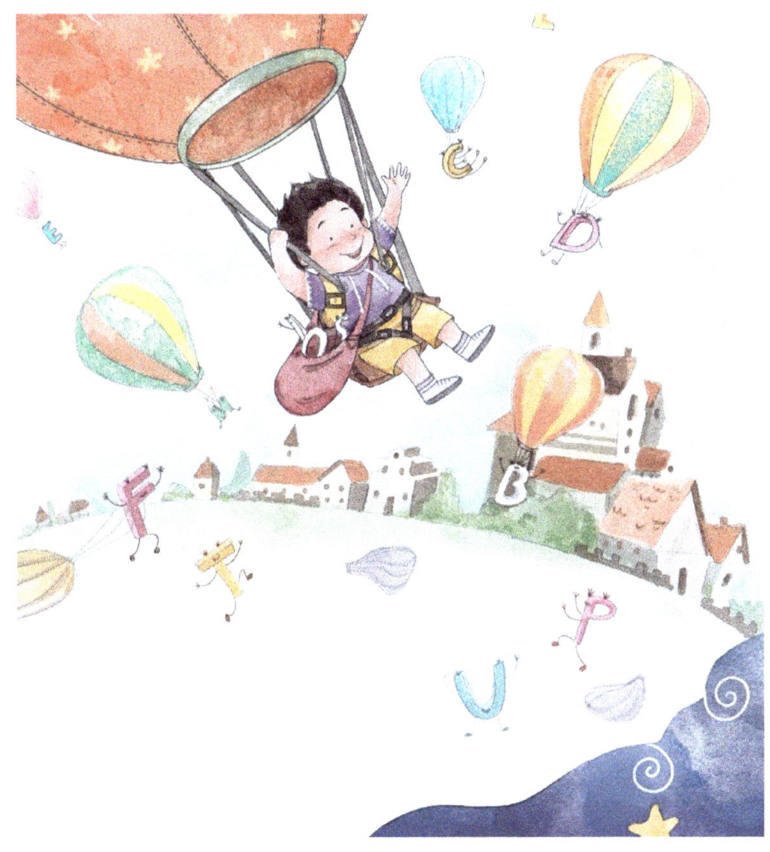

Thankful Me Using My ABCs is a title
I hope inspires young readers to be
thankful and a fun way to remember
being thankful. It can be a game.

I'm so glad you've
joined me today.
Do read on, this is
only the start.
For the many things to
be thankful for
that make us smile and
bless our hearts.
Let me share all the things
important to me,
And I'll do this by using
my ABC's!

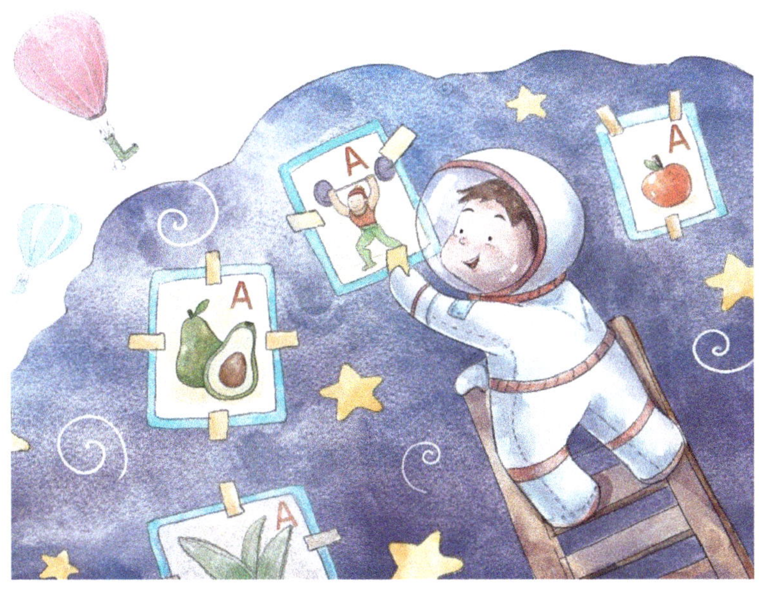

'A' is for how I appreciate
the alphabet and art,
All the ripe avocados and
sweet apples in a tart.
For awesome astronauts,
and athletes accepting
what is fair,
and aloe vera that soothes
my skin in August's
warm air.

'B' for birthdays
and bright blue
balloons, banana
splits and bees,
Blueberries and
baseball,
breakfast, and
birds high in the
trees.
I'm thankful too
for bunny rabbits,
baskets, books,
and beauty,
And all brave
friends who stand
up for others and
do their duty.

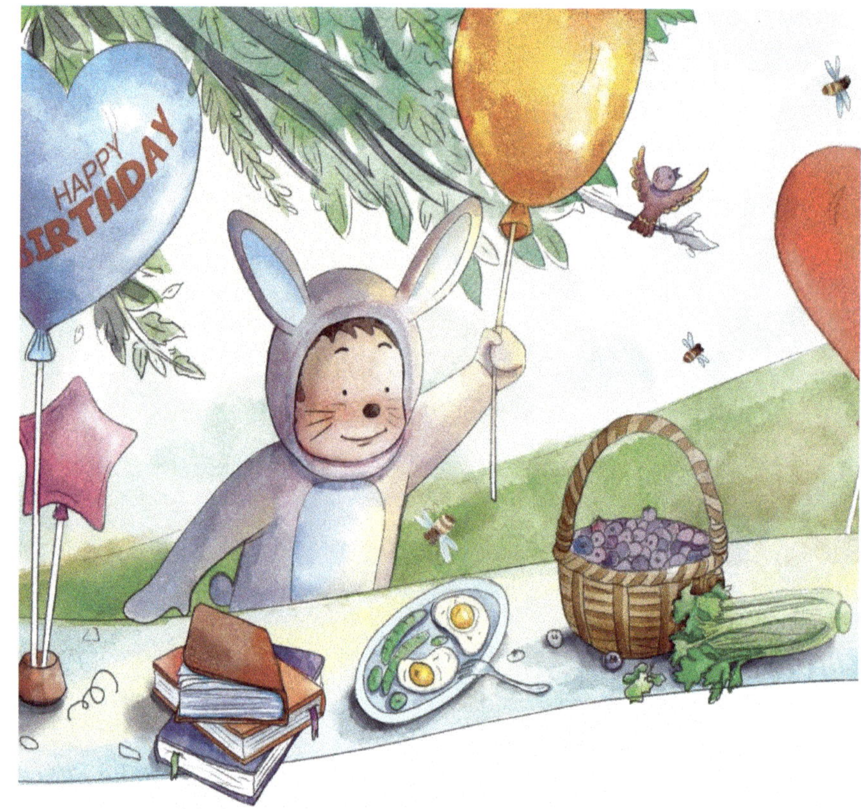

'C' is eating candy
round the campfire
with my cousins
and their cats,
Cosmic colored
crayons and clumsy
clowns in funny
hats,
Celery and carrots,
cakes and cookies
that we share,
Cheerful clothes
and Christmas
when we show how
much we care.

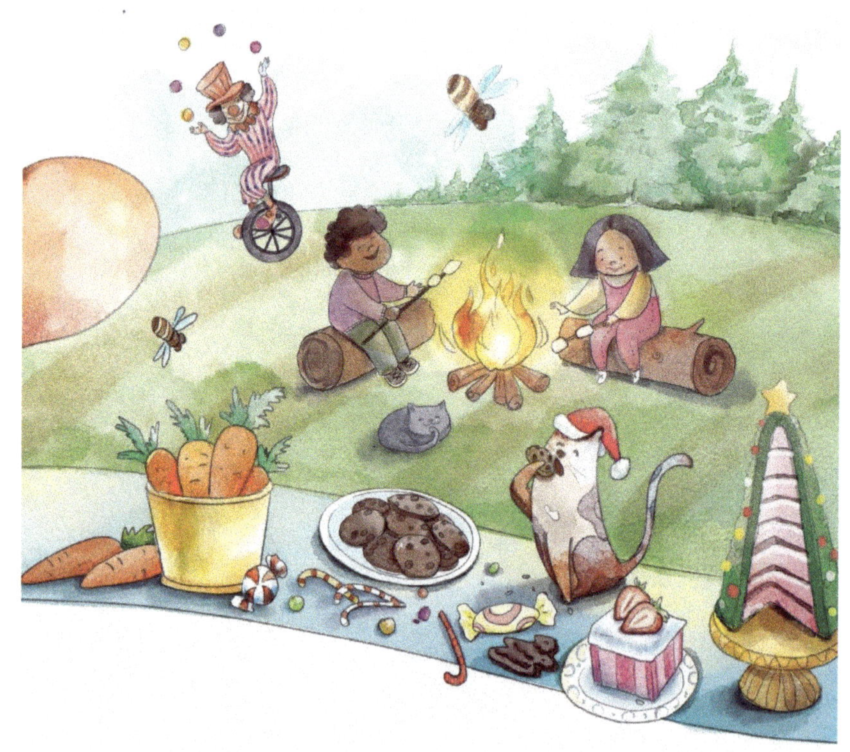

Thankful inspires ways to be thankful all the way to **XYZ** –

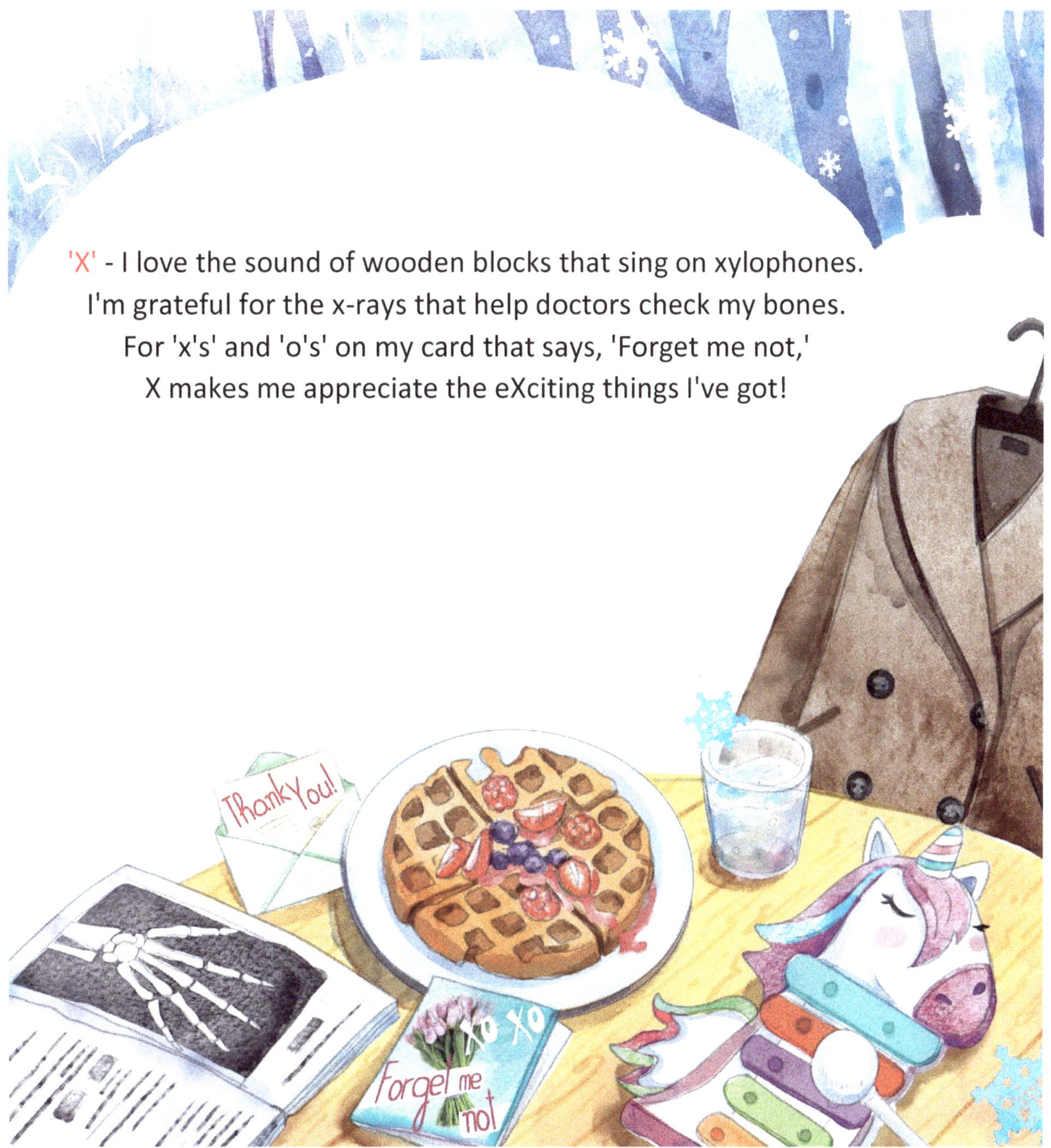

'X' - I love the sound of wooden blocks that sing on xylophones.
I'm grateful for the x-rays that help doctors check my bones.
For 'x's' and 'o's' on my card that says, 'Forget me not,'
X makes me appreciate the eXciting things I've got!

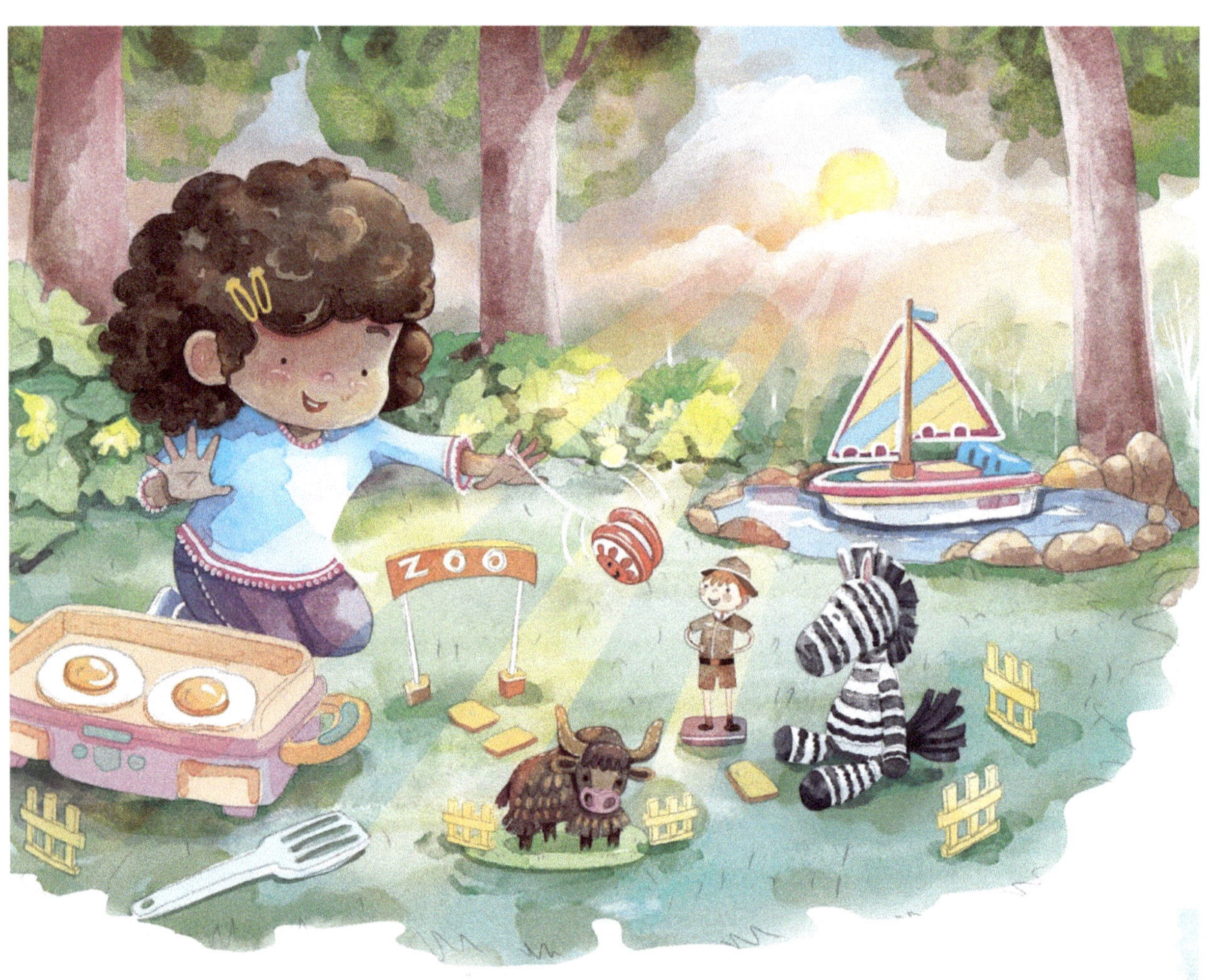

'Y' In the yard we've yelled and yodeled, then a sleepy bedtime yawn,
Yippee! The night yields to the bright and yellow sun at dawn.
There's yachts and yo-yos, yoga, yolks, and yaks down at the zoo,
But one thing I'm most grateful for in all of this is you!

'Z' - I'm grateful in my garden with zucchini and my lemon zest,
For kites that zig-zag as the zephyr wind blows from the west.
For zookeepers and zebras and zeppelins up in the sky,
And for the zipper on my raincoat as it keeps me warm and dry!

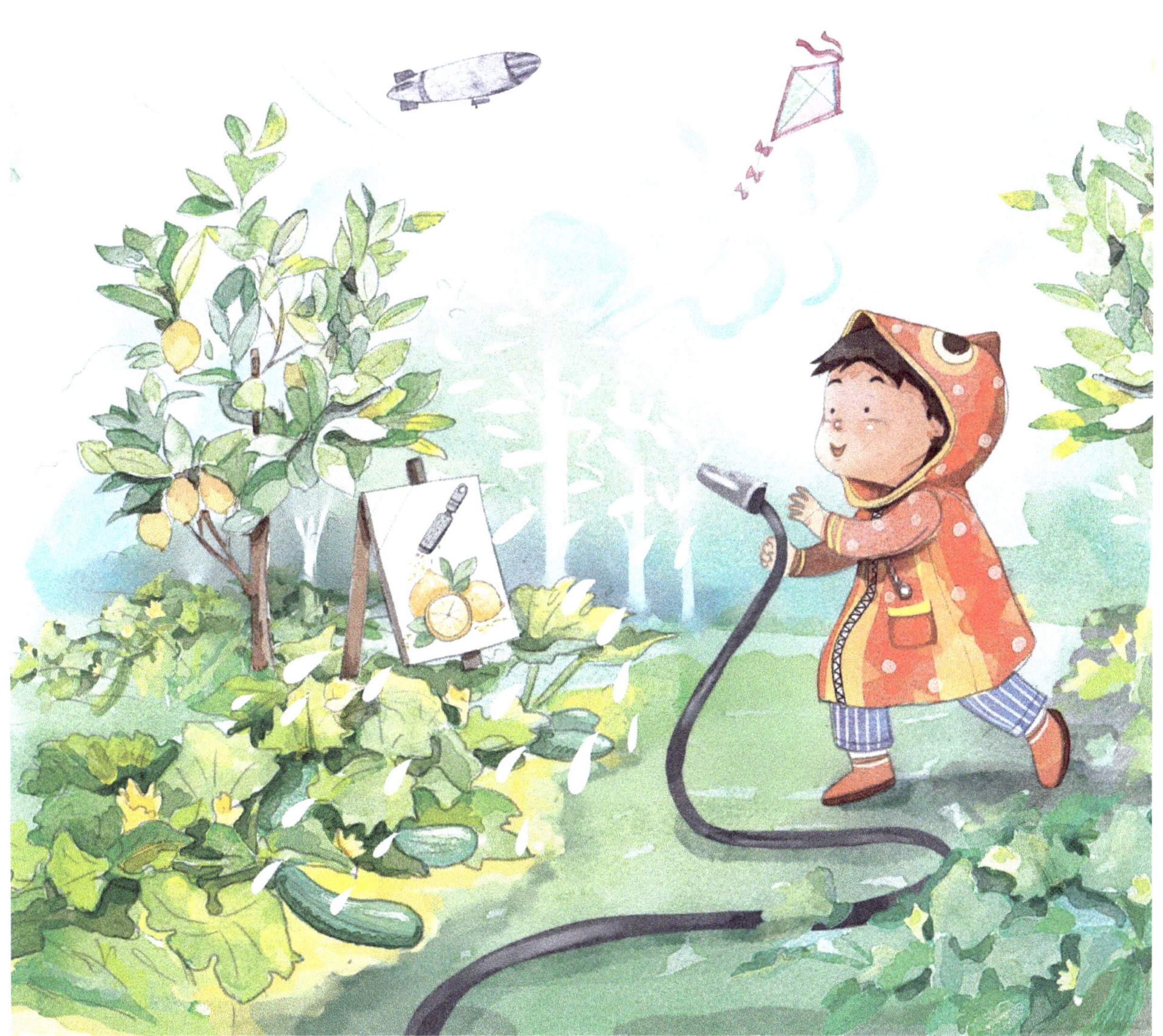

We hope picture books inspire your young reader!!

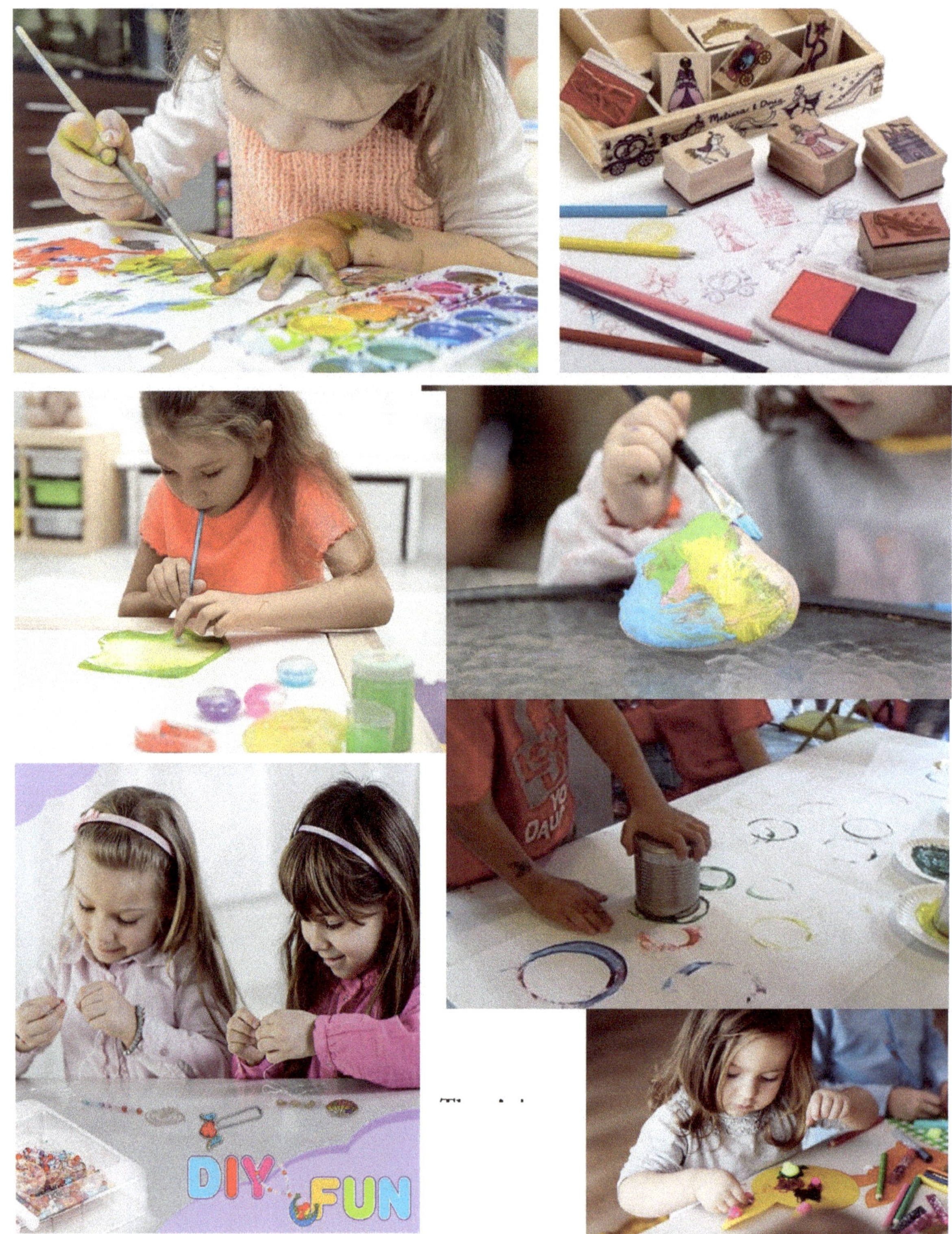

<h1 style="text-align:center">10</h1>

Great Benefits : Emotional and Social Development

Picture books help children understand and cope with many different emotions – from joy to sadness to anger or frustration. Sometimes children can see themselves in the stories and characters they read about. This helps them learn to feel and experience the world around them.

Going back to DJ Stutz's book, *Roman is BIGGER,* Roman experiences not only the heartbreak and ecstasy in chapter two, he experiences even more emotions. Let's take a look at how the illustrations help the older but still young reader identify with different emotions –

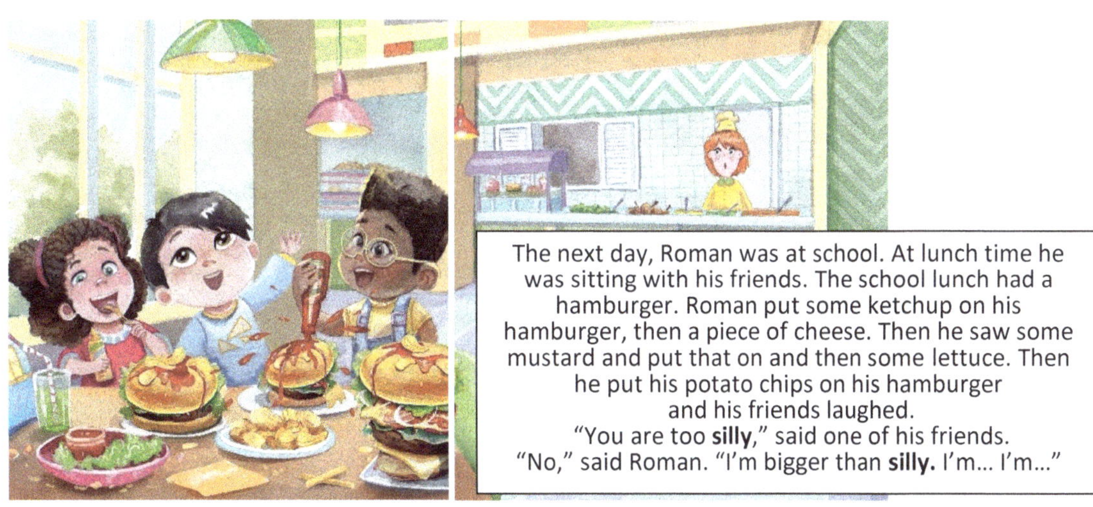

DJ's book is colorfully illustrated to match the words she places on each page. When there are many words, as in DJ's picture book, it can be more challenging to make certain the illustrations represent the story.

As for Roman's feeling SILLY, Nadii illustrates the simple and then more intense emotions Roman is feeling –

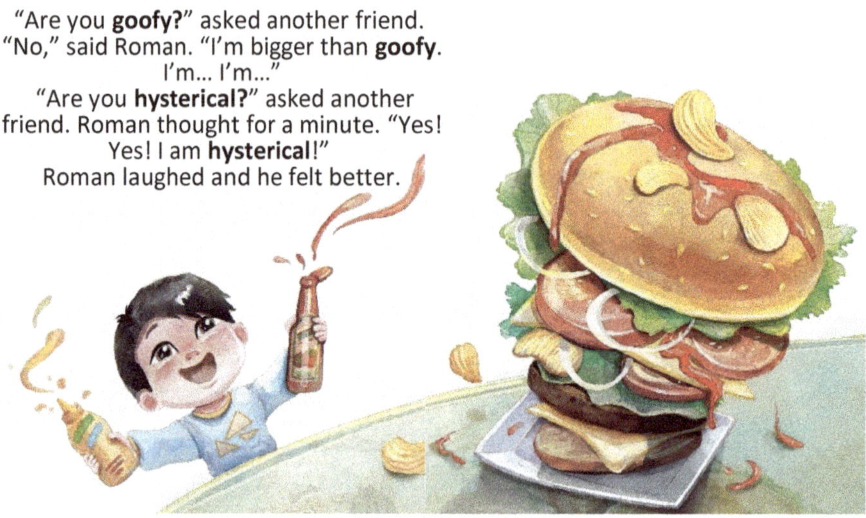

Nadii always creates illustrations that are interesting and engage the young reader. Her work is colorful and fun and full of expression. That is one BIG hamburger with all the fixins! The emotions of silly, goofy, and then to hysterical are illustrated and written well by DJ Stutz.

Scared happens for children as well -

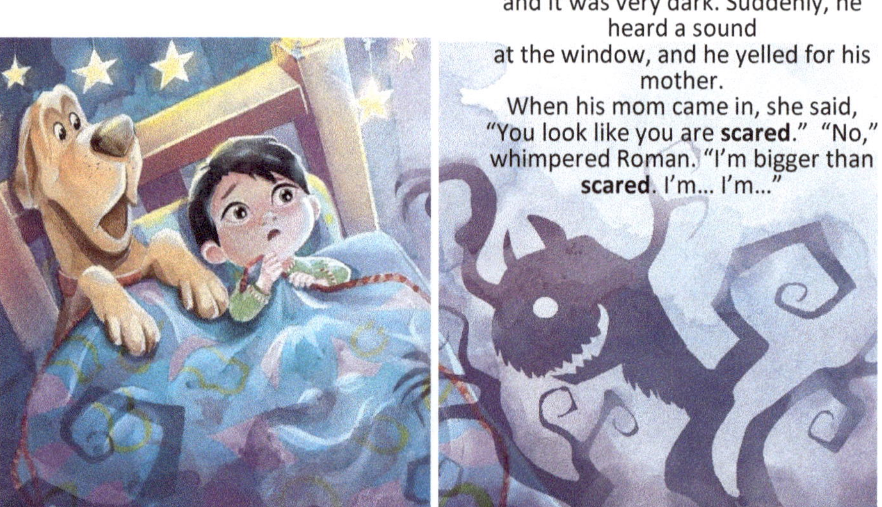

The illustrations are filled with color and detail and expression for the young reader to identify with on each page – and scared turns into the even BIGGER emotion of – let's take a look –

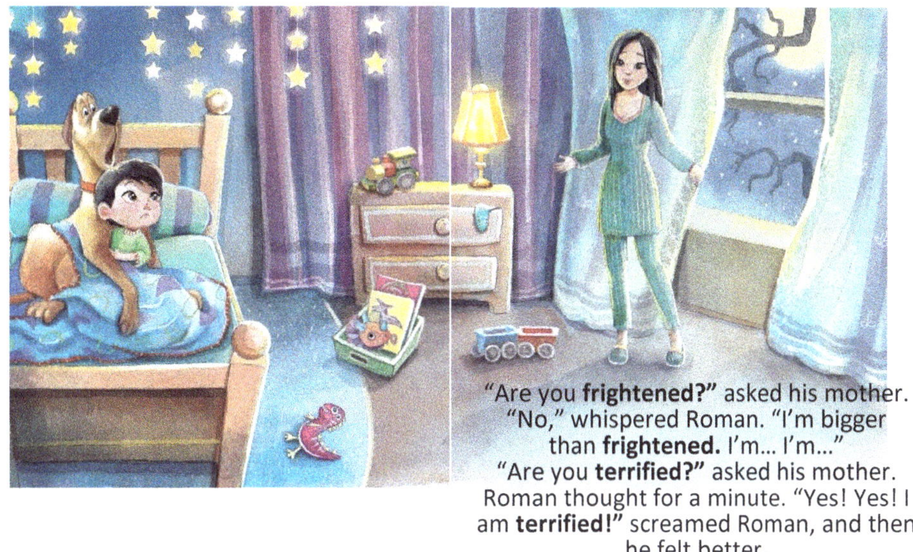

From scared to frightened to terrified! The young reader is assured their feelings are normal and they can be helped. Expressing feelings and having someone they love help them realize they don't have to be frightened or terrified is helpful for young readers, especially when it comes to night time fears.

Books provide a safe place for children to explore and understand their own emotions. They help children understand themselves and others and to think about others as well as themselves. Let's take a look into the art and words in *Just Right* -

This small, but precious book to me, starts as Eddie and his Grandpa set out to the park to meet up with Eddie's friends.

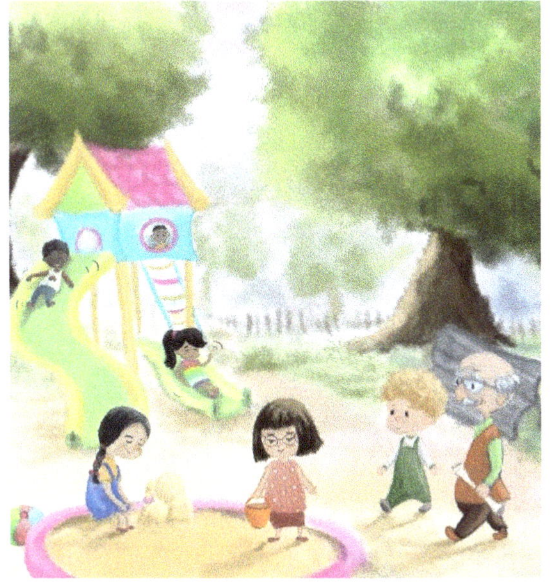

Here, the artist has set the scene in a colorful setting with different nationality children. We have a Caucasian boy, an Asian girl, an African American boy, and Indian boy, a Native American girl, and a Hispanic young man.

Picture books can help children see others as wonderful too when a book introduces a child to different cultures or perspectives. This diversity is well illustrated by Olesya in *Just Right* as each of the children ask Eddie's Grandpa about features they feel are not as 'normal' as other children's features – let's continue to look as Eddie asks first -

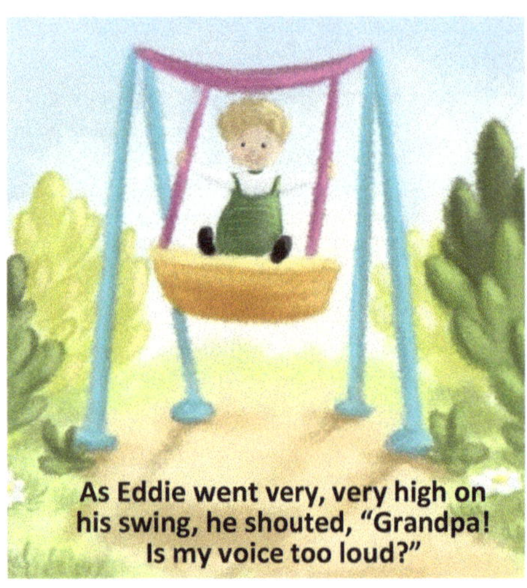

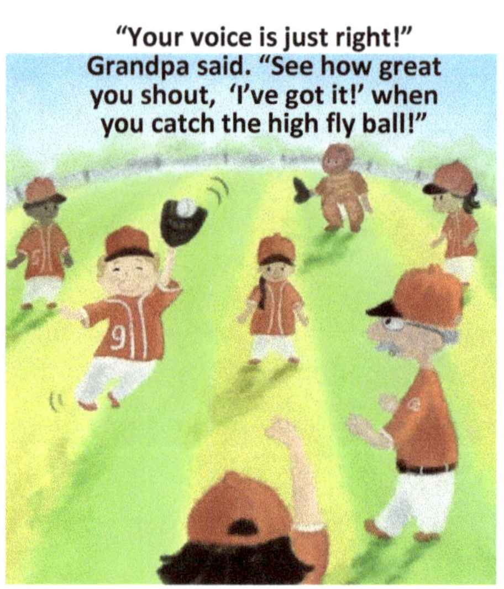

Then, after Grandpa assures Eddie he's 'just right,' Hannah asks –

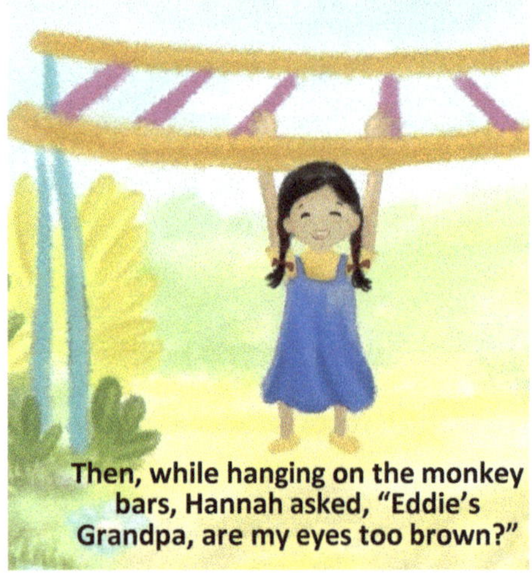

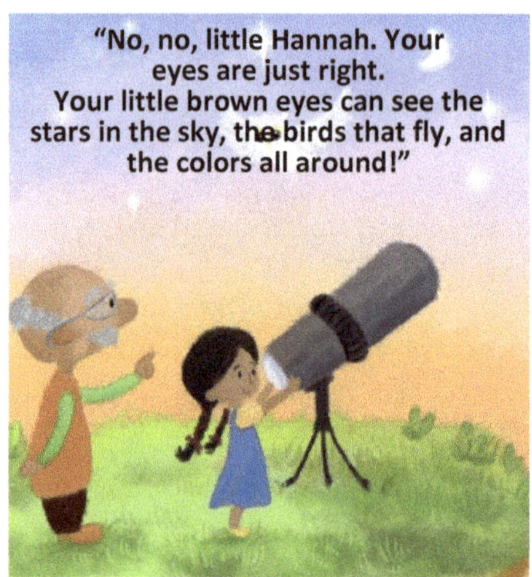

Many children feel 'bullied' for one reason or another. Grandpa helps Hannah see that her eyes are perfect for her and they have the wonderful ability to see the world around her. I realize there are visually disabled children as well and this is not intended to make them feel badly, but for children to see others feel these things about themselves-the same as a child may have things about themselves they feel are 'picked on' by others. This helps children not only develop self-esteem, it helps them be more empathetic to others and others who they may see being bullied and help stop this.

Let's take another look –

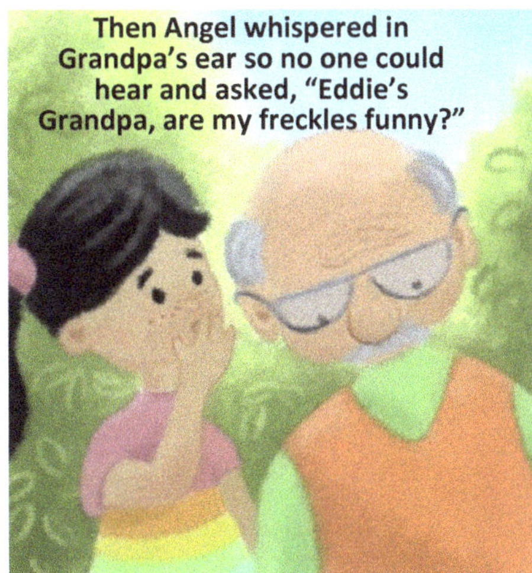

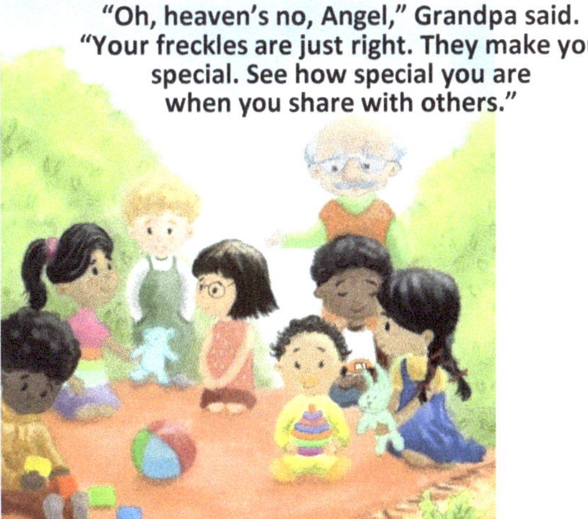

Many children find something others focus on – like Angel's freckles - negative. *Just Right* has Grandpa helping Angel embrace her 'freckles' and see her wonderful quality of being a good friend. It goes on to let the readers discover Daniel who feels he's too 'round' but Grandpa and the other children cheer him on swimming because he is a good swimmer! Also, *Just Right* makes a point of turning negatives into positives – like Jose feels 'clumsy' but Grandpa helps him celebrate how he's a great leader.

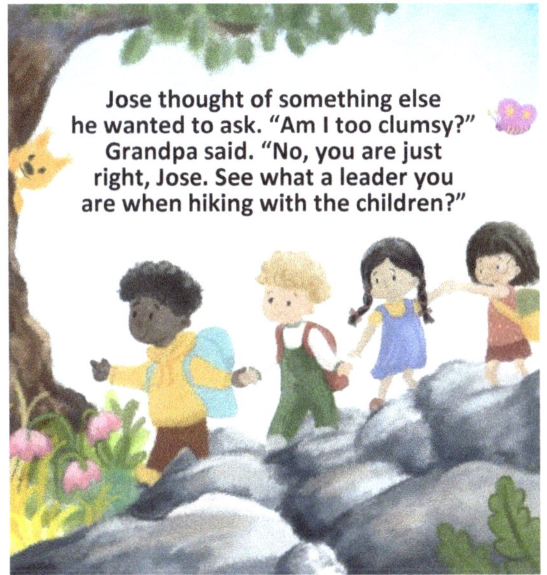

Picture books also help children relate to themes of friendship, family, community and how to get along with others and sometimes resolve conflict. When children read stories, I try to make the characters relatable as well as diverse.

In another gold-medal 'Mom's Choice Award' picture book, *The Day the Cat Said 'MOO!'* I wanted to present the message that each child has a unique and special voice and needs to celebrate who they are and not want to be something or someone else. Let's look –

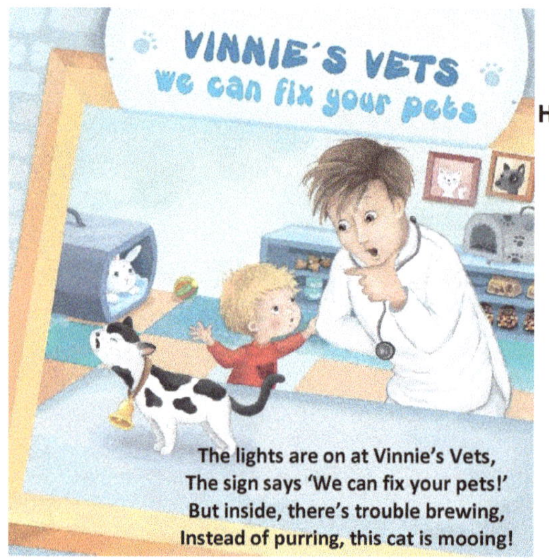

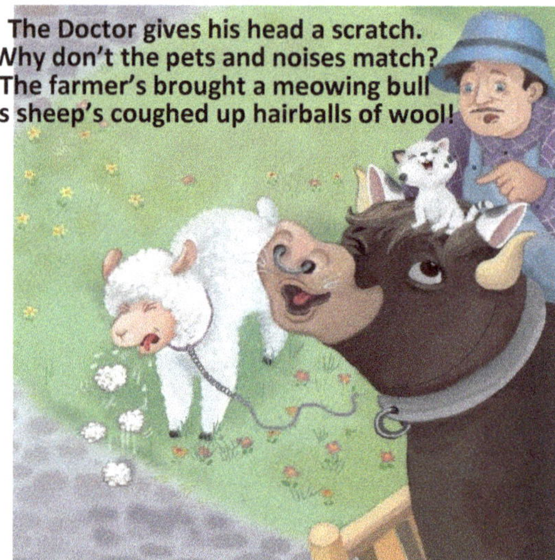

Vinnie is worried but gets help from a friendly and colorful parrot -

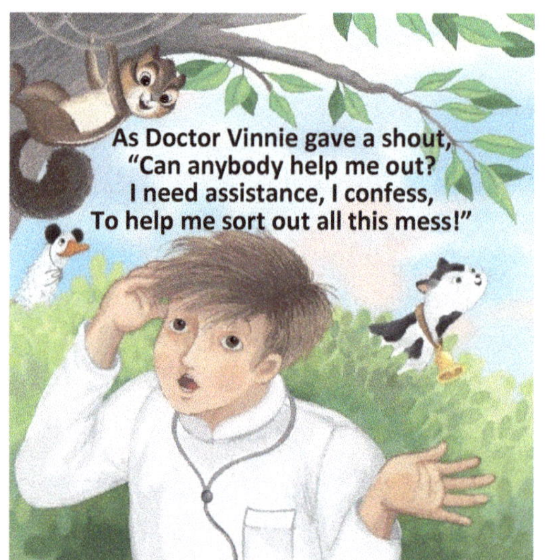

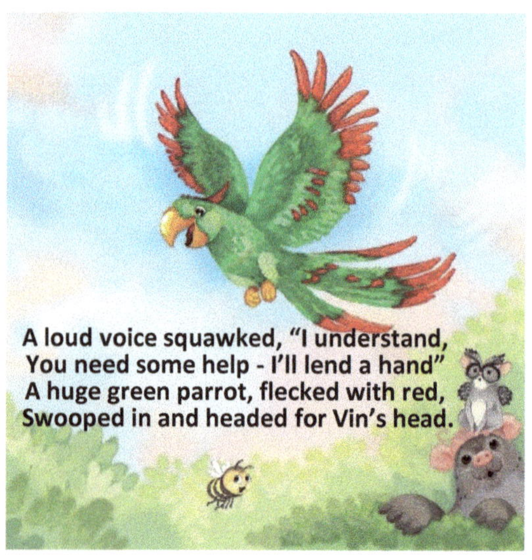

It is my hope that children enjoying *The Day the Cat Said 'MOO!'* see their voice is unique and special and to be celebrated and embraced. We were never meant to be all the same! The parrot helps Doc Vin see why the animals wanted to be different -

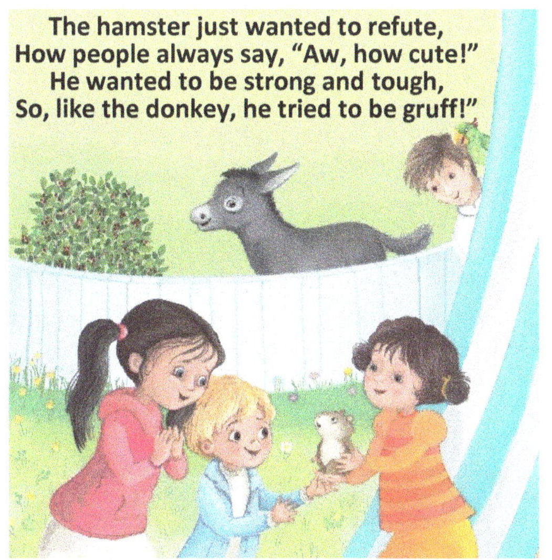

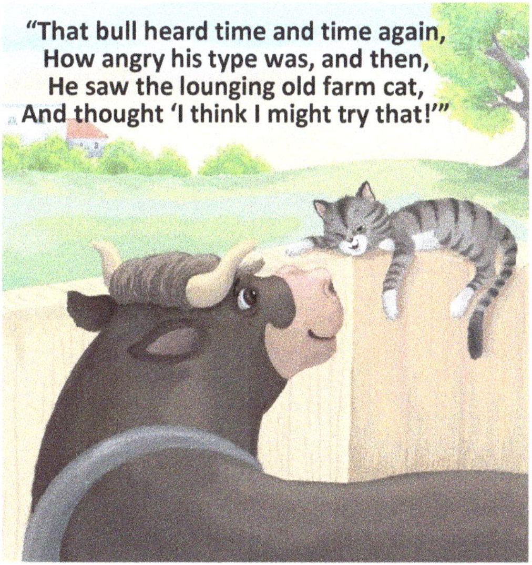

There are so many reasons to wish we were someone or something else, but the truth is we are special and the only one of *us* there is. Vin figures it out —

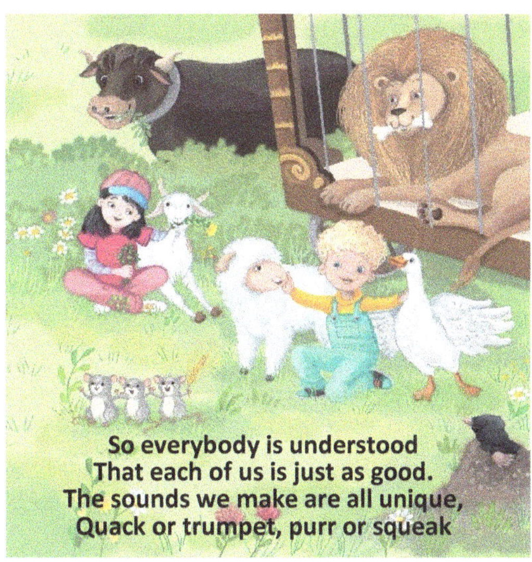

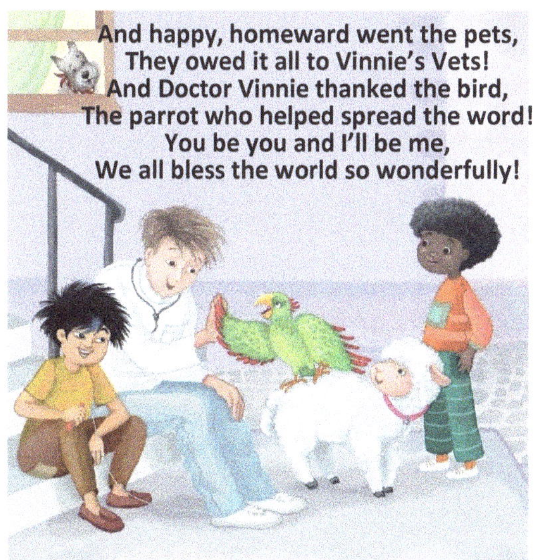

It's my hope that all children feel special and important and that who they are and what they have to say is valuable. The illustrations help bring the message home and colorful and beautiful art is always my goal. I hope you like it too.

Also, picture books help children see something before they experience it – or maybe as they are experiencing it. The award-winning book, *The Little White Kitten and Her Little Red Mittens* was illustrated by Fi Alexsandra Hilson. She did a lovely job providing cute and colorful illustrations. Let's look –

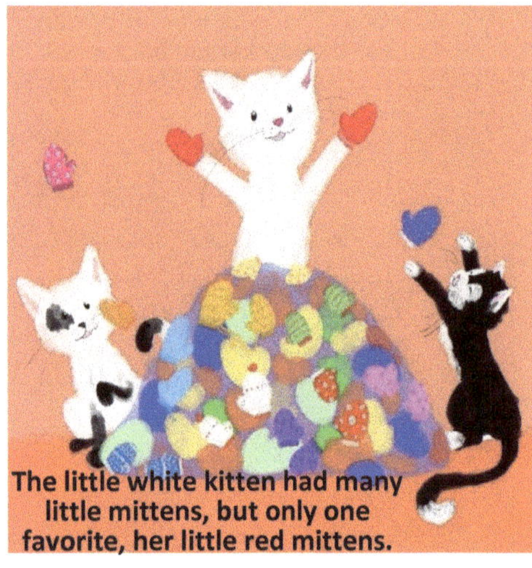

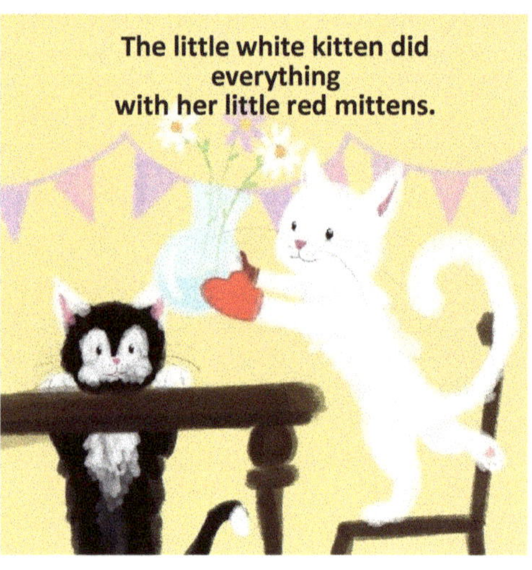

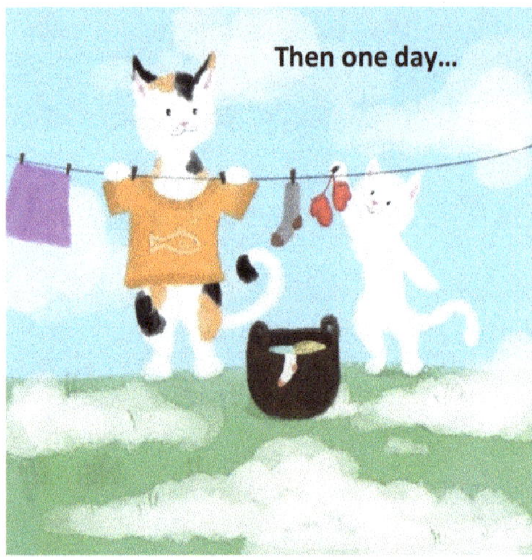

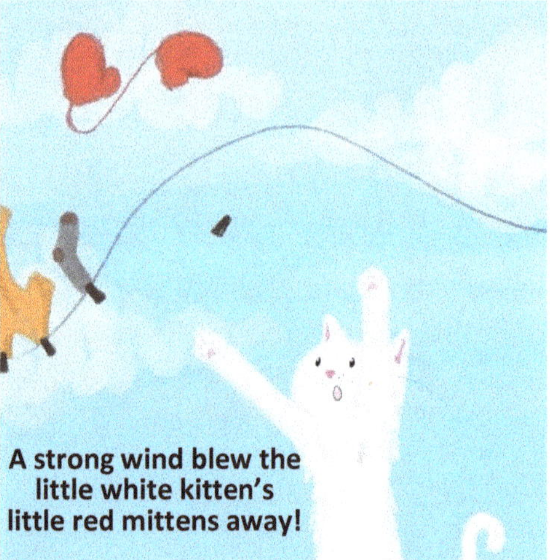

Everyone has experienced heartbreak and I hope the young readers have not had much experience in this department, but perhaps a toy has been damaged or lost like these little mittens. Some stories we store in our hearts for later times too. This may be one we do that with. Some of the illustrations are simple, but they convey what the words are sharing and that's what the illustrations are intended to do for the young readers. Let's see what the little kitten does about her loss –

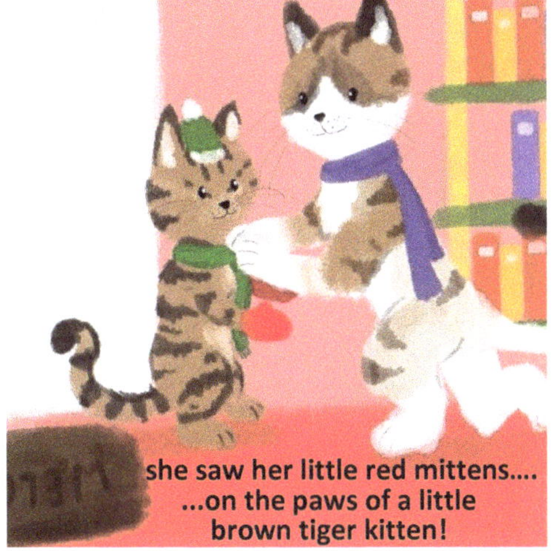

The story tells how the kitten looked and looked for her mittens to find them on the paws of this little tiger kitten. This gives her an idea and she….

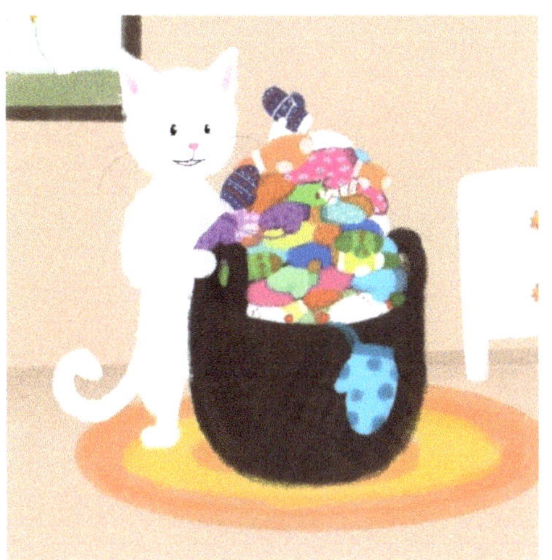

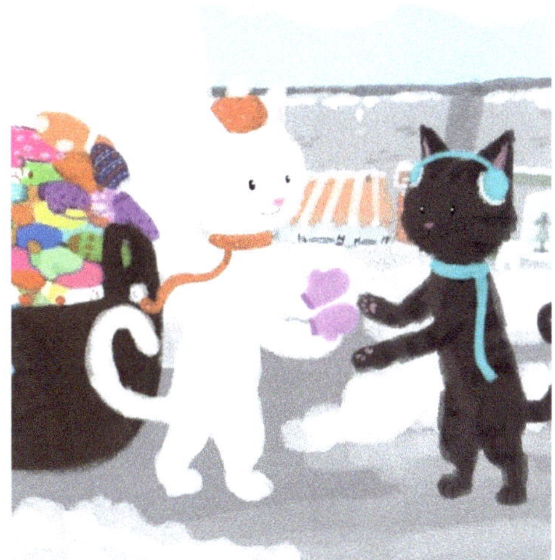

This little story has the little kitten going home and gathering all her mittens. She finds all the needy kittens in the neighborhood and gives those mittens to the others so they can enjoy their very own mittens. In the face of loss and sadness, the little kitten learns how to give and share despite her broken heart. A tremendous lesson brought to life with darling illustrations – putting the pictures in picture books is the most important aspect of the books.

Also, picture books are safe places for children to explore feelings and experiences and stories. They can read and know they are not alone with the company of their favorite little book. They can read before they experience sometimes too and develop empathy for others around them.

DJ Stutz wrote a sweet sequel to *Roman is BIGGER* about all his different emotions, she wrote *Roman is a BIGGER Brother*. This charming book helps the young readers grow emotionally and socially if they are welcoming a new brother or sister. Let's take a glance —

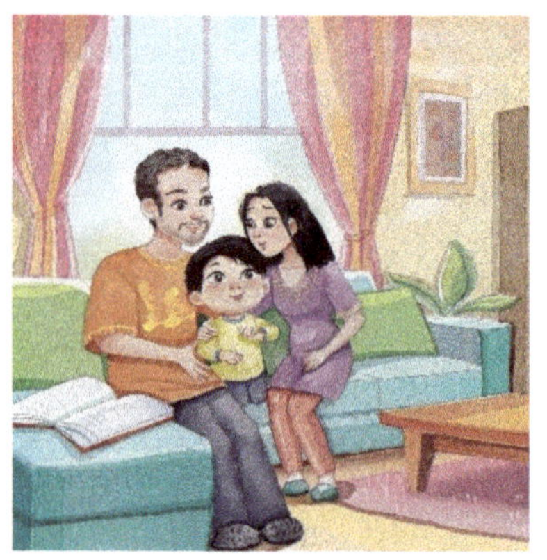

One day Roman's parents sat down with him and said, "We have some very exciting news. You are going to be a big brother soon." "Hooray!" said Roman. And Roman felt **EXCITED**, but he wasn't quite sure why.

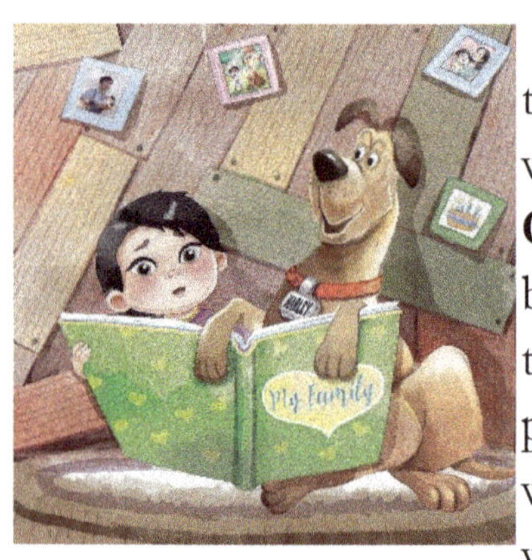

After school, Roman decided to just hang out in his tree house in the back yard. He had so many feelings. He was **NERVOUS** about this baby coming. He was **CURIOUS** if it was going to be horrible or fun. Was this baby going to be disgusting or cute? Was Mom still going to read stories and make snacks? Was Dad still going to play soccer and ride bikes? What about tickle wars? Roman was **CONCERNED**. "Oh Harley," he said, "I know you will always be my friend."

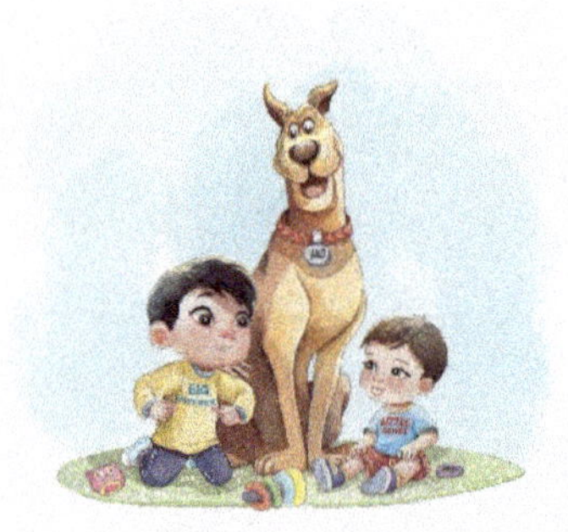

Roman thought about this and he looked at Niko. Niko looked up and smiled. Roman knew his friends Maylee and Zane were both right. Little brothers are amazing and disgusting and Roman was so glad to be a big brother.

After all the ups and downs and mixed feelings, children figure things out with our help.

More Great Benefits

Critical Thinking

Picture books help children develop critical thinking skills. This may sound far-fetched, however, picture books can be filled with information as well as stories.

The first picture books most children read concentrate on basic learning – the alphabet, numbers, how to count, different shapes, colors, things in the world like noodles, nature, science, and concepts like opposites and cheerful, meaningful messages.

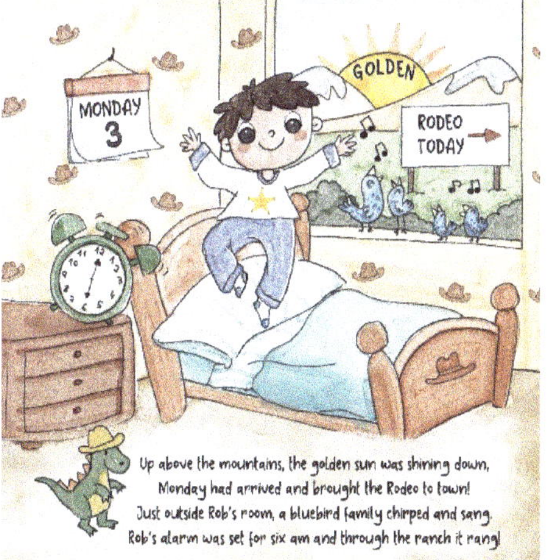

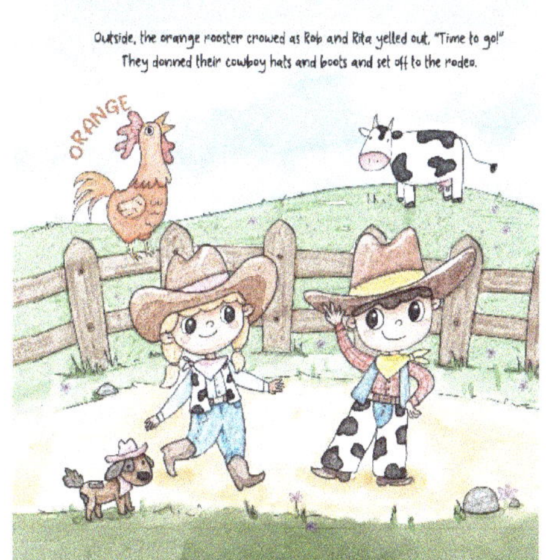

In *Rob and Rita Romp at the Rodeo,* the book is filled with numbers, colors, shapes, days of the week and times of day.

In picture books, children see how images create meaning or affect emotions in those books. This allows them to think critically about the world around them as they connect images to events in life.

Books are interactive. They demand that children think. Whether fiction or non-fiction, books widen the reader's consciousness – they provide new ways to think and new ideas.

In *Awe Inspiring Owls*, artist, Anna Naboka, brings David's words to life on the pages as she creates cute, colorful owls for the fun facts he includes. Let's look –

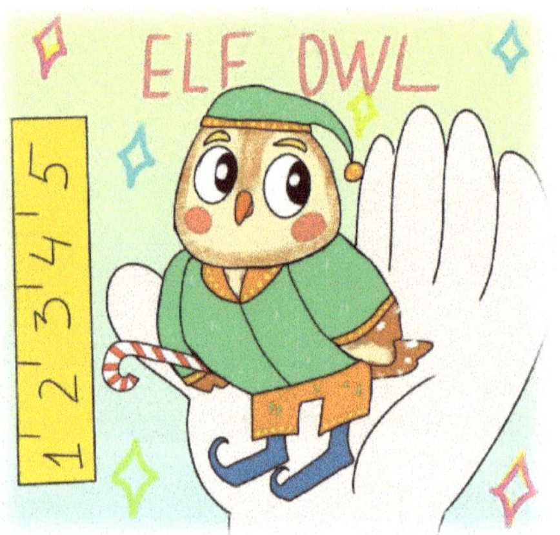

There are over 200 different kinds of wonderful owls,
With the tiniest owl being the Elf at five inches small.

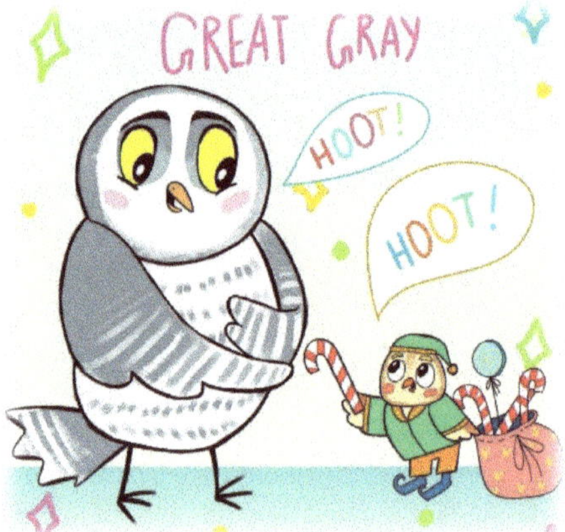

And the largest is the Great Gray
at almost three feet tall!

This book is filled with fun facts about owls to spark interest in the young reader. Owls can be seen at local zoos, Audubon societies, some parks, and around homes in the country. In the back matter of this little book is a list of fun facts about owls – such as -   1. There are over 200 different types of owls.

2. The most commonly found owl is the Great Horned Owl found in both North and South America.

3. Owls fly silently.

4. A group of owls is called a parliament. This name comes from their 'wise' and 'intelligent' depictions.

5. Owls' faces appear flattened because of the many feathers surrounding their eyes.

6. Their unusual face shape allows the owl to have great hearing because sound waves are directed to their ears.

7. An owl's large eyes allow the eye to pick up a lot of light rays and owls do not have the best color vision, but their night vision is excellent

8. Night vision is helpful because owls are considered 'nocturnal' which means they are awake and active at night and sleep during the day time.

9. A baby owl is called an owlet.

Author David R Morgan is a teacher, so he and I feel education is important for the youngsters in our lives. Making learning fun through picture books and art is an advantage because sometimes forced learning is not well-received by children. When we make learning fun and interesting, a child learns more and is excited to learn. Most of the time, they don't realize we snuck the learning in!

Picture books often present complex concepts in easily understood ways, making them ideal for introducing new ideas and encouraging children to explore their world - fostering inquisitive minds. Let's see how flowers are interesting in Sheila Marcotte's *My Grandma Has a Garden* —

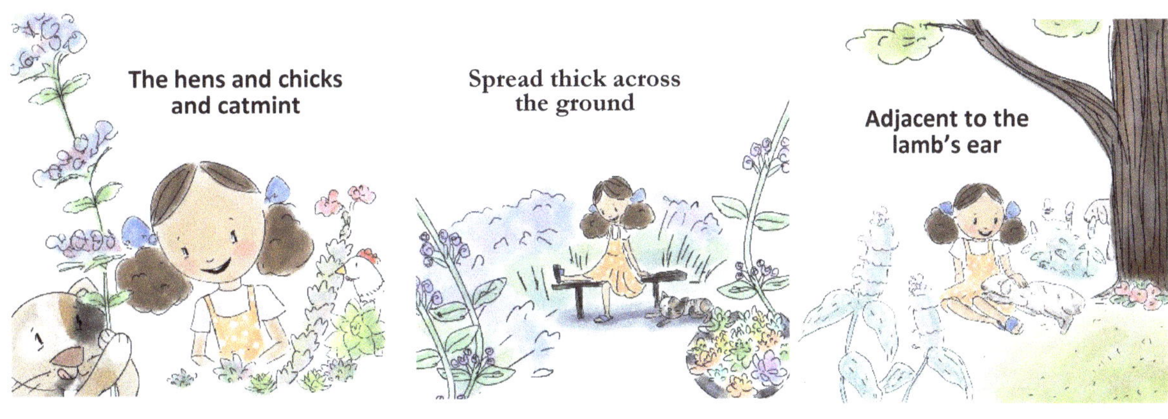

Because they're so easy to follow, picture books allow you to stop every now and again to spend time discussing the story. This is great, because it gives your child another way to engage with the story. Sheila provides engaging prose about different flowers to hold the interest of young readers and hopefully to inspire them to want to learn more about different flowers.

Picture Book Improve Listening

Because children can follow the stories visually as they listen to the story being read, it makes listening easy because the story holds their attention – especially with great illustrations.

Picture Books are Building Blocks

Picture books are usually a child's first exposure to language and learning to read and speak. Picture books are a child's first exposure to storytelling and characters, emotions, fun concepts, their alphabet, words, how pictures help them figure out all the things around them, and more.

As referred to earlier, most first books are simple with few words but lovely illustrations. These illustrations are always colorful and fun! Then, books begin to include more words, more concepts, more challenges for the young reader.

On a personal note, my step-daughter was developmentally behind due to her parents' divorce. As I spent time helping her 'catch-up,' we utilized children's picture books. She loved them! She thought she was tricking me into staying up late reading one after another, but I was tricking her to learn to read and more!!

As we read, she began to be able to read a few words and then more and more. After we utilized the picture books, she advanced to children's chapter books and then became a better reader than I!! I owe it all to the picture books!! Never underestimate them. They are worth their weight in gold!

Picture Books Promote Learning

I have been blessed to publish many children's books. Some are just for fun but many have valuable information for children to be inspired to learn more and more.

Books help teach the young reader about history, the arts, science, religion, nature, mathematics, and technology. Just about anything and everything in our world and beyond has been captured in picture books! These topics also help a child understand the effects of all the things around us, on us personally, and as a community. It has been exciting for me to learn about all the interesting topics my authors have presented for publication. Let's take a look at David's book, *Winnie and Her Wonderful Wheelchair's Terrific Time Trip* where he includes famous women in history –

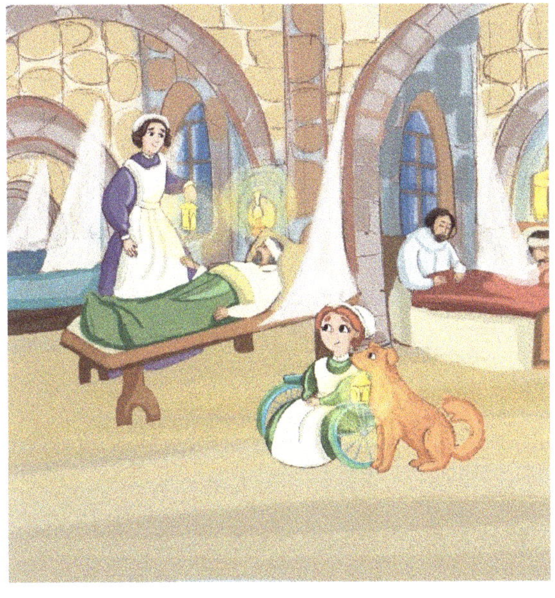

Winnie takes a time travel trip to the past and she meets Florence Nightingale.
He includes her to inspire young readers to want to know more about her.

In addition to Florence Nightingale, David includes Helen Keller, Cleopatra, Emmaline Pankhurst, Nellie Bly, Marie Curie, Amelia Ehrhart, Rosa Parks, and more famous women who have made a great difference in our world as well as

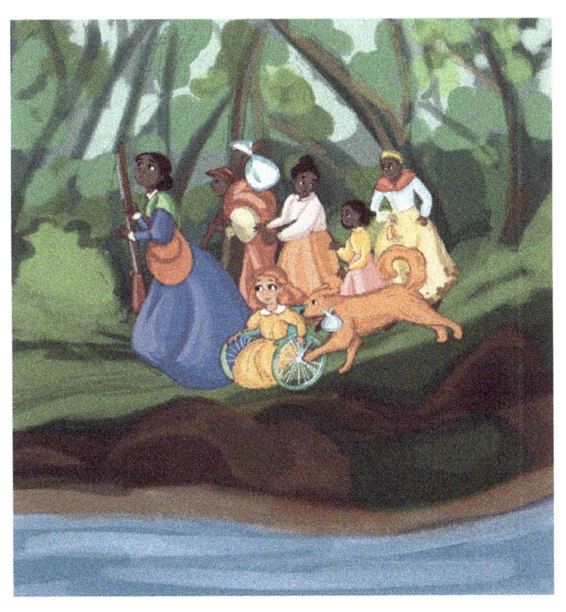

Harriet Tubman and her famous underground railroad as she helped many to freedom in a brave way.
David helps young girls see they can make a difference in this world.

I have mentioned so many books in the chapters in this small book about putting the pictures in picture books – books I have published teach about ants, worms, spiders, bees, wasps, turtles and tortoises, frogs and toads, owls, bats, eels, squids and octopi, crabs, and many more educational topics.

So, if you have a young reader who would be fascinated by *Some of the World's Weirdest and Wackiest Animals* you might want to check out David's book –

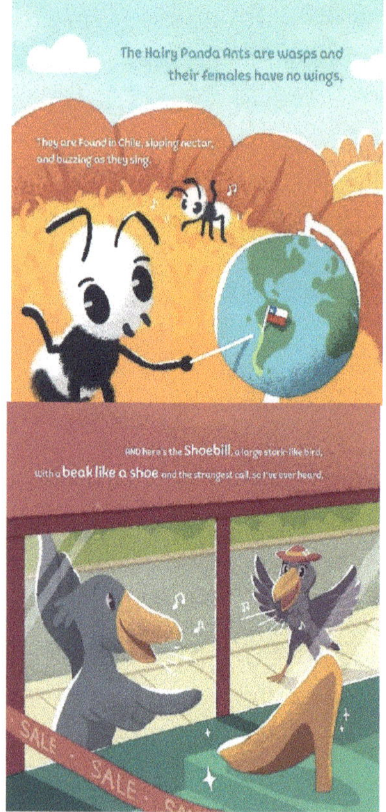

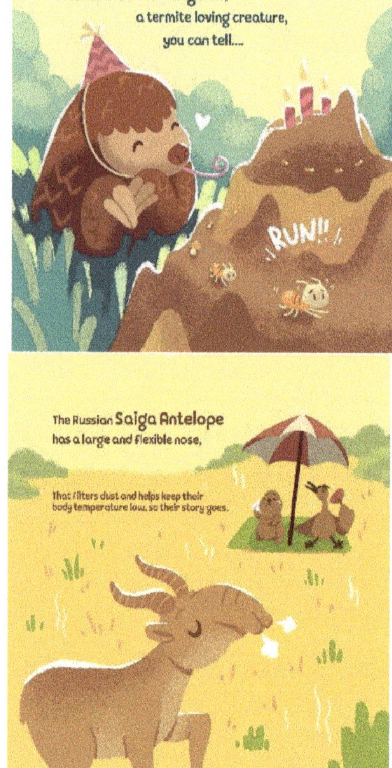

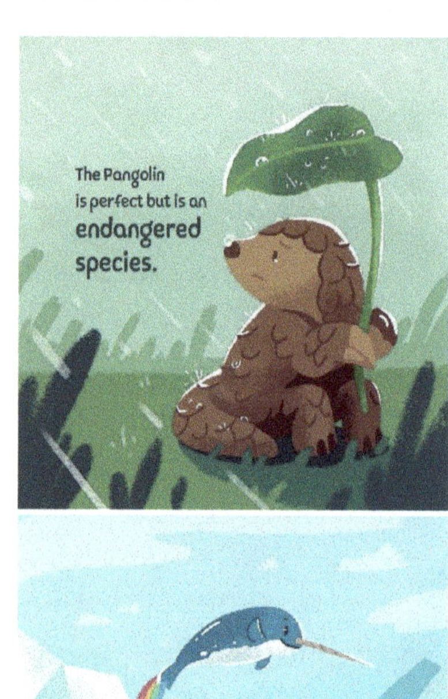

So, there are so many topics that may interest the young reader, but I hope you see how the pictures in the picture books make all the difference. The pictures keep the child's attention as we slip in the *words* to the stories. Remembering seeing the pictures will also be the helpful item in the book for the child to remember the words as well!

Have fun reading and learning and being inspired by the world around us – far around the world and as near as our bedrooms where we cuddle up to read our fun stories with amazing pictures.

12

Adult-Child Bonding

Picture books provide an opportunity for parents or any adult to have precious quality time with a child. What better way to end a day or have a special time than to open a classic or a newly discovered picture book!! See how happy the children are to spend time –

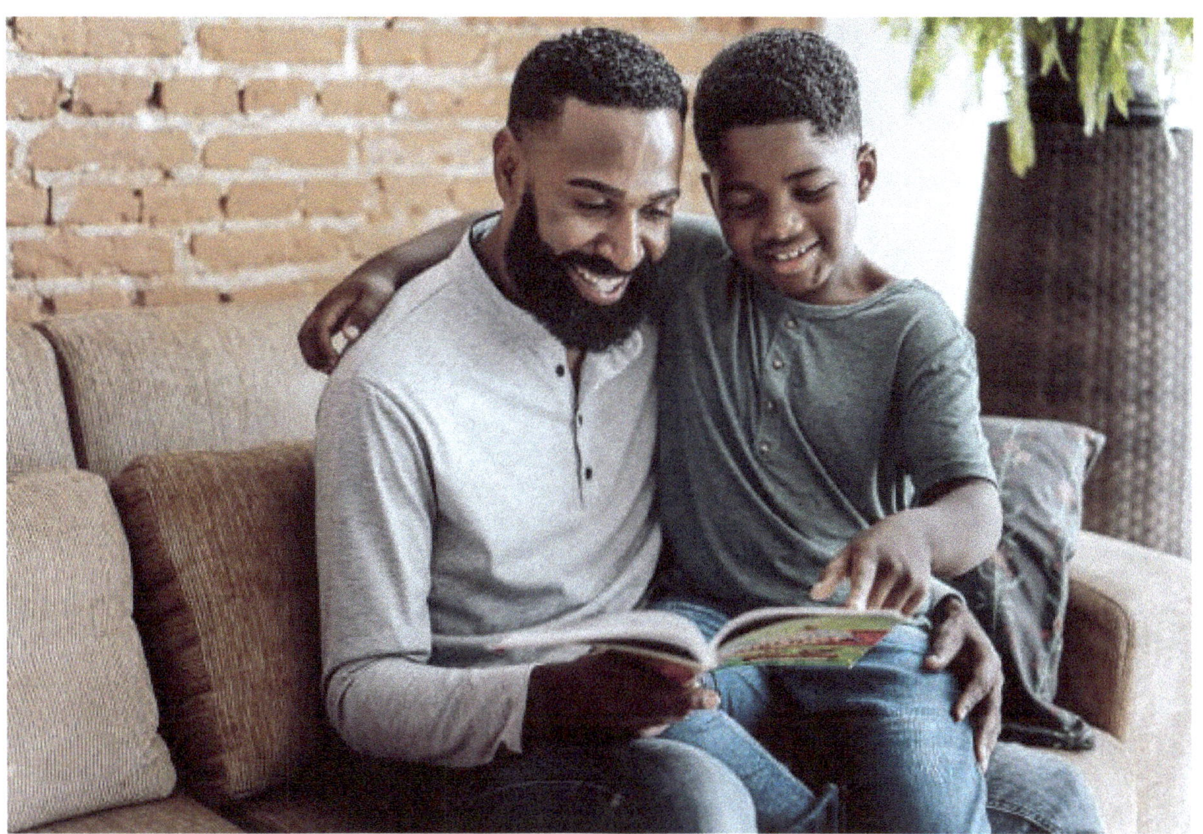

Be on the look-out for your next adventure –

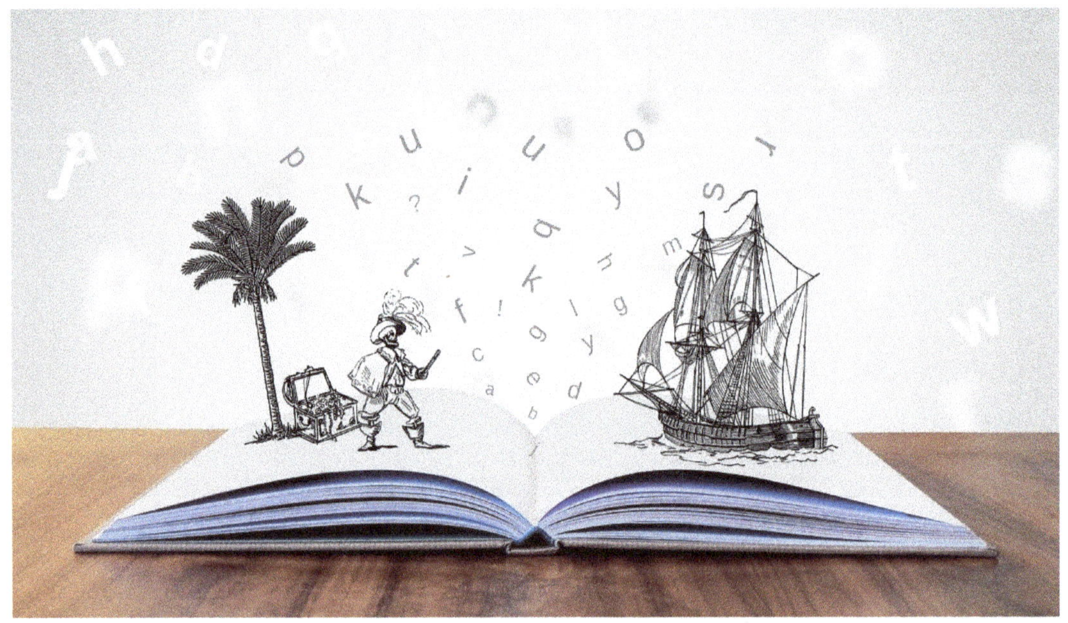

And have a sweet and special time with your little ones –

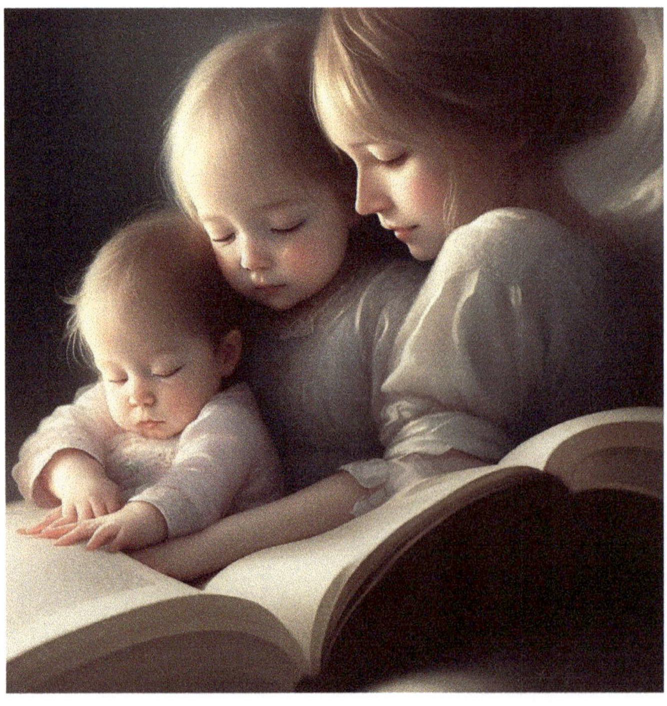

No matter if you are alone or in a group, story time is always GREAT time –

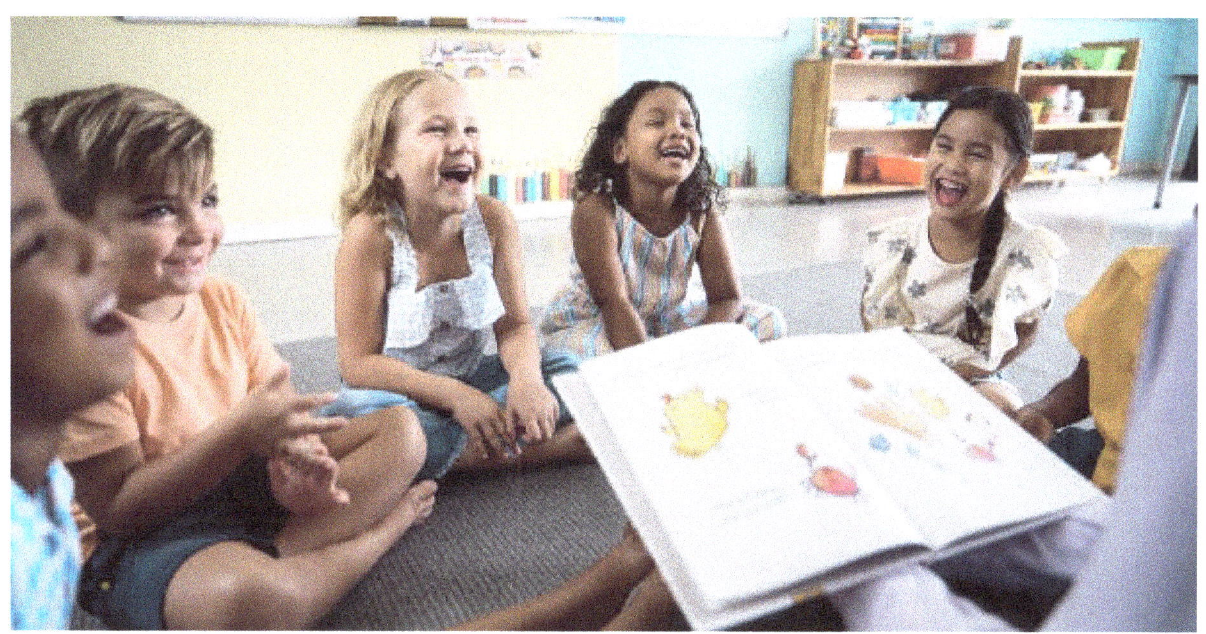

And builds social connections !

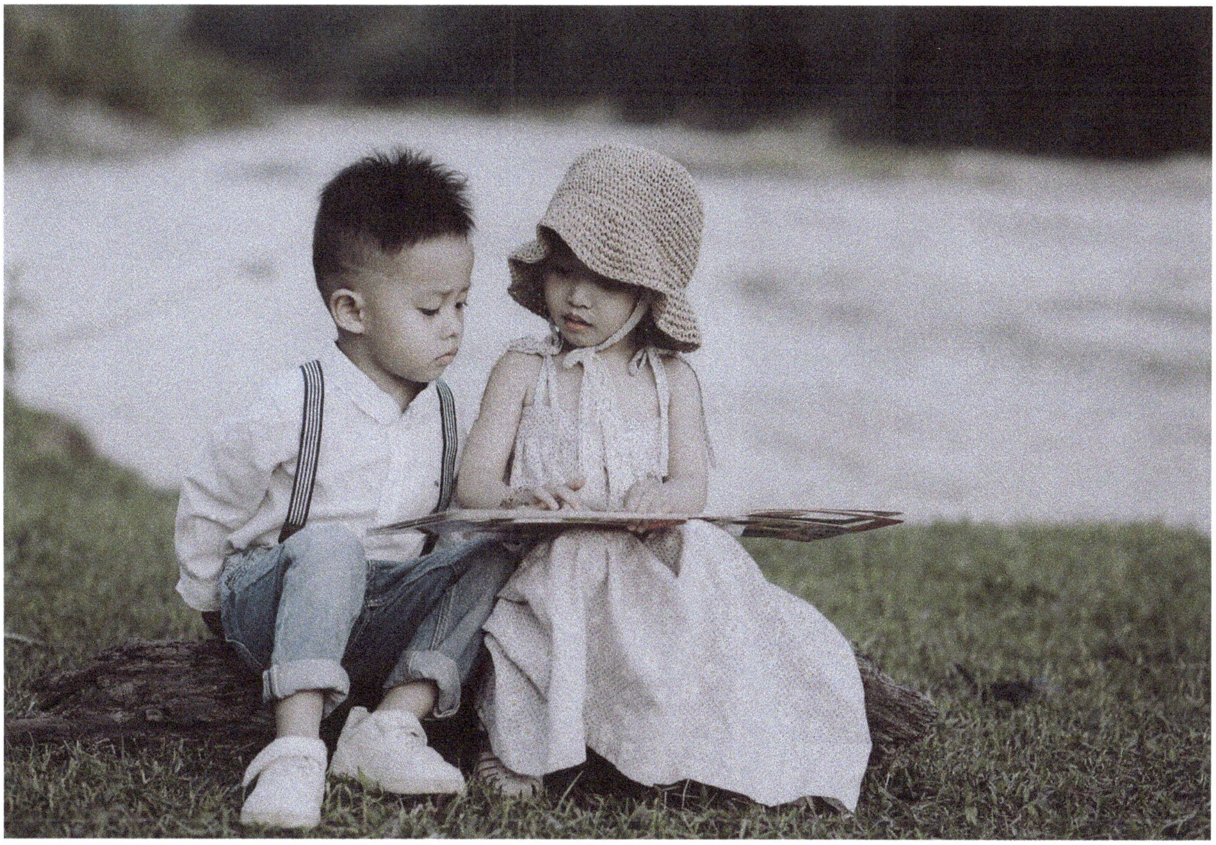

..... and remember – it's all about the pics

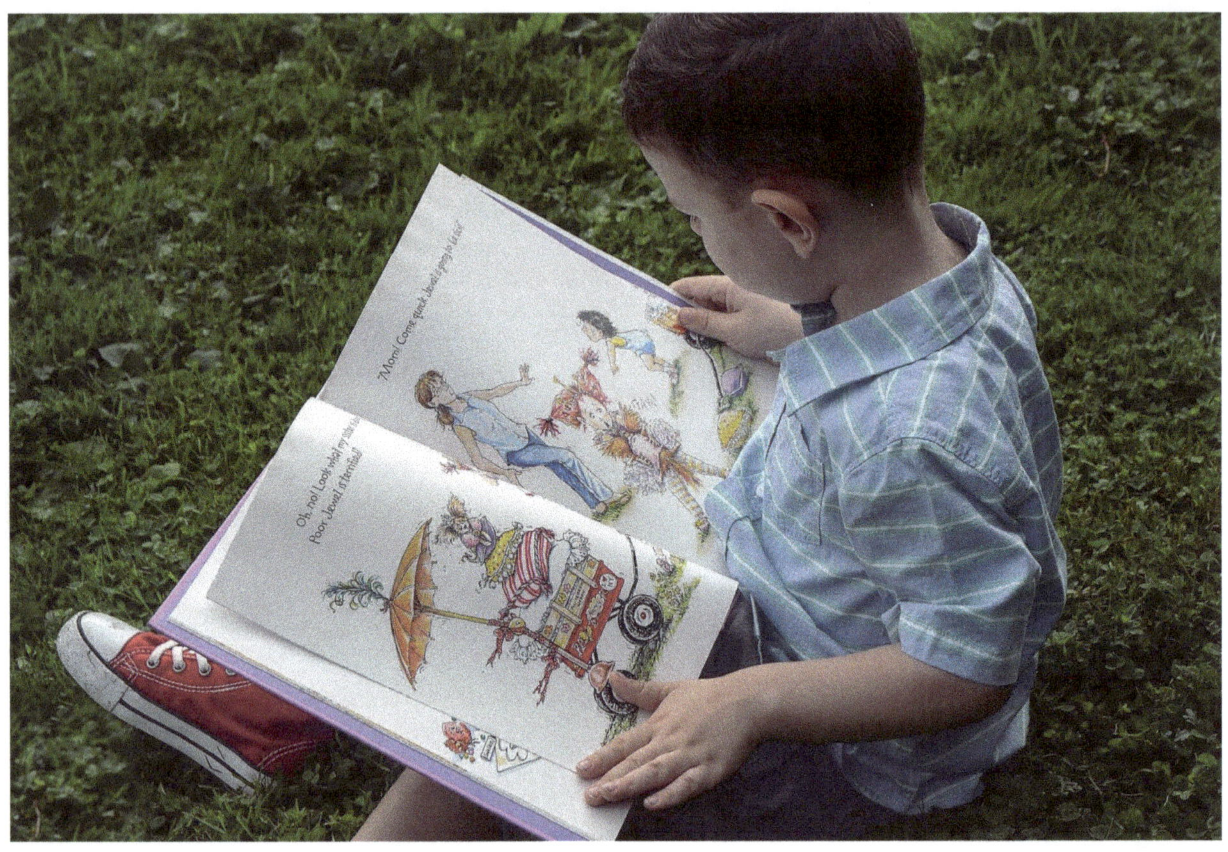

Have fun creating!

www.ingramcontent.com/pod-product-compliance
Lightning Source LLC
Chambersburg PA
CBHW041031050726
47599CB00018B/1929